D1474805

LIBRARY OF LATIN AMERICAN
HISTORY AND CULTURE

GENERAL EDITOR:
DR. A. CURTIS WILGUS

Revolutionaries, Traditionalists, and Dictators in
Latin America

Other Books by Harold Eugene Davis

THE AMERICAS IN HISTORY
GARFIELD OF HIRAM
MAKERS OF DEMOCRACY IN LATIN AMERICA
GOVERNMENT AND POLITICS IN LATIN AMERICA
LATIN AMERICAN LEADERS
SOCIAL SCIENCE TRENDS IN LATIN AMERICA
LATIN AMERICAN SOCIAL THOUGHT
THE UNITED STATES IN HISTORY
(also editions in Spanish in Mexico, in Portugese in Brazil, and in English in India)
HISTORY OF LATIN AMERICA
HINSDALE OF HIRAM: PIONEER EDUCATOR
LATIN AMERICAN THOUGHT: A HISTORICAL INTRODUCTION

(with Harold Durfee)
THE STUDY AND TEACHING OF PHILOSOPHY IN THE UNITED STATES

In collaboration with other authors:

NEW VIEWPOINTS IN COLLEGIATE INSTRUCTION
TWENTIETH CENTURY POLITICAL THOUGHT
HISTORY'S HISTORY
CONTEMPORARY SOCIAL THOUGHT
ORIGINS AND CONSEQUENCES OF WORLD WAR II

Revolutionaries, Traditionalists, and Dictators in Latin America

BY HAROLD EUGENE DAVIS

With contributions by
Donald J. Mabry, Keith L. Miceli,
Eduardo J. Tejera, and Anne Dart de Yanes

The American University,
Washington, D.C.

COOPER SQUARE PUBLISHERS, INC.
NEW YORK   1973

Copyright 1973 by Harold E. Davis
Published by Cooper Square Publishers, Inc.
59 Fourth Avenue, New York, New York 10003
International Standard Book Number 0-8154-0420-4
Library of Congress Catalog Card No. 72-77988

PRINTED IN THE UNITED STATES OF AMERICA
by SENTRY PRESS, NEW YORK, N. Y. 10013

To my students and colleagues in the Americas

PREFACE

The publication of this book offers the pleasant opportunity to thank Henry Chafetz, Sidney B. Solomon, and the Cooper Square Publishers for sponsoring it as an original to accompany two earlier works of mine, LATIN AMERICAN LEADERS and MAKERS OF DEMOCRACY IN LATIN AMERICA, long out of print, which they have reissued. I am especially grateful for this chance to present, to readers who are interested in the phenomena of Latin American politics and thought, my ideas of the relationship of the authoritarian political systems of the region to both revolutionaries and traditionalists and their ways of thinking.

It is my hope that this little book will contribute in a small way to dispelling two persistent misconceptions that distort our view of Latin American political reality. One of these false conceptions is that authoritarian regimes always originate in conservative and reactionary elements of society. The historical truth appears to be, rather, that such regimes more commonly have had their origin in revolutionary movements. A second persistent misconception is that devotion to tradition, as represented in the Church, the family, and systems of land ownership and use is the source of most of the conservatism in Latin American politics. Again, the truth is not this simple. Historical traditions have indeed motivated forces of the political right. But they have also inspired some of the most revolutionary movements and their leaders, as we shall see.

I am indebted to four talented young scholars who assisted in the writing of this book, at my invitation, and gratefully acknowledge their help. Anne Dart de Yanes wrote the chapter on Túpac Amaru; Eduardo J. Tejera contributed the discussion of his grandfather, Diego Vicente Tejera and that of Hugo Blanco; Donald J. Mabry treated Manuel Gómez Morín; and Keith L. Miceli drew on his M.A. thesis for the chapter on Rafael Carrera. It is my hope and expectation that more will be heard from all of them in the future.

Chevy Chase, Maryland
July 24, 1972

HED

ix

CONTENTS

INTRODUCTION:

REVOLUTIONARIES, TRADITIONALISTS, AND DICTATORS IN THE LATIN AMERICAN EXPERIENCE

Historians and philosophers, as almost everyone must know, have been concerned with the nature of political leadership since very early times. They have written about it in various ways. Chinese proverbs, for instance, offer such advice as this: "The greatest conqueror is he who overcomes the enemy without a blow." Aristotle tutored Alexander the Great in the Socratic and Platonic tradition, how successfully one must judge for himself. The prophet Samuel prepared David to be king of Israel in accordance with God's instructions. In his *Parallel Lives*, Plutarch compared Greek and Roman leaders in one of the classic essays on political leaders. Hindu *Ramayana*, in addition to its religious significance, describes the mythical prince who follows *dharma*—those principles of duty particularly requisite to leadership. The *Koran* and the commentaries on it provide advice to Islamic rulers, most notably in the model of Mohammed, "the trustworthy."

In the sixteenth century the *Adages* of Erasmus brought the wisdom of the ages to the eyes of would-be leaders. In his *Institutio*, Erasmus advised the future Charles V on the duties of the Christian prince. Niccolai Machiavelli, in *The Prince*, stated rational and secular principles that were even more clearly in accord with the spirit of the Renaissance for creating, gaining, using, and keeping power. Spain has preserved such proverbs for the aspiring leader as: "If you would be Pope, you must think of nothing else" and "Tyrant kings make treacherous subjects." In early nineteenth century Venezuela, the Rousseau-like Simón Rodríguez tutored young Simón Bolívar in the elitist character and responsibility of leadership in Spanish American independence.

In all ages and in all countries political leadership has had certain common characteristics. Successful leadership responds to needs, to popular aspirations that are sometimes being voiced, but more often are unvoiced. At the highest level, it has a prophetic quality, in the sense of showing an understanding of the basic trends, dangers, and possibilities of the times. It displays moral as well as physical courage and has the will to persist in the pursuit of the objectives it defines. It has the ability to communicate its objectives, its enthusiasm, and something of its will power to its followers; an essential element in this communication capacity is the ability to dramatize the making of essential decisions. Above all, leadership seems to require an intuitive understanding of the political culture within which it works, a sense of the changes going on within the system, and an appropriate political style.

The differences among leaders are of course great, and they arise at various points along the spectrum of left-right radicalism. Nor is it surprising to find conservative, revolutionary, and moderate leaders active at the same point in time and space. Without falling back on either the Hegelian or the Marxist dialectic for the explanation, it may be pointed out that an effective leader on one side often seems to call forth his opposite number. To be successful both must have an intuitive sense of the meaning of their times—of the trends and issues—together with the courage to pursue objectives that they can successfully communicate to their followers. Most important of all, they will need to understand the relative prospects of success of the forces they evoke and lead within the trends of their times. For it is one of the more obvious facts that emerge from the study of history that certain eras are more favorable than others to movements of radical change.

The present age, in Latin America as elsewhere in the world, appears to be an era favoring change, one in which men and women seem to be driven by forces in contemporary culture to follow leaders of radical revolutionary movements of either right or left. Paul Roazen, commenting recently in a new English translation from the German of William Reich's *The Mass Psychology of Fascism* (banned in Nazi Germany in 1935), makes the pertinent point that "modern man is torn by contradictory impulses toward conservatism and revolution. He craves authority and fears freedom, but is simultaneously rebellious."[1] Roazen could well have been describing the psychological basis of political leadership in Latin America at any time since independence, but particularly in the twentieth century.

Among the distinguishing characteristics to be noted in examining this political leadership in Latin America are matters of personal style and of a leadership style that is part of the culture. Personalism, which is part of this style, is not unique to Latin America; but it has acquired special characteristics (not all alike) there, seemingly derived from the various Spanish, Portuguese, French-African, British-African, and indigenous cultural backgrounds. In general, these cultural elements seem to have formed an authoritarian, personalist type of leadership. In Spanish America this element is often simplistically identified as *machismo*—the "he-man" quality expected of leaders. It is assumed that the leader will make all decisions and be all-powerful. Machismo is part of the Latin American style. But other elements in all of these varying cultural backgrounds add other characteristics and often give support to more democratic types of leadership.

The nature of leadership has also changed in the course of national history. The Argentine sociologist, Gino Germani, has distinguished six stages in the evolution of politics in Latin America since independence, stages that have special relevance to an understanding of the types of political leadership, at least in Hispanic America. The stages he describes are as follows:

1. Revolutions and wars of independence and the proclamation of nationhood.

2. Civil wars, "caudillismo," and anarchy.

3. Unifying autocracies.

4. Representative democracy with "limited" participation, or "oligarchy."

5. Representative democracy with enlarged participation.

6. Representative democracy with total participation, or as a possible alternative to these traditional democratic forms, the "national popular revolution" with "total" participation.[2]

The rather amazing sixth stage set forth in Professor Germani's analysis is formulated in broad terms that seem to embrace contradictory trends of the present era. His language may be interpreted to include Juan Bosch's *dictadura con respaldo popular* to which reference will be made later, the Leninist dictatorship of the proletariat, Maoism, Castroism, or Trotzskyism. Or it may be read as describing some kind of broad, vaguely formulated populism, within the norms of representative democracy.

The author has not consciously tried to relate the studies that follow to this Germani analysis. He had in fact written this book before noticing Germani's challenging formulation of stages. But the reader may well notice in these pages some ideas consistent with those of the distinguished Argentine scholar.

This book is conceived as a sequel to two earlier works, *Makers of Democracy in Latin America* and *Latin American Leaders*. Like these volumes, it is a series of studies of important Latin American leaders, biographical in form, noting the experiences of youth and education which influenced their formation, the principles or objectives which they espoused, and how they applied these concepts to concrete problems of their times. In general, the personages are some of those not included in the two previous volumes, but it has been necessary to include one or two of the figures studied earlier in order to round out the theme of this work. Each essay will be followed by a brief bibliographical note, referring the reader to some of the major writings on the subject.

Elsewhere, this author has written that the mainstream of Latin America's thought has been concerned with revolutionary social change and its leadership has been revolutionary.[3] This revolutionary character is most obvious since the movements for independence. But in a certain basic sense it has been true since the discovery of America, for the European, and particularly the Spanish, conquest of America may well be the most thorough revolution Latin America has experienced.

But traditionalists have continuously challenged this revolutionary call for giving substance to utopianism. In colonial days it was the traditionalism of the medieval theology and "scholastic" philosophy, as in the great sixteenth century debate between Bartolomé de las Casas and Juan Ginés de Sepúlveda, or in the eighteenth century controversy over the Jesuit addiction to the ideas of Francisco Suárez. In the nineteenth century, Latin American traditionalism assumed many of the aspects of that of Jaime L. Balmes of Spain and his compeers elsewhere in Europe, although it also reflected in many ways the French traditionalist, Joseph de Maistre. It also had its own Hispanic sources, however. The Latin Americans rejected the part of the European traditionalism that expressed the Spanish and Portuguese addiction to absolute monarchy and the privileges of the nobility. But they accepted from the Europeans the general idea of the authority of an older social order and the primacy of the Church in social life.

Another kind of Latin American traditionalism is observable in the major centers of the pre-Conquest civilizations and occasionally in areas where less advanced pre-Conquest populations survive. This is a traditionalism rooted in the cultures conquered and revolutionized by the Conquest; it expresses itself in reactionary patterns of culture that resist absorption into the Christian-European societal and cultural forms. As the first ideology opposed to the Conquistadores and missionaries this indigenous traditionalism is comparable in importance to the scholastic traditionalism in Spain and Portugal, just mentioned, as displayed by Sepúlveda.

In succeeding centuries this indigenous traditionalism finds some expression in Indian uprisings inspired more by old values and old socio-political systems than by the contemporary revolutionary ideas of Western (European) culture. Only occasionally, when assumed by such criollo (European-American) leaders as the Mexican priest, Miguel Hidalgo, or the Europeanized Peruvian Inca nobleman, Túpac Amaru, is this traditionalism transformed into something more genuinely revolutionary. Perhaps this transformation occurs to a degree in twentieth century Mexico and Bolivia? Although the historical link is not direct, indigenous traditionalism is involved indirectly in another phase of independence ideology. Study of the Spanish Laws of the Indies, which had aimed to preserve native laws and institutions in the Andean communities, inspired such criollo independence leaders as Mariano Moreno and Bernardino Rivadavia of Argentina.

Since colonial days, and even more particularly since independence, revolutionaries have challenged the traditionalists. Rejecting the authority of the European tradition, they have optimistically insisted on the right of the New World to base its case on New World historical experience and have asserted freedom to pursue their own destiny in accordance with natural law. Twentieth century revolutionaries are no exception to this general trend. Their revolt against the evolutionism of the nineteenth century was obviously a challenge of the authority of the past. Like the Spanish youth of today in their relationship to Spanish Republicanism and the Civil War, they say, *"Eso no me dice nada."* ("This says nothing to me.") Yet, paradoxically, they are inescapably a part of their past, in so far as they are cognizant of it. For whether or not they realize it, the key issue of the revolutionary twentieth century, in Latin America as elsewhere, is precisely this question of the meaning of their history.

Dictators are also a recurrent phenomenon in the politics of Latin American countries, though more common in some countries than in others. Dictators have been of various types and represent various ideologies. In the most fundamental political aspect, they are the product of weakness in the governing elites—their inability to form an effective power structure to guide the nation. But dictators do not necessarily come *from* these elites. They have sometimes arisen from the masses. They may come from the right or from the left though, on the whole, as we shall see later, they have come most frequently from the revolutionary or Liberal left. Borne on the flood of Liberal protest, they have all too often encountered the entrenched opposition of power groups too strong for them to overcome by constitutional means. Finding themselves powerless to achieve the ends to which they were committed, they have then succumbed to the ever present lure of power for its own sake. Sometimes they have actually sought dictatorial power as a means to carry out a revolution. But traditionalists have also set out to make themselves dictators.

These various types of dictators will be described more at length in a later chapter in which one of the principal objectives will be to show the relationship of these dictatorial types to the kinds of revolutionaries and traditionalists that are also described in the following pages. Here, it may be sufficient for the author to invite the reader to keep his mind open to the possibility that authoritarian rulers may be either revolutionaries or traditionalists.

NOTES

1. *Saturday Review*, February 13, 1971, pp. 48–49.
2. *Política y sociedad en una época de transición* (Buenos Aires: Ed. Paidos, 1965) p. 147.
3. The following, among others:
   Latin American Revolutionary Thought, American University Faculty Research Lecture, May, 1962; "Revolutions and Revolutionary Thought in Latin America," in Alberto Martínez Piedra, ed., *Socio-economic Change in Latin America* (Washington, D.C., Catholic University of America Press, 1970) 199–203; and "Sources and Characteristics of Latin American Thought," *TOPIC: 20. A Journal of the Liberal Arts* (Washington and Jefferson College) Vol. X (1970) 12-20. The concept is also developed in the author's *Latin American Thought: A Historical Introduction* (Baton Rouge: The Louisiana State University Press, ·1972).

PART I

REVOLUTIONARIES

2

TYPES OF REVOLUTIONARIES

Revolutionary thought and revolutionary leaders stand out as characteristics of Latin American political and social history. From the earliest days of the Conquest, the relations of Europeans to America have had this revolutionary quality. For the European Conquest of America, and especially the Spanish part of it, was in itself a profound revolution. It replaced the basic power structure of the pre-Conquest civilizations. It revolutionized their agriculture and other aspects of their economies. It substituted new value systems in all areas through the vigorous and successful Christian missionary activity. The theory and ideology animating this conquest-revolution were those of Renaissance humanism and of Christian missionary thought, including in some respects the concepts of the Catholic Counter-Reform.

During the colonial period a number of native uprisings and slave rebellions occurred. Of the former the most notable was led by Túpac Amaru (1780–81), a rebellion which spread from the highlands of Peru northward into present day Colombia and southward into Bolivia. The career of Túpac will be treated in the next chapter. Here it may be noted merely that unlike most of the indigenous uprisings, which had limited objectives of social change, that of Túpac projected a far reaching revolution. But, paradoxically, this revolution also had a traditionalist basis in the sense that it sought to restore certain aspects of the pre-Conquest regime.

Among the numerous slave insurrections of the colonial period may be mentioned the movement in Brazil which produced the escaped slave "Kingdom of Palmares," the unsuccessful rebellions of slaves in Coro, Venezuela, and of the maroons in Jamaica in the 1790's, and the successful slave insurrection in Haiti—the insurrection that brought independence to that island kingdom in 1804. Haiti exhibited the strange phenomenon of three quite distinct and simultaneous movements of rebellion, one of white planters, one of freedmen, and one of slaves. This threefold character of the independence movement in Haiti reflects its ideological links with the French-American revolution and with the upsurging European slave emancipation movement, as represented in the French abolitionist organization *Les Amis des Noires*. In its inner contradictions it also resembled, if it did not have actual ideological links

9

with, the turbulent chaotic mass uprising of Indians and mestizos led by Miguel Hidalgo in Mexico in 1810 and that of Túpac Amaru in Peru.

Spanish and Portuguese settlers also rebelled occasionally during the time of Iberian colonial rule. But on the whole these movements had little genuinely revolutionary significance. One of the earliest and most dramatic of them was the uprising of Diego Almagro, companion and partner of Francisco Pizarro. This rebellion brought the death of both leaders and a new Spanish viceroy to suppress the civil war. Equally sensational was the erratic rebellion of Lope de Aguirre in the sixteenth century. Killing the leader of his exploring expedition in Ecuador, he built river boats to sail down the Amazon river, up the Rio Negro, and down the Orinoco river to the Atlantic. He then sailed northwest along the coast to Margarita Island off the coast of Venezuela, of which he proclaimed himself Prince. Another rebellion involving a colorful leader in sixteenth century Spanish America overthrew the government of Alvear Núñez Cabeza de Vaca in Paraguay. Similar criollo uprisings occurred in the eighteenth century, for example in Paraguay and Colombia.

The independence movements produced some of the greatest revolutionists in Latin American history. The movements and their leaders expressed in a general way the Liberal, anti-authoritarian (though usually aristocratic) theories and ideologies of the Enlightenment, as filtered through the exciting experience of the American-French Revolution and the disillusioning experience of the Napoleonic Era. But, these movements exhibited great variety in their ideologies. Some of the precursor uprisings, such as that already mentioned of Túpac Amaru in Peru and that of Gual y España in New Granada (Colombia) (1798) had a traditionalist basis. Though genuinely revolutionary, they defended an older order of things and even opposed the centralizing reforms of Charles III of Spain. In Mexico, the curate of Dolores, Miguel Hidalgo, was intrigued with the ideas of Rousseau, Raynal, and other Enlightenment writers; but he directed his 1810 rebellion essentially against the *Gachupines* (Spaniards) in a manner that could be interpreted as aiming chiefly to undo the Spanish Conquest.

Even the confirmed leader of criollo independence, Juan Germán Roscio, found the basis of the New Granada movement of 1810–1811, as we shall see, in principles of the medieval Spanish legal code of Alfonso the Wise, the *Siete Partidas*, and in the principles of the natural law of God as developed by Spanish theologians. He said The Council of Regency in Spain had violated these principles in failing to consult the American colonies after the imprisonment of King Ferdinand in France.

Another element of traditionalism in the independence revolutionary leaders is their monarchism. Most of them advocated the establishment of separate, constitutional kingdoms under European princes. Monarchism was also one of the earmarks of the contemporarry European traditionalism. But the Latin American monarchists among the independence leaders sympathized with the Liberalism of the French Revolution as stated in the Declaration of the Rights of Man, believing that this Liberalism was to be based on constitutional monarchy. Every colony also had its Francophiles who saw the French Revolution as an expression of Liberalism that went beyond monarchy. But many of them came to be disillusioned by the excesses of the Reign of Terror and even more by the authoritarianism of the Napoleonic regime.

When confronted with the Napoleonic occupation of Spain, most of the Spanish American Liberals, including at least some of this French party, rejected the agents Napoleon sent to America to assert his claim to the Spanish colonies. In doing so, the Spanish American Liberals sided with the Liberals of Spain who were rising against Joseph Bonaparte in the name of Ferdinand. They later broke with the leadership of the Spanish resistance of 1810, partly because the resistance cause appeared to be defeated and partly because the regency council did not include colonial representatives, but not because of its monarchism.

Thus the Spanish American revolutions of independence had in them more than a little traditionalism. Except for a few out and out Francophiles, their leaders asserted the right of self-determination by opposing the agents of Napoleon and they rejected the authority of the Spanish Council of Regency on the grounds that it violated the traditional Spanish constitution. The Liberal Spanish Constitution of 1812 won back much of the colonial Liberalism, even though it failed to recognize colonial autonomy. Thus Ferdinand VII's rejection of this constitution after his restoration tended to put the American revolutionists more clearly in opposition to Spanish traditionalism as interpreted by the party supporting the monarch. But at this stage, too, colonial opposition had a paradoxical aspect. In Mexico, and to some extent in Peru, some of the leaders of independence in this final stage of the movement were really reactionaries opposing the Liberal Spanish revolution of 1820.

Brazilian independence was the least revolutionary of the independence movements, effecting relatively little change in the institutional and power structure. The principal leaders there were monarchists, although the *Inconfidencia* movement in Minas Gerais (1789–90) had republican tendencies, and an unsuccessful rebellion in Pernambuco in 1817 proposed a republic. In contrast to the experience in French and Spanish

America, independence did not bring slave emancipation in Brazil. Yet the Brazilians, including José Bonifacio de Andrade e Silva, the so-called Patriarch of Independence, and the first monarch, Pedro I, were confirmed Liberals, as evidenced by their connections with the Masonic order and the "Apostolate" within which plans for independence were developed.

The revolutionary leaders of Spanish America in the quarter century following independence found their program in opposing the conservative political regimes which had taken over in most countries after relatively brief periods of government under Liberal independence leaders. A similar development may also be seen in Brazil, as in the opposition of the radical Liberal priest, Father Diogo Feijó, to the regency regimes that preceded and followed his own during the 1830's. Opposition to Conservative aspects of the Rosas regime explains much of the program of the "Generation of 1837" (The Association of May) in Argentina including Esteban Echeverría, Juan Bautista Alberdi, Bartolomé Mitre, and Domingo F. Sarmiento. It is also true of such Mexican Liberals as Melchor Ocampo, *"El negromante"* Ignacio Ramírez, Sebastián and Miguel Lerdo de Tejada, and Beníto Juárez. In Chile, the generation of young intellectuals that gathered around Andrés Bello, the most radical of whom was Francisco Bilbao, had the same general character.

These post-independence Liberals were anti-monarchists, although monarchism was already dead in most of Spanish America. They opposed such aristocratic privileges as the *fueros* of the military. The major target they attacked, however, was the wealth and power of the clergy, still the most powerful institutionalized force in Spanish American society in spite of its having been whittled down during the wars of independence. The thought of these early nineteenth century leaders, as expressed in Echeverría's *Dogma Socialista*, was utopian, romantic, idealist, and anarchist. When they adopted the principles of the evolving "scientific" history and the closely related historical philosophy of law, they found themselves in the dilemma that Leopoldo Zea has pointed out in his various works.[1] If they accepted history as a source of legitimacy of laws and institutions they were impaled on the traditionalist horn of the dilemma. If, on the other hand, they rejected this authority of history they were impaled on the horn of anti-historicism. The obvious solution, seen most clearly perhaps by Alberdi, was to assert an autonomous American historical experience.[2]

By the late nineteenth century Liberal thought had lost most of its revolutionary character, becoming positivist, evolutionary, pragmatic, scientific, psychological, and sociological. Yet, by the end of the century, some revolutionary voices had again been raised out of this very background. These were such voices as those of José Martí and José Varona in Cuba, Juan Montalvo in Ecuador, Valentín Letelier and Luis Recabarren in Chile, Manuel González Prada in Péru, and Camilo Arriaga in Mexico.

These protests against the evolutionary social theory and the institutions from which it emanated often had a negative, sometimes an anarchist tone. But they also expressed new and constructive trends. One of these was a broad trend in socio-religious philosophy that embraced Krausism and spiritualism—a neo-Kantian idealism and religious humanism. Krausist philosophy was introduced by Julián Sánz del Rio into the University of Madrid in the mid-nineteenth century and soon achieved a predominant position there. Some Spaniards say it produced the leadership of the Second Spanish Republic in the 1930's. It spread from Spain to Portugal and to most of the university centers in Spanish America and Brazil, merging in Brazil with the earlier Kantian stream from the Center at Itú and elsewhere. Neo-Thomist and Christian democratic or socialist thought, following the patterns suggested by the papal encyclicals, beginning with the *Rerum Novarum* of Leo XIII in 1891, provided another such current.

Closely related to these spiritual trends as a source of revolutionary thought was the broad stream of neo-idealist thought—much of it German in origin—which was finding its way to America, especially through the writing of Ortega. Marxist thought was another revolutionary source, coming in by way of the incipient labor movement and the labor press. By the early twentieth century Marxist ideas were finding expression in the press and in the political activities of such leaders in Mexico as the Flores Magón brothers and Antonio Díaz Soto y Gama, to mention only two of a large number.

Revolutionary leaders have appeared in the twentieth century in even richer variety than in the past, if that is possible. They have been labor leaders, agrarian reformers, school* teachers, lawyers, professional soldiers, amateur generals, guerrillas, and rebel priests. Their social theories have ranged from fascism, through liberal democracy, Christian socialism, Marxist-Leninism, and anarchism to contemporary Maoism and Fidelism. Some leaders operate on a clearly defined, realistic power theory, in which the disciplined party (Leninist or fascist) becomes the basis for dictatorship, gathering all power into its hands and maintaining itself by police intelligence, or when necessary by systematic terror. Others seem to rely more on creating anarchy, within which they hope to create a power structure and a program.

Three main streams of theory appear to define contemporary concepts of social revolution: neo-idealist existentialism, neo-Thomism or neo-Christian thought, and Marxism in its various forms. The forms of the revolutions themselves are also varied. The Mexican Revolution is in many ways the prototype of the later forms, but other influential models are those of Uruguayan *Batllismo*, Argentine *Peronismo*, the Vargas *Estado novo*, the Bolivian Revolution of 1952, and the Cuban Revolution.

Since 1960, both new and old revolutionary groups have more frequently than in the past called for the destruction of the established social system, especially in its capitalistic aspects. Many of these groups, though not all, have called for the use of violence in the form of rural or urban guerrilla warfare. Most of their recruits are young, many from well-to-do middle class families. They are often university students. But they also include a significant number of university professors, rebel priests, and other professionals. One of the trends of the times is for Christian youth to move toward this more radical position, often embracing one of the varieties of revolutionary Marxism in doing so. Three leaders of this generation of guerrilla revolutionaries are treated in this section of the book: Ernesto "Che" Guevara of Argentina, Cuba, and Bolivia; Hugo Blanco, a Trotskyist agrarian revolutionary of Peru; and Camilo Torres, rebel priest and guerrilla of Colombia.

If these contemporary varieties of revolutionaries have a common denominator, it is that of a revived optimism which rejects the various forms of determinism, both Marxist and non-Marxist. They seem to agree in viewing man as the master of his destiny and in seeing the need to make over the social order on some more just and efficient basis. The sketches which follow can not possibly represent all the varieties and forms of contemporary revolutionists, anymore than those of the past. Hopefully, however, they will give a fair view of the variety which exists.

The reader who is familiar with Latin American history will find that many important revolutionary leaders, both past and present, are not included among the very select group here presented. In some cases this is because the author has written of them in the companion volumes to this book. This accounts for the omission of such major figures as Francisco Miranda, Simón Bolívar, José de San Martín, Bernardo O'Higgins, Bernardo de Monteagudo, José Bonifacio de Andrada e Silva, José Julián Martí, José Batlle y Ordóñez, Francisco Madero, José Carlos Mariátegui, Víctor Raúl Haya de la Torre, Toussaint L'Ouverture, Mariano Moreno, Bernardino Rivadavia, and Diogo Antônio Feijó. For these major revolutionary figures the author can only regretfully refer the reader to these companion volumes or to their biographies. Fidel Castro was reluctantly omitted from this section, simply because the author decided it was more meaningful to treat him in the third section of the book as a revolutionary become dictator.

The exclusion of many others was an even more arbitrary decision. One reason is simply that this is a small book and the number of Latin American revolutionaries is large. The history of Mexico, to mention just one country, abounds in guerrilla leaders largely unknown to the outside world. Another limiting factor has been the lack of adequate biographical studies of many leaders of popular uprisings, especially the leaders of slave rebellions and of Indian revolts. Some day an enterprising student of political leadership may provide us with a definitive study of the history of Latin American revolutionary leadership. This little book has the much more modest objective of presenting a few examples of the various varieties that revolutionary leadership has assumed.

NOTES

1. See his *Dos etapas del pensamiento hispano-americano* (México: El Colegio de México, 1949). Also in translation by James H. Abbott and Lowell Dunham, *The Latin American Mind* (University of Oklahoma Press, 1963). See also his later two volume *El pensamiento latinoamericano* (México: Pormaca, 1965).
2. Zea points out, in terms reminiscent of José Ortega y Gassett, that only as they relived and experienced this past could they transcend it.

BIBLIOGRAPHY

In the author's judgment, the Latin American historical literature does not include an adequate treatment of revolutionary leadership. The biographies are the best source, but many of them, one might say most of them, lack adequate perspective. Volume III of D.M. Condit, Bert H. Cooper, Jr. and others, *Challenge and Response in Internal Conflict* (Washington: The American University, 1968) provides some perspective for the twentieth century, but treats only a few examples in Mexico, Colombia, Cuba, and Venezuela. Luis Mercier Vega, *Guerrillas in Latin America: The Technique of Counter-State* (New York: Praeger, 1969) is also useful, as are the writings of "Che" Guevara (see note at end of his sketch) and Regis Debray, *Revolution Within Revolution* (New York: Grove Press, 1967). Richard Bourne, in *Political Leaders of Latin America* (Baltimore, London, and Victoria, Australia: Penguin Books, 1969) offers helpful ideas, as does Carleton Beals in *Great Guerrilla Leaders* (Englewood Cliffs, N.J.: Prentice-Hall, 1970). Irving Louis Horowitz, ed., *Latin American Radicalism, a Documentary Report on Left and Nationalist Movements* (New York: Random House, 1969) is useful, but only for contemporary leaders. Richard Gott, in

Guerrilla Movements in Latin America, sketches a variety of leaders. The work of Carlos M. Rama, *Revolución social y fascismo en el siglo xx* (Buenos Aires y Montevideo: Palestra, 1962) has a useful chapter (3) "Ensayo sobre el hombre revolucionario."

3

TUPAC AMARU II (1742–1781)
by Anne Dart Yanes

It is difficult to name a more revolutionary figure in the history of Latin America than Túpac Amaru, leader of the Indian uprising that swept through the ancient Inca realm in South America in the years 1780–1781. As in the case of other native rebellions against Spanish colonial rule, this one was vigorously and cruelly suppressed. In fact, no such Indian rebellion led to national independence in Spanish America; instead, independence was won by the American born Spanish elite, the *criollos*.

José Gabriel Condorcanqui, known as Túpac Amaru, was a descendant of the last Inca ruler, Túpac Amaru I, who had defied Spanish authority from his mountain stronghold in the Andes after Pizarro's conquest of the Inca' Empire. This first Túpac was finally captured in 1571 and, like his namesake two centuries later, was executed in the main square of Cuzco. For this execution the Viceroy Toledo was later reprimanded by King Phillip II in words that became legendary, "I sent you to serve kings, not to kill them."[1]

Two centuries later, José Gabriel Condorcanqui, having dropped his family name and adopted that of his Inca ancestor, began a revolt that developed into the greatest native uprising in the history of the Americas. Beginning in the Vilcamayu Valley town of Tinta, some eighty miles to the south of Cuzco, the rebellion burgeoned in all directions, fanned by the underlying discontent of criollos and mestizos, as well as of Indians. Ultimately it extended through Peru, Bolivia, northwestern Argentina, and part of Ecuador.[2] Before the insurrection was brought under control, it had exacted a great toll in human life; the exact magnitude of the toll will never be known, although it has been estimated as high as 80,000.

José Gabriel was the second son of the Inca cacique, or *curaca*, (Quechua term), Miguel Condorcanqui and his wife Rosa Noguera. He was born in Tinta, probably in 1742, and baptized in Tungasuca, his father's birthplace. His year of birth appears in various accounts as 1740, 1741, and 1742. Lillian Fisher cites a baptismal certificate, submitted by José Gabriel in 1777 to the Lima audiencia during a dispute over his right to the marquisate of Oropesa, that seems to fix the date in 1742.[3] His mother died shortly afterward, as did his older brother Clemente, leaving José Gabriel as his father's heir. His father soon remarried, to Ventura

Monjarras, and in 1747 José Gabriel's half-brother, Juan Bautista, was born from this marriage. Juan Bautista was to live to write his memoirs in Argentina after forty years of exile, giving us one of the important, though not always dependable accounts of the rebellion. Another brother, Diego Cristobal, sometimes referred to as the cousin of Túpac Amaru, was also a half-brother, possibly of illegitimate birth. There was also a half-sister, Cecilia.

When his father died in 1750, José Gabriel, then a boy of eight years, inherited the title of cacique and the extensive feudal land holdings granted by Viceroy Toledo in 1572 to Juana Pilcohuaco, daughter of Túpac Amaru I and wife of Diego Felipe Condorcanqui. During his boyhood, his paternal and maternal uncles exercised the cacique's powers on his behalf and arranged for his education. Like other caciques, he was educated by private tutors. His first teachers were Dr. Antonio López de Sosa, the curate of Pampamarca, and Dr. Carlos Rodríguez de Avila, the curate of Yanaoca. The former was a native of Panama, the latter of Guayaquil. José Gabriel later attended the Colegio de San Francisco de Borja, founded in Cuzco in 1619 by Viceroy Esquilache for caciques and other Indian nobles and run by the Jesuits. He was noted by his professors as an able student. He learned to read Latin, to speak and write Spanish fluently, while continuing to speak Quechua " with peculiar grace."[4] Beyond this meager knowledge of his education, we know only that during visits to Lima he occasionally attended lectures at the University of San Marcos.[5]

Boleslao Lewin, one of the best biographers of Túpac, confesses that he has not been able to identify clearly the ideological or philosophical currents that influenced the thought of the Inca leader. Lewin is not even certain that Túpac read the *Comentarios Reales* of Garcilaso de la Vega, although the indirect influence of Garcilaso in Túpac's thought would seem to be obvious.[6] The Jesuit historian, Guillermo Furlong, insists that the Jesuits played a decisive role in the intellectual conformation of Túpac Amaru. Lewin is skeptical of this influence;[7] but since the Jesuits conducted the Colegio in Cuzco which Túpac Amaru attended, they must have had an influence upon his education.

Lewin thinks that the most formative influence on Túpac was that of the Bishop of Cuzco, Juan Manuel Moscoso y Peralta, whose Enlightenment ideas were those of the criollos and hence not necessarily rebellious. Some writers have charged that the bishop supported the rebellion of Túpac, but Lewin is convinced that the bishop was not directly involved, citing in support of his judgment the decision of King Carlos III that freed the bishop from charges of involvement and appointed him Archbishop of Granada. But this royal exoneration was qualified in a curious way, however, for the King also "imposed upon him perpetual silence concerning matters in Peru."[8] Thus, the question of the influence of the Bishop of Cuzco is involved in the controversial question of his alleged complicity in the insurrection itself. But whatever the degree of the bishop's involvement, as Lewin points out, the whole episode had the effect of directing attention to the "social and political importance of the movement headed by the last Inca."[9]

In general, Túpac Amaru's education and ideological formation seem to have been like that of most upper class Spanish American colonials of the eighteenth century. In Lima, as elsewhere, the criollos were caught up in vigorous philosophical discussions, pitting their old prejudices against the new ideas of the Enlightenment. As an educated mestizo of the Inca nobility, Túpac Amaru had intimate acquaintances among Peninsular Spaniards and within the criollo society, both in Cuzco and in Lima. Through these contacts he was certainly aware of the eighteenth century natural law theories so much in vogue.

José Gabriel always spoke of himself as a devout Catholic, who had never gone against any of the precepts of the Church. Always professing undying loyalty to the Spanish Crown, he contended that he disagreed only with administrators and functionaries who refused to observe the directives of the King that the native populace be accorded fair treatment. Contemporary writers felt that his actions disproved his words; but later students, with more historical perspective, tend to view him more as he saw himself. Thus, the Peruvian historian Daniel Valcárcel states that Túpac Amaru was "profoundly religious" and that he also had great respect for the "authentic mandates of the Crown."[10]

But although his philosophy was more criollo than revolutionary, and his person was more cosmopolitan than provincial, something set him apart. In large measure it was a legitimate pride in his ancestry and a sense of the uniqueness of his position as the cacique most clearly derived from the Incaic tradition. As his awareness of the social injustice around him increased, so too did this sense of his responsibility as the heir of the Inca tradition grow upon him.

In physical appearance and manner of dress, José Gabriel was far-removed from any present day notion of a native chief. As described in 1780 by Colonel Pablo Astete, a criollo from Cuzco, he was approximately five feet and eight inches tall, "well proportioned" and "sinewy"; his features included a "handsome Inca face, a slightly aquiline nose, full black eyes, and a countenance intelligent, benign and expressive." His attire was European. He allowed his "glossy black hair to flow in ringlets nearly down to his waist." His dress included a black velvet coat, a gold waistcoat, a beaver dress hat, silk stockings, and embroidered linen; he wore gold buckles at his knees and on his shoes.[11] During the revolt this style of dress was modified somewhat. Thus, on one occasion he was portrayed wearing a blue velvet suit and matching cloak, with a three-cornered hat. Over the suit he had added a heavily embroidered *uncu*, a tunic like those worn by his ancestors; a golden sun hung as a medallion around his neck.[12]

In 1760, José Gabriel married Micaela Bastides Puyucahua, a native of Pampamarca. She was a beautiful girl and was said to be a "pure-blood Spaniard."[13] During the next ten years three sons of the couple were born: Hipólito (1761), Mariano (1763), and Fernando (1770).[14] Other members of the Condorcanqui household were Diego Cristóbal and his mother, Marcela Castro, and Jose Gabriel's nephew, Andrés Mendagure, the son of Cecilia and Pedro Mendagure. All these family members, as well as the other more distant relatives, figured in the insurrection, either as actors or as innocent victims of its repression. Micaela played a particularly important role as her husband's principal advisor and confidant.

Means describes the society in which José Gabriel moved as "the best which the region offered."[15] By colonial standards he was rich. Part of his income came from 35 teams of cargo mules that he hired out for the transport of merchandise, and he was popularly known as the "muleteer cacique."[16]

During this decade of the 1760's José Condorcanqui gave few indications that he was destined to lead a life different from that of other caciques. He was still engaged in proving his legal right to the caciqueship of Tungasuca, Pampamarca, and Surimana, all in the province of Tinta.[17] Much of this time he seems to have spent in traveling throughout Peru, on business as well as for pleasure. Whatever the reason for it may have been, this apparently casual approach toward formalizing his caciqueship stands out in sharp contrast to the conscientious manner in which he discharged his duties as cacique. According to Markham, he "governed his villages exceedingly well, and was highly esteemed by the corregidor of the province, Don Pedro Múñoz de Arjona, who admired his punctual attention to his duties, and therefore distinguished him above all the other caciques."[18]

This post of cacique carried with it privileges and responsibilities that tended to set the Indian cacique apart from his people in many ways. Since the Conquest, Spain had capitalized on the mystique of the Inca class in governing the native population. As Charles Gibson has pointed out, by concentrating the various offices and ranks of the native "nobility" into one class, that of the caciques, Spain reduced what had been a complicated hierarchical system to a society of two classes, a "society of foremen and separate masses."[19] The cacique was exempt from tribute and from personal service, but he had to aid the *corregidor* (governor) in collecting tribute from the Indians and in providing laborers for the mines and for local work projects. Unlike the corregidor, who had no fixed salary but was given exclusive trading privileges and a percentage of the tribute collected, the cacique received an established stipend for his services. In addition to his inherited titles and estates, the cacique also was allowed to wear certain distinctive clothing and other insignia of his Inca descent.[20]

In 1770 Túpac learned that one Vicente José García had submitted a rival claim to the marquisate of Oropesa. José Gabriel journeyed to Lima and presented the documents to establish his own claim to the title. The Lima audiencia (royal council) decided in his favor and he returned to his native Tinta as the official Marquis of Oropesa. Lillian Fisher concludes that this visit to Lima brought a change in his life. Before, she says, he had been "humble and devout," but upon his return "he gave added attention to his style of living" and adopted the name "Túpac Amaru."[21]

Writers on Túpac Amaru have given various meanings to his name, all of them relating in some way to the *serpent*, an especially venerated religious symbol of the Incas. The phrase was used to refer to the sun and to refer to a leader of special gifts. The Quechua dictionary of Jorge Lira defines Túpac or Thúpak as one who scrapes or grates and Amaru as serpent. Either the symbol of the rasping serpent or of the shining sun was a fit title for a revolutionary. After Túpac's death the corrupted term *Tupamaro* came to be applied by royalists in the Banda Oriental, present-day Uruguay, to rebels against Spanish authority. This tradition is, of course, what the contemporary Tupamaro guerrillas of the region derive their name from.[22]

During the decade following his confirmation as Marquis, Túpac sponsored numerous appeals on behalf of the Indians against injustices of the colonial system that required a payment of tribute, personal service for a set period of time each year under the *mita*, and the purchase of goods from the corregidors. Each corregidor had exclusive trading privileges in his domain, an arrangement that enabled him to force the Indians to purchase goods for which they had no need, at prices they could not afford. If they did not pay, they could be forced into indentured servitude. Of all these Indian grievances the *mita* system of forced labor was the most intolerable. The *mita* supplied workers for haciendas and mines, including those as far away as Potosí. By requiring men to leave their families, it often forced Indian women into concubinage or prostitution.[23] Túpac became a voice of appeal against the injustice of these practices.

In 1777 we find Túpac Amaru again defending his title to the Marquisate of Oropesa. It had been challenged by Diego Felipe Betancour whose claim, according to Lillian Fisher, was based on false information supplied by his mother. Since, as of 1780, the matter had not yet been settled by the audiencia, at the time of the insurrection Túpac Amaru apparently did not have a clear legal title to the Marquisate.[24]

Establishing residence in Lima for several months, he used the opportunity to address the Spanish Visitador (royal inspector) Areche on behalf of the Indians. He twice appealed formally to that high Spanish official, reiterating the many abuses caused by the *mita*, particularly at Potosi. Citing the Spanish law, he pointed out that if the law had been faithfully applied, such abuses would never have occurred. Indians were transported 200 leagues or more from their homes to work at Potosí, he claimed; whereas, by law, that distance should not have exceeded two leagues. The Indian population had drastically decreased in many areas through the years, he pointed out, but no corresponding reduction had been made in the quota of persons required to serve under the *mita*. The Visitador ordered an investigation, but all maltreatment was denied by the superintendent of the *mita*, and the investigation went no further. Túpac Amaru thus failed in this, as in all his subsequent attempts, to remedy the conditions of the Indians by legal action.

Antonio de Arriaga had been the corregidor in the province of Tinta since 1776; his cruelty and intransigence proved to be the catalyst that finally brought the insurrection of Túpac Amaru II, and the "execution" of Arriaga was the beginning of the rebellion. It is not clear why Túpac decided on his execution. The act was not without precedent, however. The former Viceroy Guirior, in his *Memorias*, had described disturbances relating to corregidors in fourteen provinces and had reported the assassination of three corregidors. It has been claimed that the attack upon Arriaga originated in a controversy between him and the Bishop of Cuzco. The cleavage between these two was so profound that on one occasion Arriaga was excommunicated for a two month period. Arriaga had accused the Bishop of conspiring to stir up Indian unrest and some persons believed that Arriaga had been imprisoned on the orders of the bishop. Túpac Amaru later laid the blame for the attack upon the bishop.

But Túpac also had motives for attacking the corregidor. Arriaga not only abused Indians; he dealt with persons from all classes in an arrogant manner. He resented the respect accorded the cacique and interpreted Túpac's most innocent gestures as attempts to usurp power. He had called Túpac a "fraudulent Indian," and Túpac is reported to have said, "Very soon the corregidor will pay me for this insult."[25]

No one could have forseen, however, that an attack on a corregidor would produce a general insurrection such as engulfed the Viceroyalty of Peru from 1780 to 1783. November 4, 1780, the day of the "Grito de Tinta," is an important date in the Latin American independence movement. On that date, Túpac Amaru and corregidor Arriaga were guests in the home of José Gabriel's former tutor, Dr. Rodríguez, the cura of Yanaoca. Túpac excused himself early on the pretext of having an unexpected visitor. With a small band of followers, he waited in ambush for Arriaga on the road to Tinta, seized him, and conveyed him to Tungasuca. There he held him incommunicado. The imprisoned corregidor was forced to sign an order releasing funds in the public treasury to Túpac Amaru and a letter that summoned all the inhabitants of the area to assemble in Tungasuca. Both these extraordinary measures were based on an allegation that English pirates were about to invade Peru!

With this authority Túpac Amaru collected over 22,000 pesos, a small store of muskets, horses, mules, and other supplies. More important for his purposes, however, was the crowd that assembled in Tungasuca, called together unwittingly to witness the execution of the corregidor. Arriaga was given a rudimentary trial, but when Túpac was confronted with an appeal to spare the corregidor's life, he replied that he had an order for the death penalty from a "higher authority" and that his responsibility was to carry out that order.

He later admitted he had no such order. Perhaps, since false edicts had often been circulated to support illegal acts of exploitation of the Indians, Túpac may have reasoned that his false claim of authority was justified in achieving the opposite objective. Or he may simply have presumed, as Means suggests, that Arriaga's crimes placed him outside the law so that anyone might kill him in accordance with the "higher" natural law.[26] Such thinking might have well resulted from an oversimplification of the natural law concepts that he had heard discussed in the Jesuit College in Cuzco.

On November 10, six days after his capture, Antonio de Arriaga was publicly executed. Túpac Amaru had chosen the time and circumstances. All details of the execution were carefully arranged to give legitimacy to the sentence as well as to set the stage for a revolutionary proclamation. A scaffold was constructed in the main square of Tungasuca and the Inca's followers were ranged about it armed with muskets, pikes, and treble loaded slings.[27] Before the execution Túpac addressed the assembled crowd in Quechua, explaining the crimes for which Arriaga was being punished. He also outlined his own plans, declaring a royal order gave him authority to reform the corregimientos and to seize, try, and punish corregidors and their aides. He promised to abolish the *mita*, to alleviate other abusive forms of forced labor, to suppress the corregidor's monopoly of trade, and to lessen the most exacting tax burdens. He called upon those present to join him and passed out the silver that had been confiscated, two reales to each Indian and four to each Spaniard. The people proclaimed him their Liberator and pledged their lives to him. Several days later, Novermber 26, 1780, he issued a proclamation of emancipation to include all slaves. Most of the Negro slaves were concentrated in the coastal area, however, and were probably unaware of the promised freedom.[28]

Arriaga was given a funeral with appropriate rites the next day and was buried at the Church of Tungasuca.[29] After the funeral, Túpac Amaru sent out proclamations to caciques and other leaders in the surrounding area calling for their support. He also traveled to many towns to address crowds that awaited his arrival. Obviously, he was building up his following chiefly among the Indians, yet he also seemed to be seeking the support of Spaniards and criollos. He called on the people to punish other corregidors and he constantly spoke of his devotion to the King and to the Church.

All the writers on Túpac mention a persistent myth, perhaps dating from the sixteenth century, of a temple inscription in Cuzco predicting that the Incas would one day regain control of their kingdom with the aid of the English. This myth may have circulated at the time of the Túpac rebellion with British encouragement, for Britain was at war with Spain. Or it may simply have been circulated clandestinely, possibly through criollo Masonic circles, possibly even by disgruntled Jesuits, to make capital of the obvious potentialities of the war situation by holding out the possibility of British support. Túpac may have included the reference to British pirates in the letters Arriaga was forced to sign as a means to capitalize on this myth. Daniel Valcárcel refers to documents dealing with the rebellion that mention possible British participation, one from a Masonic source and one from a priest. The possibility that British agents encouraged the rebellion is an interesting one for further study, but all that can be said at present is that proof is lacking.[30]

The insurrection spread rapidly. By mid-November (1780) the rebellion had 6,000 recruits, although only 300 muskets with which to arm them. The authorities in Cuzco, after learning of Arriaga's execution, dispatched a royalist force of some 600 Spaniards and 700 loyal Indians under the command of Tiburcio Landa to quell the rebellion. On November 17, these loyalist forces camped outside of the town of Sangararâ, some 15 miles from Tinta, with the apparent intent of attacking the insurgents the next day. But the Inca discovered their plans and attacked them while they were still asleep in the early morning, forcing them to take refuge in the church of Sangararâ with other inhabitants of the town.

Although eyewitness accounts from that point on differ, it seems clear that Túpac Amaru called on Landa to surrender and that Landa refused. A letter was then sent to the priest, ordering him to dispose of the sacrament and vacate the church. When the priest did not reply, Túpac called on the criollos and women to leave the church. But they did not leave, perhaps because stones and other missiles being thrown against the church made it dangerous if not impossible for them to do so. It is not certain that the Inca then ordered the destruction of the church; he claimed that he did not. But an explosion occurred within the church, the royalist troops fired a canon that killed a number of Indians near Túpac Amaru, and his followers responded by setting fire to the building. Almost 600 persons who had sought refuge within the church perished either in the fire or upon trying to leave; the only survivors were 28 wounded men whom Túpac Amaru ordered set free after treating their wounds.[31]

After the victory of Sangararâ, Túpac returned to Tungasuca. In a letter to Bishop Moscoso, written there, he explained why he had executed Arriaga and attacked the royalist troops sent against him. He asked for pardon on the natural law grounds that "seeking relief from oppression was not opposing God." Since Bishop Moscoso is said to have spoken of Arriaga's fate with two officials in Cuzco on the very day it occurred, it may be assumed that he had prior knowledge of Túpac Amaru's plans. But he had taken no steps to save the corregidor and did not even inform the Viceroy of Arriaga's death until a week later, on November 17. If the Bishop was involved in the action against Arriaga, as seems likely, he probably did not expect the rebellion to spread beyond Tinta. Now that it had done so he probably feared the consequences of his complicity, and particularly that it would be reported to higher authorities. Whatever the reason, he now turned against Túpac Amaru and excommunicated him for attacking Sangararâ, "for profaning its church, for being a traitor to the King and a revolutionist, and for usurping royal authority." The edict of excommunication, posted throughout the province of Cuzco, also threatened the excommunication of Túpac's followers.

After Sangarará, panic and confusion spread in Cuzco. The victory had inspired thousands to join the Inca's ranks. By early December he claimed 60,000 followers, while only 3,000 volunteers had rallied to the city's defense. In Lima, Viceroy Augustín Jáuregui sensed the seriousness of the insurrection and issued a proclamation against Túpac Amaru. He also dispatched several hundred troops to Cuzco. To quell the spirit of unrest he ordered the abolition of the corregidor's trade privileges and placed the corregidors on fixed salaries. The frightened Cuzco cabildo had already declared the abolition of the corregidor's trade monopolies and of the tributes. The fact that these actions were taken without waiting for royal orders suggests the seriousness of the crisis. It is doubtful, however, that Túpac's followers even learned of these actions of the viceroy and of the Cuzco cabildo before the rebellion was over, or that they would have believed them had they heard of them.[32]

As Túpac travelled through the area south of Cuzco, he received almost daily messages from Micaela urging him to invade Cuzco before the forces there became strong enough to resist him. Convinced by his wife, he began a march on Cuzco on December 19. This first attack was a stand off, and Túpac withdrew to Tinta to reorganize his forces. The withdrawal proved to be an error, however, giving his enemy time to get reinforcements from Lima and recruits from other provinces. The second attack, on January 8–10, 1781, was also indecisive. Again Túpac retreated to Tinta, where he remained throughout February. On both occasions he seemed to wish to avoid an all-out attack. Whatever his objective may have been, and his reasoning is far from clear, he sacrificed any advantage of surprise by waiting outside Cuzco for days while dispatching ultimatums to the city and proclamations to other provinces. On both occasions his withdrawal seems to have had no other effect than to strengthen the position of the defending forces.[33]

On February 23, 1781, the Spanish Visitador, José de Areche, arrived at Cuzco. He was accompanied by the Spanish General Del Valle, who took command of royalist forces numbering some 15,000 and including loyal Indians and some Negroes. Túpac Amaru now addressed to Areche a conciliatory letter saying that he had avoided the occupation of Cuzco to prevent unnecessary bloodshed. Appealing for justice for the Indians, he declared he would take no further action until receiving Areche's reply. Areche's answer was brutal. Even General Del Valle later protested its tone, saying that if Areche had been more moderate in his reply some later misfortunes could have been avoided.[34]

The royalist troops moved against the Inca's forces in early March 1781.

By April 6, the superiority of Spanish weapons and the failure of Túpac Amaru to use to advantage his major asset, the mobility of his poorly armed troops, combined to bring about the Inca's defeat. After several skirmishes in the Vilcamayu Valley, the rebels were pushed back on Tinta. There they were finally defeated on April 6. Túpac Amaru and his family escaped from Tinta to take refuge in a mountain hideout. But their hideout was soon betrayed. On the day of their capture, 67 of Túpac's followers that were previously captured, were hanged in Tinta. Their heads, displayed on poles along the route over which the prisoners were led, were a macabre warning of the fate awaiting the leader.

Túpac Amaru, some of his officers, his wife Micaela, two of their sons, and other relatives were paraded into Cuzco as prisoners. There they were separated, not to meet again until the day of their execution; they were tortured to exact confessions of accomplices.[35] Convicted of treason, they were sentenced to cruel forms of death. On the execution day, May 18, 1781, Visitador Areche visited Túpac Amaru early in the morning, still hoping to persuade the rebel to name his accomplices. To Areche's question, Túpac Amaru replied: "We two are the only conspirators: You, Your Honor, for having exhausted the country with unbearable exactions, and I for having wished to free the country from that very tyranny."[36]

The Inca was forced to watch the executions of his wife, his eldest son, and other members of his family. Then he was executed brutally as his ten-year-old son Fernando watched. First his tongue was torn out, and then he was pulled to pieces by four horses. After his body was burned, parts of his remains were distributed among various villages to be displayed on poles. A series of Draconian edicts followed. They forbade the use of Quechua speech in public and ordered the destruction of all "dramas," folk-tales, pictures, and books preserving the memory of ancient days, and of all objects pertaining to Túpac Amaru.[37]

The rebellion inspired by Túpac Amaru did not end with the brutal executions at Cuzco, but became increasingly violent during the months that followed. La Paz was twice besieged by an army of Indians under Julián Apaca, who had adopted the name Túpaj Katari.[38] It is estimated that this siege cost the lives of 40,000 Indians and 20,000 Spaniards and mestizos. After La Paz was liberated the insurrection lost momentum, although it continued for several years in some regions. Except for a few centers, such as Cochabamba, Sucre, Buenos Aires, and Lima, most of the interior of Spanish South America was in revolt between 1780 and 1783. To the south of Cuzco, Puno and Oruro, as well as La Paz, were major centers of the rebellion. To the north, in the viceroyalty of New

Granada, the insurrection of the so-called *comuneros*, in protest against increased taxes, was led by revolutionary juntas whose members were in direct communication with Túpac Amaru. Like some of the others, this revolt of the *comuneros* continued after Túpac's death. Abortive attempts at rebellion also occurred in Venezuela, Panama, and Chile during 1781.[39]

To pacify the rebel population, the Viceroy, Augustín Jáuregui, issued a general pardon in September, 1781. Diego Cristóbal, Mariano Túpac Amaru, Andrés Mendagure, and other members of Túpac Amaru's family who had managed to escape capture accepted the offer and surrendered. Diego Cristóbal took the oath of fidelity on January 26, 1782. His lead was followed by some 30,000 Indians and by other members of Túpac Amaru's family. Some relatives, including Juan Bautista, who had been imprisoned since early in the revolt, were permitted to return to their homes.

At first these relatives were treated well, but another Indian uprising in January of 1783 brought further punitive action against them. By April of that year most of the relatives of the Inca had been captured and imprisoned; on July 17, 1783, they were sentenced. Diego Cristóbal, who had watched his mother hung and burned, was now hung and quartered along with other relatives. Lesser offenders were strangled. Mariano and Andrés were condemned to prison in Spain and are presumed to have died at sea on their way there.

Some ninety men and women, relatives by blood or by marriage, were sent by ship to Spain via Cape Horn. Half the prisoners died before reaching Rio de Janeiro. Most of those who survived the voyage to Spain died there in prison. Fernando, the cacique's youngest son, was released from prison in 1789, however. Suffering from melancholia, he is reported to have died at the age of 26. Only Juan Bautista survived to return to the New World after forty years in exile. In Argentina, where he spent his last years, he wrote his memoirs, entitled *Forty Years of Captivity*. There he met the leader of independence, José de San Martín, who embraced the Francisco Miranda proposal for an independent Spanish American monarchy under an "Inca." Juan Bautista died at the age of eighty-five in Argentina.

The rebellion of Túpac caused great concern in Spanish officialdom. In America it was chiefly the Indians who were punished for the rebellion, but in peninsular Spain the colonial administrators themselves were judged. As Lillian Fisher has observed, all persons associated with the uprising or its repression were held accountable for their actions, and "no one directly or indirectly involved—neither Spanish officials nor churchmen—escaped censure." Visitador Areche, for example, was found "guilty of misconduct, malicious, lacking in the propriety which the laws demanded, and no longer fit to serve the King."[40]

Moreover, while the rebellion of Túpac Amaru was cruelly suppressed, many of the reforms it sought were instituted shortly thereafter by the new Viceroy, Teodoro de Croix. The abuses of the *mita* were tempered, corrupt officials were removed, the corregidors were replaced by intendants, and a separate audiencia was established in Cuzco. Viceroy de Croix was an enlightened and competent administrator and these reforms made Spanish rule more palatable. But the very nature of the larger revolt said something about a developing consciousness on the part of the Indians, mestizos, and *criollos*. Túpac Amaru had been unable to make a common cause with the Peruvian criollos, even though he got support from the criollo *comuneros* in New Granada. The Grito de Tinta, however, sparked a movement which was later to continue under criollo auspices in Peru until the completion of independence at Ayacucho some forty-four years later. In a very real sense, therefore, this revolt of the last Inca "marked the beginning of the end of Spanish colonial Peru."[41]

NOTES

1. Phillip Ainsworth Means, "The Rebellion of Túpac Amaru II, 1780–1781," *Hispanic American Historical Review*, Vol. II, No. 1 (February, 1919), pp. 1–25, at p. 9; Salvador de Madariaga, *The Fall of the Spanish American Empire*, rev. ed. (New York: Collier Books, 1963) p. 132.

2. Lillian Estelle Fisher, *The Last Inca Revolt, 1780–1783* (Norman, Oklahoma: University of Oklahoma Press, 1966), p. ix.

3. Fisher, *op. cit.*, p. 35.

4. Sir Clements R. Markham, *A History of Peru* (New York: Greenwood Press, 1968. Reprint from 1892), p. 195.

5. Fisher, *op. cit.*, p. 35; Daniel Valcarcel, *La rebelión de Túpac Amaru* (México: Fondo de Cultura Económica, 1947), p. 23.

6. Boleslao Lewin, *La insurreccion de Túpac Amaru*, 2nd ed. (Buenos Aires: Eudeba Editorial Universitaria de Buenos Aires, 1967). This work is a short and popular version of the author's previous studies of Tupac Amaru.

7. *Ibid.*, pp. 20–21.

8. Fisher, *op. cit.*, p. 384. Lewin, *op. cit.* p. 21.

9. Lewin, *loc. cit.*

10. Valcárcel, *op. cit.*, p. 25.

11. Markham, *op. cit.*, pp. 195–196; Lewin, *op. cit.*, p. 26.

12. Fisher, *op. cit.*, p. 30.

13. Means, *op. cit.*, p. 14; Fisher, *op. cit.*, p. 26.

14. Fisher, *op. cit.*, p. 27, gives these dates. Daniel Valcárcel, *op. cit.*, p. 23, gives the birth dates for the last two as 1762 and 1768.

15. Means, *op. cit.*, p. 15.

16. Fisher, *op. cit.*, p. 30.

17. Valcárcel, *op. cit.*, p. 23; Lewin, *op. cit.*, p. 18; Fisher, *op. cit.*, p. 27.
18. Markham, *op. cit.*, p. 196.
19. Charles Gibson, *The Inca Concept of Sovereignty and the Spanish Administration in Peru* (Austin: Univeristy of Texas Press, 1948), pp. 91, 98.
20. Means, *op. cit.*, pp. 10–11.
21. Fisher, *op. cit.*, p. 31.
22. *Diccionario Kechuwa-Español*, por Jorge Lira (Tucumán, Argentina: Universidad Nacional, 1944); Fisher, *op. cit.*, p. 32; Lewin, *op. cit.*, p. 106; and Emilio de Solar, *Insurreccion de Túpac Amaru, sus antecedentes y efectos* (Lima: Casa Editora "La Opinion Nacional," 1926), p. 53; Lewin, *op. cit.*, pp. 106ff.
23. Lewin, *op. cit.*, pp. 13–14; Fisher, *op. cit.*, p. 13.
24. Fisher, *op. cit.*, pp. 33–35.
25. Fisher, *op. cit.*, pp. 20, 38, 39, 42, 43.
26. Means, *op. cit.*, p. 17.
27. Markham, *op, cit.*, p. 198.
28. Markham, *op. cit.*, loc. cit.; Fisher, *op. cit.*, p. 48; Juan José Vega, *José Gabriel Túpac Amaru* (Lima: Editorial Universo, 1969), pp. 55–57.
29. Fisher, *op. cit.*, p. 48.
30. Valcárel, *op. cit.*, p. 42; Fisher, *op. cit.*, pp. 50, 115; Lewin, *op. cit.*, pp. 22–23.
31. Fisher, *op. cit.*, p. 103.
32. Fisher, *op. cit.*, pp. 104, 108; Means, *op. cit.*, p. 19.
33. Valcárcel, *op. cit.*, pp. 68–73.
34. Fisher, *op. cit.*, p. 133.
35. Markham, *op. cit.*, p. 205.
36. Lewin, *op. cit.*, p. 28.
37. Means, *op. cit.*, p. 21.
38. Markham, *op. cit.*, p. 208; Fisher, *op. cit.*, p. 240, Augusto Guzmán has written a fascinating novelized biography, *Tupaj Katari* (México: Fondo de Cultura Económica, 1944).
39. Fisher, *op. cit.*, p. 343.
40. Fisher, *op. cit.*, pp. 384–385.
41. *Ibid.*, p. 241.

BIBLIOGRAPHY

The works by Lewin, Valcárcel, and Fisher, referred to in footnotes, are the most useful sources on Túpac Amaru. Juan Bautista Túpac Amaru, *Cuarenta años de cautiverio, Memorias del Inka Juan Bautista Túpac Amaru*; Notas, comentarios y adiciones de documentos inéditos por Francisco A. Loayza; Prólogo de Carlos A. Romero (Lima: Los Pequeños Grandes Libros de Historia Americana, Serie I, Tomo I; Lib. e Imp. D. Miranda, 1941) has special value as a contemporary account, as does the anonymous *La verdad desnuda*, written in 1780, cited in the text; and a three-volume work, written in 1786 by Melchor de Paz, *Guerra separatista, Rebeliones de Indios en Sud América: La sublevación de Túpac Amaru*; con apostillas a la obra de Melchor de Paz por Luis Antonio Eguiguren (Lima: Imprenta Torres Aguirre, S.A., 1952), of which the author found only the first two volumes. Original documents are woven into the text of Jorge Cornejo Bouroncle, *Túpac Amaru; La revolución precursora de la emancipación continental* (Cuzco: Ediciones de la Universidad Nacional del Cuzco: Edit. H.G. Rozas, S.A., 1963), 649pp. A recent study by Juan José Vega, *José Gabriel Túpac Amaru* (Lima: Editorial Universo, 1969), presents some novel interpretations of the relationship of Túpac Amaru to the black population of Peru and to Negro emancipation.

4

JUAN GERMAN ROSCIO (1769–1821)

Like a number of others who might have been but are not treated in this all too short volume, Roscio was fundamentally an intellectual rebel. What distinguishes him from many of the others is that he translated his theoretical ideas into action. He has been called the jurist of Venezuelan independence, and the validity of this title is borne out by his published *Works* as recently edited by the Spanish-Venezuelan scholar, Pedro de Grases. Though seemingly incomplete, especially for the early years of his life, these *Works* constitute one of the most intelligible and impressive records we have of the evolution of independence thought. In them Roscio himself has described this evolution, showing the impact of Enlightenment thought, including the Spanish traditionalist contribution to these currents, upon his evolution from a student of canon and civil law to a republican revolutionist.

His record gives added proof to a fact too often overlooked, at least by foreign scholars—that Caracas and its university had become a center of a remarkably live intellectual life by the end of the eighteenth century. The fact that Roscio was a friend and collaborator of Francisco Miranda and Simón Bolívar, enjoying their intellectual respect, illustrates another aspect of this colonial intellectual life. As a product of Church controlled higher education in Venezuela, Roscio shows that the university was producing well educated criollo leaders who found in Christian doctrine, as well as in the more secular natural law concepts of the Enlightenment, the ideological basis for national independence and even for republicanism. He appears briefly as a revolutionary leader, but his greater significance lies in his contribution to the theory and ideology of Spanish American independence. Even more specifically his writing is important as an expression of the influence of Spanish traditionalism in the thought of the Spanish and Spanish-American Enlightenment and in the independence movement.[1]

As the author of the 1811 document declaring the independence of Venezuela "from Spain and any other foreign domination," Roscio was a revolutionary. The Venezuelan Declaration, like that of the United States, was formulated as a "manifesto to the world," stating the reasons for independence in natural law terms. But it also contained an element of Spanish scholastic and traditionalist thought, seeking the basis of the right of rebellion in a concept of social contract expressed in a traditional Spanish code, the *Siete Partidas* of Alfonso the Wise, and in the sixteenth century natural law doctrines of the Dominican Francisco Vitoria and the Jesuit Francisco Suárez. For Roscio, the war for independence was a civil war in which the Venezuelans defended the cause of legitimacy against the usurping Regency Council in Spain. In a speech to the Venezuelan Congress, June 25, 1811, he stated clearly his theory of the right of revolution. Basically it was the sixteenth century natural law theory of Francisco Súarez, but it also showed the influence of Rousseau and of Locke or Hobbes. Ferdinand, by his abdication had turned over his American subjects to the mercies of Napoleon said Roscio, and thus had lost his right to their loyalty.[2]

Several years later, in his *Triumph of Liberty over Despotism*, published in Philadelphia (in Spanish) in 1817, Roscio wrote one of the most thorough expositions of Spanish American independence thought. He was clearly committed to republicanism at this date, but his thought still bore marks of the Spanish scholastic traditionalism of his early formation.[3]

Juan Germán Roscio was born, May 27, 1763, in San Francisco de Tiznados, Province of Caracas, in present-day Venezuela. Cristobal Roscio, his father, was an immigrant from Milan, Italy. His mother, Paula María Nieves, came from a mestizo family of San Francisco, a family of at least modest means. For his early education he was sent to Caracas and entrusted to the direction of Dona María de la Paz Pacheco, daughter of the Count of San Javier, whose philanthropic care provided for the education of a select number of promising young students. In Caracas he studied in the Tridentine Seminary, from which he graduated in 1792. Two years later he received a doctorate in canon law and in 1800 a doctorate in civil law from the University of Caracas.

Meanwhile, his outstanding scholarship had been recognized in 1798 by an appointment to a professorship of civil law, a chair that included instruction in natural law as well, two years before receiving his degree in the material. But admission to the College of Lawyers, recently organized under a royal charter, was a requirement for the practice of the legal profession, and here he encountered opposition. He was refused at first on the grounds that he had not shown the *limpieza de sangre* (purity of race) required under the charter—a provision requiring proof that "parents and paternal and maternal grandparents have been old Christians, clear *(limpios)* of all evil race *(mala raza)* of Negroes, mulattoes, or other such, and with no note of moors, jews, or recent converts to our Holy Catholic Faith. . . ." The objection was obviously directed against his mestiza mother, hinting at her African ancestry. Roscio was able to demonstrate that both of his parents had proved *limpieza de sangre*, and that in any case Indians and Spanish-Indian mestizos did not fall within this legal ban. But he never forgot this insult to his family.

The more serious obstacle then presented to his admission was based on the "subversive, heretical, sacrilegious" views he had expressed in a paper addressed to the municipal council of Valencia, defending Isabel María Páez against the charge that she had illegally used a prayer rug in church, a privilege limited to upper class criollos. This paper, unfortunately, is not published in the *Obras* of Roscio, presumably because it is lost. But the language of the charges against him show quite clearly that he defended Señora Páez, a mestiza, on Christian natural law grounds that denied any basis for the racial and class prejudice expressed in regulations such as she was charged with disobeying. The importance of these charges must be seen in the light of the recently suppressed republican and independence conspiracy in Venezuela. This conspiracy, headed by Manuel Gual and José María España in 1798, was inspired by a group of Spanish political exiles, condemned for their participation in the pro-French and republican San Blas conspiracy in Spain, who had been landed in La Guaira on their way to imprisonment in various places in America.

Roscio successfully defended himself against these charges, as well, and no evidence was produced to show that he was really a revolutionary at this time. August Mijares concludes that Roscio was not a revolutionary then and that he had no direct connection with the supporters of Gual and España, despite certain resemblances of their ideas to those Roscio had expressed in defending Isabel María Páez. Later, in a letter to Francisco de Paula Santander written in 1820, Roscio spoke of himself as having been "servile" in the old Spanish administration, defending the rule of Carlos IV. Even as late as the revolutionary movement of 1808, when news of Napoleon's invasion of Spain arrived, he did not appear openly in support of those who advocated independence, although his writings give some evidence that he sympathized with the movement. Later he came to believe that this was the time when independence should have been declared.

His action as a revolutionary first appeared clearly in 1810 when he and others entered the meeting of the Cabildo of Caracas as it was considering the new crisis arising from the defeat of the Spanish forces opposing

Napoleon. He and his friends opposed accepting the call for loyalty to the Council of Regency that had taken refuge in the Isle of León. Roscio was the spokesman and the intellectual leader of these self-proclaimed "deputies of the people" and he continued to play those roles during the following months of intense revolutionary activity. He was a member of the *junta* that took over the government of the Captaincy-general of Venezuela and was named Secretary for Foreign Relations. Soon thereafter he was put in charge of all the ministries of the revolutionary government. In this capacity he drafted the major public papers of the new regime, including regulations for the election of the first Venezuelan Congress.

Elected a deputy to this Congress from Calabozo, he participated actively in its deliberations. His role was particularly notable in presenting cogent arguments, both political and constitutional, for declaring Venezuelan independence. The pledges of loyalty given to King Ferdinand in 1808 and 1810 were a great mistake, he urged. "There is no doubt," he said to Congress on July 5, 1811, "that it is the work of God that America should begin to take its place *(figurar)* in the world." Nor should Venezuelans wait for the assurance of an alliance with Britain. In 1810 Venezuelans simply told the British what had been done; the same course should now be followed, he urged. The international situation, he believed, was not what stood in the way of independence; the real obstacle was in Venezuela herself.[4]

After the Congress decided for independence, on July 5, 1811, Roscio and the Secretary of the Congress, Francisco Isnardy, were given the task of drawing up what became Venezuela's "Manifesto to the World . . . of the Reasons on Which it Has Based its Absolute Independence from Spain and from Any Other Foreign Domination." Roscio is the acknowledged author of this document that fills forty-two pages in his *Obras.*[5]

The North American reader may find Roscio's document lacking in that rare quality of condensation in which every word carries a new meaning, the quality that makes Thomas Jefferson's much briefer Declaration a universally recognized literary masterpiece. But in its own way that of Roscio is a worthy successor to the U.S. Declaration, and in one major respect it surpasses the U.S. Declaration. For it is on the whole a sober, carefully analyzed examination of the sequence of events beginning with the involvement of the Spanish court and Ferdinand in the agreement under which Napoleon entered Portugal, driving the Portuguese Court to Brazil. This history Roscio presents as a breach of natural law and of the social contract, not only that of the people of Spain with the Bourbon monarchs, but also that between the people of America and their monarchs.

The critical student, while recognizing that Roscio's theoretical basis, like that of Jefferson in his masterpiece, is a social contract theory, will see that the peculiarly pragmatic character of the Venezuelan reflects the Spanish legal tradition as well as Spanish scholastic traditionalism in legal and political theory. He will also find in Roscio's work one of the best contemporary analyses of the effects of European developments of the era upon the Spanish American independence movement.

Roscio also participated with Francisco Javier de Ustáriz, Gabriel de Ponte, and Isnardy in drawing up the first constitution of Venezuela. He was a member of the triumvirate executive provided for under this overly liberal and federal constitution, and in this capacity helped to direct the short-lived First Republic. When the Republic was overthrown a few months later, after the debacle under Francisco Miranda, Roscio and other leaders capitulated, were imprisoned, and were sent to Spain in chains. Imprisoned in Ceuta, he escaped to British controlled Gibraltar in 1814. There he was at first turned over to Spanish authorities; but in 1815 he was released from prison upon British demand. In 1816 we find him in Jamaica and in touch with Bolívar concerning the latter's plans to renew the war for independence. From Jamaica he went to New Orleans and from New Orleans to Philadelphia. One of his biographers (Ramón Azpurúa) says he left Jamaica because he disagreed with Bolívar's political ideas, but this is far from certain. In Philadelphia, as noted, he published his *Triumph of Liberty over Despotism* in 1817.

This work, an all too little recognized classic of the Spanish American independence movement, deserves further notice here as a statement of the theory of that revolutionary movement by one of its keenest intellectual leaders. One may dismiss Roscio's bequeathal of this work in his 1817 will to the cause of independence as a romantic gesture. But the number of editions through which it went is in itself a measure of its importance to the cause of independence, as is the fact of its being burned by the public hangman in Caracas. It is rewarding reading for any serious student of the history of Spanish American independence, and especially important for students of Spanish American intellectual history.

Its autobiographical and apologetic tone may mislead the casual reader. Roscio states in the *Prologo* that his book is a "confession" of "political errors." But it soon appears that this "confession" is only a rhetorical or literary device for presenting his ideas. Spanish religious tradition gives special poignancy to such a "confession of errors," making it an effective vehicle for presenting ideas that are based as largely as those of Roscio are upon Christian concepts of natural law, supported by examples from the Bible.

Man is naturally free, he wrote, because Adam was created in the image of God. Roscio often refers with approval to Rousseau's concept of the social contract; but Roscio's version of the contract is one more traditionally Christian than that of Rousseau, one in which natural law is the perfect reason of God, the first principle of all things. Only within this natural law is the authority of government legitimate, whatever its form. Following his rhetorical device, he "confesses" to have once held the false belief that sovereign power resided only in the monarch. Now, he says, he sees that sovereign power rests in the people because man, created by God, is a natural sovereign.

Although he once believed that punishment for the violation of natural law should be left to God, Roscio goes on, he has now come to see that when God's natural law is violated man has the right to use force against force. To repel force with force is a natural right and in some cases it is a duty. Here we have the basis of Roscio's theory of the right and duty of revolution. "Any popular movement," he writes, "or that of persons capable of saving the people from oppression . . . will be meritorious and glorious whenever it is directed toward breaking the yoke of tyranny, toward recovering national independence and liberty. . . ."

In the scholastic tradition within which Roscio moved and thought, such ideas lead naturally to a theory of the right of regicide and tyrannicide, as given classical form in the writings of Francisco Suárez. Roscio indicates the importance of this theme of tyrannicide in his thought by devoting to it three chapters of his book.[6] In these chapters, too, the basis of the argument is biblical. He first cites the example of Moses, following this example with those of Joshua and other great figures of the Old Testament, including notable women tyrannicides. These chapters constitute one of the notable Spanish-American expressions of a theory of tyrannicide, a revolutionary concept that is more common in the Spanish American revolutionary literature than in that of French or English America. These latter tend to give greater emphasis to the idea of submitting the tyrant to legal process. Spanish Americans, it must of course be added, also urge this legal process. In some respects they go further in their constitutions than their British and French contemporaries in providing for the trial of presidents who have acted arbitrarily, after their terms of office have expired. But the writing of Spanish Americans on this topic of tyrannicide has given a distinctive characteristic to their political thought that is not duplicated in other parts of America.

When Roscio approached the controversial question of Negro slavery and emancipation, he turned again to the Bible for his arguments. Commenting upon Saint Paul's well-known advice to servants to obey their masters, he pointed out that to Christians this obedience must be understood as obedience in accordance with natural, that is to say Divine, law. According to natural law the master has only the right to command what is just. In the Hebrew tradition, as Roscio pointed out, servitude was limited to six years and was carefully surrounded with provisions for the protection of the rights of the servant. Moses rose to leadership by avenging the maltreatment of Hebrew slaves in Egypt. Roscio concluded this discussion of Old Testament precedents with the revolutionary observation (for the slave owning society of Venezuela) that both Christian doctrine and natural law forbade slavery. Saint Paul and Saint Peter temporized on this question, he believed, only because they did not wish to involve themselves in questions of political reform unconnected with their apostolate. The apostles could not have approved chattel slavery, because it was contrary to the law of nature. This discussion of slavery concludes with congratulations to Great Britain for her leadership in abolishing the international slave trade. "A thousand thanks to the English nation because it has taken in charge the abolition of this inhuman commerce." It is interesting that, although Roscio was publishing this book in Philadelphia, he did not even mention the simultaneous action of the United States in abolishing the international slave trade. Was this because he saw that slavery still existed in many parts of the United States?[7]

Roscio returned to Venezuela in 1818, in time to participate the following year in the Congress of Angostura that drew up the constitution of the indepenent Colombia (Gran Colombia). Bolívar, under whose leadership the new republic was established, had always recognized the intellectual pre-eminence of Roscio and this respect was mutual. Although Roscio had been a major author of the federalist constitution of the first republic, and thus had differed earlier with Bolivar on federalism, he now accepted the Bolivarian concept of a more highly centralized Gran Colombia with a unipersonal executive. Elected vice-president for Venezuela, he served in this capacity, and for a time as vice-president for the whole republic, until his death two years later. He remained in Angostura, in charge of the government, until the transfer of the seat of government to Bogotá in 1821. In that year he composed the last public paper that appears in his *Obras*, a proclamation to the people of Cúcuta, February 15, 1821, announcing the extension of the Colombian constitution to include New Granada after the patriot victory in the Battle of Boyacá. Roscio was to have been the president of the Congress that assembled in Cúcuta to effect this extension of Gran Colombia, but died on March 10, 1821, before the Congress assembled.

Two years before his death, at the age of fifty, he had married. There were no children of this marriage. Rather, the progeny of this illustrious Venezuelan revolutionary were the ideas that joined the Spanish scholastic and Christian tradition with the newly vital concept of the nation-republic.

NOTES

1. Augusto Mijares, "Prólogo," in Juan Germán Roscio, *Obras*. Compilación de Pedro Grases. 3 vols. (Caracas: Xa Conferencia Inter-americana, 1953) I, xi–xcviii. See also Enrique de Gandía, *Historia de las ideas políticas en la Argentina* (Buenos Aires: Depalma, 1960 —) V, chs. 34–36; and O. Carlos Stoetzer, *El pensamiento político en la América Española durante el período de la emancipación, 1789–1825*, 2 v. (Madrid: *Instituto de Estudios Políticos*, 1966).
2. The speech is in the *Obras*, II, 23–25.
3. *El Triunfo de la libertad sobre el despotismo*. Six editions had been published by mid-nineteenth century, three in Philadelphia and three in Mexico. The second edition, by M. Carey e hijos, Philadelphia, 1821, is included in Volume I of the *Obras*, pp. 1–489.
4. *Obras*, II, 23–36.
5. *Obras*, II, 41–83.
6. Chapters 45, 47, and 48.
7. *Ibid.*, pp. 303–316.

BIBLIOGRAPHY

The best general source on Roscio is the three volume *Obras*, prepared by Pedro Grases, with a Prólogo by Augusto Mijares, and published in Caracas in 1953 under the auspices of the Secretariat of the Tenth Inter-American Conference. Pedro Grases has given a good brief interpretation in *Un hombre del 19 de abril: Juan Germán Roscio* (Caracas, 1952) 16 p. Other useful works include Pedro Grases, *La Conspiración de Gual y España y el Ideario de la Independencia* (Caracas: Comité de Origines de la Emancipación, Instituto Panamericano de Geografía e Historia, 1949); *La colonia y la independencia* (Caracas: by the same Comité, 1949); Hector García Chuecos, "El real e ilustre Colegio de Abogados de Caracas" in his *Relatos y comentarios sobre temas de historia venezolana* (Caracas: Imprenta Nacional, 1957), pp. 164–185; Ramón Azpurúa, *Biografías notables de Hispano-America*, 4v. (Caracas: Imprenta Nacional, 1877); *Diccionario biográfico de Venezuela*. (Madrid: Editores Garrido Mezquita y Compañía, 1953); and José Gil Fortoul, *Historia constitucional de Venezuela*, 3v. (Caracas, 1930).

5

TWO MEXICAN INDEPENDENCE LEADERS: VICENTE GUERRERO (1783–1831) AND JOSE MARIA MORELOS (1765–1814)

Guerrilla warfare and guerrillas are nothing new in the Spanish and Spanish American experience, as has been noted in preceding chapters. The very word, *guerrilla*, seems to have evolved in early nineteenth century Spain and some of the earliest examples of guerrilla activity come from the Spanish American wars for independence and the civil wars that followed.[1] Fundamentally the tactics of irregular warfare employed by these guerrillas of a century and three quarters ago do not seem to have differed in fundamentals from those of the current age. Then as now they avoided pitched battles, concentrating on hit and run tactics. Then as now they relied on the friendliness of the population to provide them with food and to hide them when necessary. They captured their weapons and ammunition from their enemies.

Several of the Mexican independence leaders were such guerrilla leaders. Vicente Guerrero, with the appropriate surname of the warrior *(guerrero)* is an excellent, although a tragic, example. Another was the first president of the republic of Mexico after the overthrow of the Iturbide empire. This was Guadelupe Victoria (Manuel Félix Fernández) (1791–1845). The original movement for Mexican independence, a rebellion of the Indian and mestizo masses, was led by two priests, Miguel Hidalgo and José María Morelos. After the defeat and execution of Morelos in 1815, Guadelupe Victoria, like Guerrero, carried on resistance against Spanish rule as a guerrilla. He later emerged, in alliance with Santa Anna, to overthrow Emperor Augustín Iturbide and to become the first president of republican Mexico.

The second president of republican Mexico, Vicente Guerrero, with whom we are here concerned, is one of the most tragic figures in Mexican history, a history that abounds in TRAGEDY. All that the universally respected and usually informative *Nuevo Larousse Ilustrado* manages to say of him is that he was a "Mexican general and politician, president of the Republic in 1827"! Mexicans do better, having named for him the state in which his military activity centered. His historical reputation is confused by the partisan controversies of the times between the political parties of the the Scottish rite and York rite masons and by the bitter

40

vendettas that brought about his overthrow as president and his subsequent assassination. But the Guerrero record is one that many Mexicans and non-Mexicans believe deserves the highest level of national recognition.

In 1810 he joined José María Morelos, the lieutenant of Miguel Hidalgo, in the successful attack on Tixtla, near Chilpancingo. After Morelos was defeated in 1814 at Valladolid, Guerrero rallied the forces of independence in the essentially Indian area of southern Mexico. There he successfully maintained a guerrilla resistance movement until after the Spanish Revolution of 1820. Then he met with Augustín Iturbide at Iguala and agreed to the latter's plan for organizing Mexico as an independent Catholic monarchy, one in which all Mexicans, as Americans, would have equal rights.

Thereafter Iturbide, in making himself emperor, seems to have double-crossed Guerrero. Later, when the empire of Iturbide was overthrown and a republic established in 1824, Guerrero might have expected to be president. But Santa Anna gave his support to Victoria. Guerrero was thereupon elected vice-president, with Guadalupe Victoria as president.

As vice-president Guerrero was caught up in the conflict between the conservative Scottish rite and the more radical, federalist, and secular York rite masons. He was elected to the presidency in 1828 with Yorkino support, to be overthrown a year after he took office as president by a revolution led by the vice-president, Anastasio Bustamente, a conservative caudillo of the Scottish rite party. When Guerrero put himself at the head of rebellious forces in southern Mexico, his enemies engaged an Italian naval captain and friend of Guerrero, Francisco Picaluga, to lure him aboard his ship *Colombo*, stationed off Mexico's southern coast. Picaluga turned Guerrero over to the Mexican Captain Miguel González, who took him as a prisoner to Oaxaca. There he was shot on February 24, 1831 in Culiapán. The issues involved in Guerrero's tragic end are obscure. They were probably more personal and partisan than anything else, and Guerrero generally emerges in Mexican histories as the victim of partisan strife.

José María Morelos (1765–1814) can only be discussed here briefly, not because of his lack of importance, but because this author has treated him in his *Latin American Leaders*,[2] to which the interested reader is referred. Morelos did not play the role of a guerrilla, although he might well have done so if he had escaped after his defeat at Valladolid (present day Morelia, capital of the state of Michoacán). But he is in fact one of the most important revolutionary leaders in Latin America and a Diego

Rivera mural portrays him carrying a standard reading, *"Paso a la eternidad"* ("I pass to eternity").

Little is known about the family background and origins of Morelos. He was born José María Teclo Morelos y Pavón, September 30, 1765, in the city of Valladolid, the city where he was to meet his ultimate defeat. His father was Manuel Morelos, a carpenter, and his mother was Juana María Pavón, the daughter of a school teacher. José was baptised as the legitimate child of Spanish parents, but the certified *limpieza de sangre* (pure race) in this case, as Mexican historians agree, concealed a mestizo or mulatto parentage.

Left an orphan at an early age, he was brought up by an uncle. His education was meagre since, as he relates, most of his boyhood was spent as a shepherd on a hacienda in Apatzingán. Later he drove mule pack teams between Valladolid, Mexico City, and Acapulco. At an advanced age, he had studied in the seminary at Valladolid presided over by the initiator of Mexican independence, Miguel Hidalgo, and upon graduation became a parish priest.

Morelos was a born leader, displaying an extraordinary capacity to evoke the loyalty of the Indians, negroes, mestizos, and mulattoes of Mexico. But although he was committed to the liberation of these depressed masses, he refused to allow the war for independence to become racial. An illustration of this racial neutrality, frequently cited, was his condemnation to death for treason, at the same time, of a Mexican of African origin, a Spaniard, and a citizen of the United States.

His natural military genius appeared in the campaign he undertook in 1810 in southern Mexico at the direction of Miguel Hidalgo. Hidalgo directed him to capture Acapulco, the major center of the trade with the Orient, and on that basis to organize the independence of all of southern Mexico. The genius of Morelos appeared in the intuitive understanding of the strategic importance of Acapulco that he displayed in his conduct of this military campaign; it appeared even more clearly in his understanding of the key significance of Acapulco for the cause of independence in southern Mexico.

The brave defense of Cuautla (1812) against a much larger loyalist force than his own, and his subsequent brilliant evacuation of that closely besieged city, show him at his best as a military leader. This courageous action at Cuautla will never be forgotten by Mexican historians. His final defeat and capture at Valladolid has sometimes been ascribed to amateurish leadership and to the difficulty he experienced in disciplining his Indian, mestizo, and Negro troops. Viewed in larger perspective, however, this defeat is seen to be more largely due to the turn of events in Europe that had brought Ferdinand VII back to the Spanish throne. Spanish Americans mistakenly assumed that the return of the king they had fondly spoken of as *el deseado*, the desired one, would permit the Spanish world to live under the Liberal constitution of 1812. This was a tragic misconception, as Mexicans were soon to learn. For the time, however, it was a premonition of this coming tragic disillusionment that Morelos was captured and executed. Like Guerrero and such other widely differing independence leaders as Hidalgo and Iturbide, Morelos paid with his life for his temerity in undertaking to lead a rebellion that did not evoke the united support of the ruling criollos.

The concern of Morelos for the revolutionary south of Mexico is a major link with Guerrero, who fought there under Morelos's command and later kept the independence movement alive in the area by guerrilla activity, after Spanish authority was restored in most of the viceroyalty. Both of these leaders, moreover, had links with the popular and ethnic basis of the Hidalgo rebellion that had aroused the subject masses, Indian mestizo, and Negro, of southern Mexico in 1810. Both Morelos and Guerrero enlisted Indian, mestizo, and black soldiers in their armies, to the point where it came to be assumed that the independence armies would be dark skinned. This southern Mexican aspect of rebellion continued to be a political fact in Mexico for several decades thereafter, ultimately producing both the triumph of Juárez and the rise of Porfirio Díaz to power.

Like Morelos, Guerrero was of humble origin, with a dark complexion and the thick lips that suggested negroid ancestry. The son of a poor agricultural worker of Tixtla, near Chilpancingo, he had no formal schooling as a child. Unlike Morelos, he did not seek formal education as an adult and was barely literate. Like Morelos he was a muleteer, often entrusted with such valuable cargo as silver bullion, along the route between Acapulco and Mexico City. He had pride in this work, courage and confidence in his ability to confront difficulties, and an inquisitive mind that led him to query even perfect strangers about the districts they lived in. The detailed knowledge of the Mexican countryside gained in this way was of inestimable value in his later guerrilla activity. Another of his assets was that he had gained the confidence of the Bravo and Galeana landowning families of the area. They furnished him with supplies and recruits, supporting him in his rise to a position of the highest confidence in the ranks of Morelos's army.

Like Morelos, Guerrero had an intuitive sense of strategy, combined with courage and the capacity to lead men. After the defeat of Morelos, and during the dark days of the restoration of Spanish control after 1815, he emerged as the major symbol of the continued drive for Mexican independence, even excelling the popular Guadalupe Victoria in this respect. These two were the major guerrilla leaders who refused the pardon offered to all rebels by the new viceroy, Juan Ruiz de Apodaca, representing the restored King Ferdinand.

Like Morelos, Guerrero suffered from the stigma of his lower class origin and supposed African blood. This appeared in his relations with Ramón Sesma, with whom Guerrero was soon leading a band of a thousand guerrilla warriors in southern Mexico. Sesma was jealous of Guerrero's popularity and showed his prejudice by ordering Guerrero to Tehuacán, with five hundred unarmed men and with a note to his superior, General Juan Nepomuceno Rosainz, to keep a close watch on the *negro*.

Guerrero rose above this racial-class stigma however, one which was not very strong in any case, to become the major independence leader with whom Augustín Iturbide found it necessary to come to terms in 1821. He supported Iturbide until the latter declared himself emperor. Then he joined with Nicolas Bravo and Santa Anna in the movement that brought about Iturbide's overthrow and the establishment of a republic. Guadalupe Victoria's election to the first presidency of the republic, as we have seen, was due in large measure to Santa Anna's support. By the end of Victoria's presidency, however, the Yorkino, anti-clerical, federalist and popular party had gained power to the extent that the the criollo leadership had to accept a political compromise that made Guerrero president and the Scottish rite and centralist Anastasio Bustamente vice president.

The sequel, as we have seen, was a major tragedy of Mexican history—Guerrero's execution by a firing squad after the betrayal by a supposed friend! In his death he joined the select company of Hidalgo, Morelos, Iturbide, and other Mexican patriots who paid with their lives for their dedication to forming the Mexican nation. Does any other modern nation have a more tragic guilt complex in relation to its independence than Mexico has?

NOTES

1. Literally, *guerrilla* means a little war, and the correct Spanish term for a guerrilla leader is *guerrillero*. But the English adaptation of the term (guerrilla) has come to be used generally, and so is used here.
2. See the author's *Latin American Leaders*, pp. 40–47.

BIBLIOGRAPHY

The author has written of Morelos in his *Latin American Leaders*, pp. 40–47. See also Alfonso Teja Zabre, *Morelos* (Buenos Aires: Colección Austral, 1946); Justo Sierra, *Evolución política del pueblo mexicano* (México: Fondo de Cultura Económica, 1940), pp. 169–175; James A. Magner, *Men of Mexico* (Milwaukee, Bruce Publishing Co., 1942), ch. ix; Rubén Hermesdorf, *Morelos, hombre fundamental de México* (México: Ed. Grijalbo, 1958); and Ubaldo Vargas Martínez, *Morelos, siervo de las nación* (México: Ed. Porrúa, 1966).

On Vicente Guerrero see: Manuel García Purón, *México y sus gobernantes* (México: Manuel Porrúa, 1964); J.N. Lagragua, in E.L. Gallo, ed., *Hombres ilustres mexicanos*, 4 v. (México: Imp. de I. Cumplido) IV, 297–378; Lucas Alamán, *Historia de Méjico desde los primeros movimientos que preparon su independencia en el año de 1808 hasta la época presente*, 5 vols. (México: 1849–1852); Antonio Magaña Esquivel, *Vicente Guerrero* (México, 1946); W.R. Sprague, *Vicente Guerrero, Mexican Liberator* (Chicago: R.R. Donnely and Sons, 1939); and Alejandro Villaseñor y Villaseñor, *Biografías de los heroes y caudillos de la independencia*, 2 vols. (México, 1910).

6

TWO PRECURSORS OF THE MEXICAN REVOLUTION: ANTONIO DIAZ SOTO Y GAMA (1880–1967) AND RICARDO FLORES MAGON (1873–1922)

During the last decade of the Porfirio Díaz regime (1900–1910), Mexico produced a vigorous group of intellectuals and activists who were precursors of the revolution to come in 1910. Among this group were journalists, literary critics, artists, lawyers, farmers, engineers, labor organizers, and school teachers. Their political theories covered a wide range, including radical revolutionary anarchism-syndicalism, traditional Liberalism, the moderate humanistic-spiritualism of Francisco Madero and the Bergsonism or neo-Kantian Krausism of others. Some were even developing ideas that led them later to adopt radical rightist political ideologies.

In Mexico City a group of young intellectuals under the leadership of the philosopher Antonio Caso, formed the *Ateneo de la Juventud* (Youth Atheneum). This *Ateneo* included such diverse figures as the lawyer-philosopher-politician, José Vasconcelos, the painter Diego Rivera, and the literary critic Pedro Henríquez Ureña. A number of others, not strictly members of the group, were closely associated with them. Félix F. Palavicini was a prophet of an intellectual revolution to come. The lawyer-school-teacher Luis Cabrera became the author of the original proposal of a national law for *ejido* (communal) land grants and of President Venustiano Carranza's labor and agrarian decrees of 1914–15. Martín Luis Guzmán was to become one of Mexico's great writers and for a time secretary to Pancho Villa. Otilio Montaño helped Emilio Zapata write his revolutionary agrarian reform proposals in the Plan of Ayala of 1911.

Another group, in the city of San Luis Potosí, centered around the Liberal Club Ponciano Arriaga that was named for a nineteenth century Liberal and supported by his wealthy son, Camilo Arriaga. The Mexican Liberal Party, founded in 1905, absorbed this San Luis Potosí group and in some respects grew out of it. After the formation of the Party, the Liberal Club of San Luis Potosí began to move away from its traditional anti-clerical Liberalism toward frank criticism of the social and economic injustices of the Díaz regime. Attacking the monopoly of land ownership and the predominance in Mexico of "money, power, priest, and foreigner," they were soon discussing tactics for the revolution by force that they had come to think was necessary. These young radical intellectuals supported a number of revolutionary causes before the Madero Revolution of 1910, thus earning the right to be called precursors of that movement. Their right to this title appeared most clearly in the support they gave to a peasant uprising in the eastern part of the state of San Luis Potosi in August 1910.

Antonio Díaz Soto y Gama (1880–1967) was one of the ablest among this San Luis Potosí group. During the most violent phase of the Mexican Revolution, a few years after supporting the San Luis Potosí peasants, he shocked the Congress meeting at Aguascalientes (1914) after the overthrow of Victoriano Huerta with a gesture that some contemporary agrarian revolutionaries might envy. Braving the pistols leveled against him in this meeting of armed militants, he crumpled the Mexican flag in his hand, saying it represented "the lie of history" because independence had not been won for the Indian but only for the criollo.

Díaz Soto y Gama's activity in the Liberal Party (1905–1911) led him into the anti-Reelectionist Party *(Partido Nacional Anti-Reelectionista)* that supported Francisco Madero's presidential candidacy in 1910 and 1911. Although he parted company at this time with Ricardo Flores Magón, the anarchist-syndicalist journalist leader of the Liberal Party who joined the I.W.W. in the United States and led an anarchist rebellion in lower California, his personal loyalty to this former colleague made him a link between the mainstream of the Mexican Revolution and the anarchist fringe.

Emerging first as a student leader, Díaz Soto y Gama next became a lawyer who defended the poor and supported radical causes. He was a brilliant writer on labor and agrarian problems. He has been called the Danton of the Mexican Revolution and like his French prototype, was a fiery orator. Like Danton, also, and despite such dramatic gestures as that at Aguascalientes in 1914, he stood between the mainstream of the Mexican Revolution and the more radical and doctrinaire wing led by Ricardo Flores Magón.

Born in San Luis Potosí in 1880, Antonio Díaz Soto y Gama was one of sixteen children. His father Conrado Díaz Soto was a lawyer of anti-clerical Liberal views; his mother, Concepción Gama, was a devout Catholic. Their modest middle class home boasted a portrait of the Liberal president Sebastiano Lerdo de Tejada, and Antonio's father "lectured him," as the son later said, on Liberal principles. Despite the poverty of his family and the overwhelming problem of providing for such a large number of children, Antonio attended the local Instituto

Científico y Literario, graduating as *Licenciado* in law. His thesis was on municipal government reform; in it he argued the abolition of the office of *jefe político*, a reform later to be accomplished by the Revolution. He became a friend of the wealthy Camilo Arriaga who introduced him to works on the French Revolution, to the writings of Karl Marx, and to those of the anarchists Pierre Joseph Proudhon, Michael Bakunin, and Peter Kropotkin. These were the writers whose influence may be seen most clearly in Díaz Soto y Gama's development as a revolutionary. He made his earliest appearance as a student agitator in 1899, at the age of 19. With two other students he led a street demonstration that ended in front of the San Luis Potosí military zone headquarters, shouting "Death to Porfirio Díaz."

On September 13, 1900, as a student leader, Díaz Soto y Gama helped Camilo Arriaga to organize the *Club Liberal "Ponciano Arriaga,"* named, as noted above, for the father of the founder. The club was begun as a protest against what its members charged was "resurgent clericalism" in open violation of provisions of the 1857 Constitution. The next day Díaz Soto y Gama presided over a meeting of the Student Liberal Committee in which it appeared that the Club members were now prepared to raise issues other than that of anticlericalism. One member went so far as to link "intriguing clerics and usurious capitalists."[1]

In general, however, the Liberal Club, and the Liberal Party which it spawned did not go much beyond anti-clericalism in these early years. At the first Congress of the party, held in San Luis Potosí in 1901, the resolutions adopted were largely those of this nineteenth century position. Yet even in this 1901 meeting a new note was introduced when Díaz Soto y Gama read his law thesis, calling for the abolition of the *jefe político* system. As a result, the party Congress adopted a resolution condemning the system.

During the three years following the organization of the Liberal Party, the Club "Ponciano Arriaga" and the Liberal Party both moved from their traditional anticlerical posture to a clear position of protest against the Díaz system. They adopted a platform calling for no reelection to the presidency, emphasizing the social injustices in Mexican life, and attacking what they called the monopoly of land and the predominance of "money, power, priest and foreigner." Diaz Soto y Gama was a leader in this radicalizing trend, although he did not move as far to the left as the brothers Ricardo and Jesús Flores Magón. The Flores Magóns were arrested when the Liberal Clubs were closed down by the authorities. Díaz Soto y Gama escaped arrest at this time, but shortly thereafter he made a speech in Pinos, Zacatecas, in which he criticized the Díaz regime as "narrow, unpatriotic, and dictatorial." This speech landed him in jail and he stayed in prison until the end of 1901.

Two years later he joined with Camilo Arriaga in drawing up a protest to the Federal Congress against Governor Bernardo Reyes for his harsh suppression of a demonstration held in Monterey to protest the governor's re-election. When the Congress cleared Reyes and adopted a resolution charging the signers of the protest with subversive acts, Díaz Soto y Gama fled to El Paso.

His dramatic condemnation of the criollo leaders of independence at Aguascalientes portended what turned out to be the ultimate significance of his revolutionary career, his defense of the cause of land distribution. Unlike Ricardo Flores Magón, his friend and early collaborator at whom we shall next look, Díaz Soto y Gama went on to play an important role in the later development of the Mexican Revolution, especially as a theoretician of agrarian reform. With Rodrigo Gómez and Felipe Santibáñez he founded the National Agrarian Party (PNA) in 1920, during the provisional presidency of Adolfo de la Huerta. This party, with other parties, supported the candidacy of Alvaro Obregón. True in the main to the agrarian principles of Emiliano Zapata, Díaz Soto y Gama continued to support Obregón in the Congress, and later Calles. He was always a voice for land reform and lived to enjoy in a ripe old age the renown of being one of the founders of the new Mexico.

Ricardo Flores Magón (1873–1922). Other principal leaders of the San Luis Potosí group, in addition to the wealthy founder Camilo Arriaga and Díaz Soto y Gama, were Juan Sarabia, self-educated journalist, Jesús Silva Herzog, historian and economist, Aurelio Monrique, later governor of San Luis Potosí, and Librado Rivera, school-teacher and son of a small farmer. Rivera was typical of primary school teachers (Plutarco Elías Calles the most famous) who became revolutionaries. Though not a native of San Luis Potosí, nor an original member of its Liberal Club, Ricardo Flores Magón became one of the principal leaders among the group of revolutionaries that emerged from it to form the new Mexican Liberal Party. His role was to lead the new party in a more revolutionary direction than some of its founders anticipated.

Like many other Latin American Leaders of protest at this time, especially in labor circles, Flores Magón was committed to an ideology of revolutionary anarchism and employed tactics of violence that alienated many of his colleagues. Paradoxically, his career had success only in its contribution to the revolutionary reforms of the Mexican Revolution with whose leadership he disagreed and ultimately broke. He was imprisoned many times, both in Mexico and in the United States, for his revolutionary activities and his last years were spent in the U.S. federal penitentiary at Fort Leavenworth. The mystery surrounding his death there, under circumstances that left some question as to whether it was a suicide, death from natural cause, or murder by fellow prisoners, provided a tragic climax to a life also tragic in other respects, a life filled with frustration, suffering, and bitter disappointments.

Ricardo Flores Magón was born in the village of Teotitlán del Camino, in the mountains of the state of Oaxaca, Mexico. By an irony of history, this future leader of internationalist anarchism was born on September 16, 1873, the anniversary of Mexican independence. Both of his parents, like their fellow countrymen whose followers they were, Benito Juárez and Porfirio Díaz, were of Indian-mestizo ancestry. His father may have served in the Mexican army in the War of 1846–48 against the United States—the evidence is not clear. He certainly served later in the army against the French intervention and Maximilian. The family was prosperous enough to give Ricardo and his brothers, Enrique and Jesús, a good education in Mexico City. Both of these brothers, incidentally, played a prominent part in the Revolution, parting company ideologically with Ricardo.

Nineteen-year-old Ricardo was studying law in the national University when he joined in his first public protest, leading a group of students in a demonstration against the election of President Porfirio Díaz. This demonstration was in the year 1892 and his participation in it, combined with publication of an opposition journal, landed him in jail briefly. It was the first of a long series of imprisonments for political activity. Eight years later he joined the Liberal Party that was founded, as previously noted, by Camilo Arriaga; and he assisted in starting the party's journal, *Regeneración (Regeneration)*, in whose pages some of his best writing appeared. Imprisoned again in 1903, he fled to the United States when released; there he was soon joined by others of the Liberal Party. In 1905 these young rebels organized a Junta of the Party, with Ricardo as its head, and renewed publication of *Regeneración*, which thereafter was usually published in the United States. This Junta is recognized by Mexicans as the revolutionary nucleus of the movement later led by Francisco Madero, and *Regeneración* is thus one of the Mexican Revolution's early ideological voices.

The revolutionary role of this little group of young Mexican political exiles is expressed significantly in the program of reform proposed in a manifesto they issued from St. Louis, Missouri, on July 1, 1906. Drawn up by Ricardo Flores Magón and Juan Sarabia, its program of social, political, and economic changes reads like a list of the innovations in the

Mexican Revolutionary Constitution of 1917. It goes far beyond the changes proposed in the Plan of San Luis Potosí with which Francisco Madero initiated the successful move against the Díaz regime five years later. Among other things, this 1906 manifesto proposed a one term presidency, restrictions on the influence of the Church, especially in education, the breaking up of large landed estates by extensive distributions of land to the peasantry, the establishment of minimum wages, workmen's compensation, and the abolition of child labor. The document had an anticapitalist flavor, but the tone was mild in general, for Flores Magón was still conforming to the views of his less radical associates. Their program was for reform, not for marxist or anarchist revolution. Their motto was "Reform, liberty, and justice."

The Junta was revolutionary, however, and stimulated sporadic but generally unsuccessful uprisings in several parts of Mexico; it also was credited with encouraging strikes in the growing textile industry in the years 1906–1908. Because of these activities the Junta's mailing privileges were revoked in the United States. Flores Magón and some of his friends were arrested in Los Angeles in 1907 and imprisoned for violation of the neutrality laws. Their imprisonment, incidentally, stirred the resentment of liberals in the United States, who voiced their protest in Congressional hearings in 1910. The Mexican prisoners were released in that year and were given an enthusiastic welcome by their friends when they made a brief visit to Mexico in August, in the midst of the excitement of the electoral campaign.

By September, 1910, they were back in Los Angeles, renewing publication of *Regeneración* and stirring up guerrilla movements in the border states of Mexico. It is not clear what the objective of Flores Magón was in his revolutionary activities during these next months. Was he really giving support to the Madero movement or was his object to establish some kind of opposition force? His major move was an attack upon Lower California. Some of the little band that crossed the border for the initial attack on Mexicali were Mexican members of the IWW from the U.S. portion of the Imperial Valley, which also extends into Mexico. The valley had recently been irrigated from the Colorado River. After capturing Mexicali, Mexican recruits from there were added, as well as a scouting force of Cocopa Indians, who lived on both sides of the border in the lower Colorado river valley.

Either because of lack of resources or lack of leadership, the initial victories of the invaders were not followed up. The rebellion thus had only mixed success. It gained ill repute in some quarters because it accepted the leadership of a soldier of fortune, Carl Ap Rhys Price, who captured Tijuana, but seemed to be playing the role of a filibuster rather than a revolutionary. Richard Wells Ferris, actor and publicist, also gave the enterprise an atmosphere of annexationism by publishing filibuster plans that were never carried out.

These anarchist rebels in Lower California, directed by Ricardo Flores Magón, refused to come to terms with Madero after his triumph in 1911, even though Madero sent Ricardo's brother Jesús and his erstwhile collaborator, Juan Sarabia, with offers to share power in the new government. Thereafter the Magonista forces in Lower California were eventually defeated by a combination of Maderista diplomacy and the military actions of a Díaz army officer who had also refused to accept the victory of the Maderista forces.

Back in the United States, Flores Magón and other leaders of these ill-starred ventures were again arrested and convicted of violation of neutrality laws in 1912. Ricardo was released from prison in 1914, but was arrested and convicted again, two years later, for his activities connected with the IWW. He was out on bail, awaiting the outcome of an appeal on this conviction, when he was arrested again in 1918 for violating the Espionage Act of that year by publishing in Spanish an appeal to anarchists of all lands to rebel. This arrest, at the beginning of the "red hunt" of the post-War years, was his last encounter with the law. He was convicted and sentenced to a twenty year prison term in the Fort Leavenworth federal prison. But on November 21, 1922, long before this term was completed, he was found lying dead at the door of his cell. The cause of his death remains an unsolved mystery.

His increasingly clear commitment to a largely anarchist theory that accepted violence, even in collaboration with ideological enemies had gradually alienated Flores Magón from his youthful colleagues, even when, as in the cases of Juan Sarabia and Antonio Díaz Soto y Gama, they retained for him a kind of personal loyalty. Antonio Díaz Soto y Gama, for example, eloquently supported in the Mexican Congress a resolution memorializing him on the occasion of his death. It was in the anarchist oriented Industrial Workers of the World (IWW) organized among migratory workers of California, that Flores Magón had found support for his revolutionary plans for Mexico. Eventually he had joined their ranks, committing himself to their world revolutionary ideology, an ideology in which Mexican nationalism had little place.

As Lowell L. Blaisdell had pointed out, he thought of the IWW and of his Mexican followers as "a phase of world wide revolution."[2] When the Mexican Congress offered him a pension in 1920, in recognition of his service of the Revolutionary cause and to ease his life in prison, he had refused it, saying that he did not believe in the state because it was "an institution created by capitalism to guarantee the exploitation and subjugation of the masses," and that he fought "for the universal brotherhood of man." On similar grounds he refused to ask for a pardon, although the request would have been supported by many liberals in both the United States and Mexico who did not share his anarchist theories.

The life of Ricardo Flores Magón is thus a complex of contraditions difficult to reconcile, as well as a tragic and in some respects ironic mixture of successes and failures. As a leader of the rebellion in Lower California he must be judged a notable failure. He has even been accused of physical cowardice because he did not join the guerrilla forces personally. On the other hand, he achieved international prominence as an ideological leader and he had the moral courage to face the almost constant threat of imprisonment for his actions. Paradoxically, though an anti-statist and an anarchist internationalist, he was also one of the major ideologues of the Mexican Revolution. Among Mexican historians he has an assured reputation as one of the precursors of Francisco Madero and Venustiano Carranza, both of whom he detested, as well as of Emiliano Zapata and "Pancho" Villa, both of whom he admired. It was a kind of crowning irony to a life with a number of ironic aspects, that the Mexican Government in 1945 placed the remains of this anarchist revolutionary in the Rotunda of Illustrious Men in Mexico City. Imagine what this anarchist and internationalist revolutionary would have thought of this superbly nationalist tribute!

NOTES

1. Quoted in James D. Cockcroft, *Intellectual Precursors of the Mexican Revolution 1900–1913* (Austin: University of Texas Press, 1968), p. 94.
2. *The Desert Revolution* (Madison, Wisconsin: University of Wisconsin Press, 1962), p. xiii.

BIBLIOGRAPHY

For a general treatment of the Mexican precursors see the work of James D. Cockcroft cited in footnote (1) above and Charles C. Cumberland, "Precursors of the Mexican Revolution of 1910," *Hispanic American Historical Review* XXII, No. 2 (May, 1942), 344ff. On Camilo Arriaga, see an article by José Vasconcelos in *Novedades* (Mexico), July 9, 1945. On Díaz Soto y Gama see Eugenio Martínez Núñez, "Antonio Díaz Soto y Gama, caballero del ideal," *El Universal* (Mexico), Oct. 15, 1958, and "Precursores de la Revolucion: Antonio Soto y Gama," *Boletín*

Bibliográfico de la Secretaría de Hacienda y Crédito Público, Nov. 20, 1964; also Díaz Soto y Gama, *La revolución agraria del sur y Emiliano Zapata* (México: Inprenta Policromia, 1960).

The published works of Ricardo Flores Magón have geen gathered by his admirers in *Ricardo Flores Magón, vida y obra*, 6 vols., published by the Grupo Cultural "Ricardo Flores Magón" in 1923–25. Early speeches and articles of Ricardo and Jesús Flores Magón are found in *Batalla a la dictadura* (México: Empresas Editoriales, 1948). See also Antonio Díaz Soto y Gama, "Ricardo y Enrique Flores Magón," *El Universal* (México), Nov. 10, 1954; Ethel Duffy Turner, *Ricardo Flores Magón y el Partico Liberal Mexicano* (Morelia, Michoacán: Editorial Erandi, 1960); Rafael Carillo, *Ricardo Flores Magón, esboza biográfico* (México, 1945); Diego Abad de Santillán (a fellow anarchist), *Ricardo Flores Magón, el apóstol de la revolución social mexicana* (México: Grupo Cultural "Ricardo Flores Magón", 1925); and Lowell L. Blaisdell, *The Desert Revolution* (Madison: University of Wisconsin Press, 1962).

7

DIEGO VICENTE TEJERA (1848–1903)
by Eduardo J. Tejera

Diego Vicente Tejera, founder of the Cuban Socialist Party, lived through and participated in fifty-five decisive years of the Cuban struggle for independence. For him, as for many of his generation, the achievement of independence was a personal mission. Like his fellow Cuban and admired friend, José Martí, he was a sensitive poet. Thus the prestigious dictionary, *Nuevo Pequeño Larousse Ilustrado,* identifies him as a poet and "painter of the rural landscape." But like Martí, also, he was a revolutionary, joining liberation movements in Spain and other parts of the Spanish world as well as in his native Cuba. It was the inspiration of Martí that led him into the Cuban revolutionary movement of 1895. After the achievement of his nation's independence he founded the Cuban Socialist Party, believing that Socialism would add social and economic emancipation to political independence.

Tejera was born on November 20, 1848, in Santiago, in the eastern Cuban province of Oriente. His father, Diego Vicente Tejera y Piloña, was a lawyer and judge in his native Santiago and later in Puerto Rico. Ascensión Calzado y Portuondo, his mother, also came from Santiago. There young Tejera received his primary education in the parochial school of San Basilio. His family and teachers wished him to enter the priesthood but, as he later wrote, he felt he could not accept the rigid discipline and dogmatism of the seminary life. From San Basilio he went on to the Institute of Secondary Education to prepare for the University.

In 1866, at the age of eighteen, he was sent to Paris to begin the study of medicine. Thereafter, his life was one of the unceasing agitation and travel of the revolutionary. After a short time in Paris, he visited England, Belgium, and the Netherlands. It was a time of social, political and cultural agitation in Europe, and Tejera quickly absorbed this spirit of rebellion. Back in Paris, he enlisted under General Pierrad y Contreras in an army organized to invade Spain in a move to overthrow the monarchy. Shortly after the rebels entered Spain they were discovered and dispersed. Having no friends in Spain, Tejera lived in Madrid in misery until his father sent him funds from Puerto Rico. This early and Quixotic participation in an ill-planned invasion illustrates Tejera's temperament as a youth eager for romantic ventures and willing to risk his future and his life for a cause in which he believed.

Shortly afterwards he returned to Puerto Rico and joined in the separatist movement in Lares. When this uprising was defeated, Tejera fled to the (Danish) Island of Saint Thomas. Upon arriving there he joined the insurrectional forces led by Doctor Ramón Betances that were planning an invasion of Puerto Rico.

When this plan failed, Tejera went to Venezuela to resume his postponed medical studies (which he never completed). In Caracas he wrote a poem, *En la Hamaca*, which won him literary fame. But the bucolic tranquility of life in Caracas that produced this poetry was soon broken. At the outset of a rebellion led by Antonio Guzmán Blanco in 1871 against President José Ruperto Monagas, Tejera enlisted with other youths of Caracas in a volunteer force to defend Monagas against the army of Guzmán Blanco. Wounded and defeated, Tejera fled first to Puerto Rico and from there to Barcelona, Spain, then under the short-lived Liberal rule of the Italian King Amadeo.

During his brief stay in Barcelona, Tejera published two books of poems: *Consonancias* and *La Muerte de Plácido*. The spirit of the young poet was restless, however. Discontented and driven by his revolutionary convictions, he left Spain to join the Cuban revolutionary leaders gathered in New York.

There in 1876, he helped to found the official organ of the Cuban independence movement, *La Verdad*. The Cuban Ten Years War (1868–78) for independence was nearing its tragic end. The Mambises rebels had fought hard and persistently for eight years, but they had been unable to win a decisive victory. The people of Cuba were tired and disillusioned. When the War with Spain ended with the Peace of Zanjón in 1878, Tejera refused to accept the settlement. Instead of returning to Cuba, he began another period of wandering through Central America, Mexico, and the United States.

The following year he returned to Havana, where he was introduced to the select audience of the Atheneum to recite his poem, *En la Hamaca*. The performance gained him immediate acceptance in the intellectual community of Havana and he began to write in the principal newspapers of the nation: *El Triunfo, La América, La Habana Elegante, El Almendares,* as well as in the literary *El Fígaro.* In 1883 his life seemed to take on more stability when he married María Teresa García. But two years later, discontented with what he considered the decadence of colonial life, he moved again to New York and began to work intimately with José Martí. He remained in New York for several years, earning his living as a journalist, translator, and proof reader.

But the real Cuban revolutionary movement had not yet begun; ten more years were to pass before Martí could initiate the final emancipating epic. From 1891 to 1893 Tejera was in Paris, publishing the literary magazine, *América en París*. There his revolutionary conception changed to embrace the socialist doctrine of the Second International. The numerous ideological currents in Paris at this time included the Utopians who continued the ideas of the earlier Saint Simonians, Anarquists led by Proudhon and Kropotkin, the syndicalists of George Sorel, as well as revolutionary groups of other tendencies. As a way of introducing himself to the Marxist socialists of the day, Tejera wrote *Un sistema social práctico; sus grandes líneas*, stating his idea of a socialist structure of society. In all his revolutionary activity and in his earlier writings, Tejera had always expressed a deep social sensibility. But now he was expressing a clearer revolutionary theory and doctrine as well as a better understanding of the social forces of society derived more from his experience than from systematic study. For although he had studied for two professional careers, Law and Medicine, he had finished neither. His real schooling had been his travels, his unsuccessful participation in rebel groups, and his extensive reading.

In 1893 his son Paul Louis died. In that year, also, Tejera returned to Puerto Rico to see his ill father, who as if merely awaiting his son's coming, died upon his arrival. Saddened by the double tragedy, he sailed to Havana to find a new sphere of activity. The city was in the state of turbulence that preceded the independence movement about to begin. But the revolution was being organized from the United States under the leadership of Martí, and Tejera soon realized that he could render better service from abroad. So in 1895 we find him again in New York, working as a propagandist in the Cuban revolutionary organization, writing in *La Patria*, the organ of the Cuban Revolutionary Party.

Ill health led him to Key West, where he continued his proselytizing efforts. This island had a large colony of immigrant Cuban workers who gave enthusiastic support to the independence movement. In ten speeches to Key West workers, Tejera outlined the future of the labor movement in a free Cuba, pointing out the necessity of creating a workers socialist party to advance the democratic nature of the new Republic. Among the lecture topics were: "A Practical Socialist System," "The Future of the Political Parties in the Republic," "Education in Democratic Societies," "Cuban Socialism," "The Cuban Women," and "Cuban Society." His lectures were a kind of sociological analysis of the Cuban character and society upon the basis of which he projected his views of the future politics of the new nation. He advocated a thorough democracy, with universal adult male suffrage. But his principal concern was for a Cuban workers party which by its sheer numbers and moral pressure could influence, perhaps even direct, the political process of the new republic.

Returning to Cuba after the War of 1898, Tejera and many other patriots who had dedicated their lives to the ideal of independence suddenly found that their emerging nation had come under another foreign power—the United States. This control, Tejera and his friends believed, thwarted the aspirations of the Cuban revolution.

The Platt Amendment, imposed in a treaty with the United States and in the Cuban Constitution of 1902, made Cuba a protectorate. Within this limited sovereignty, however, Tejera and other Cuban labor leaders undertook to work. As he had promised the labor migrants in Key West, he founded the Cuban Socialist Party on February 19, 1899. The party called for giving a larger share of the income from production to the workers and advocated a more equitable distribution of the national wealth, both for humanitarian reasons and to insure political and social stability. Its program also called for an eight hour work day, pensions for the elderly, a social security system, and other workers' benefits.

In sum, the program of the Socialist Party founded by Tejera called for regenerating and transforming the inherited colonial, social, and economic structures of the nation in order to bring national life into accord with the democratic ideals of Martí. Most Cuban leaders of the time had conceived the struggle for independence merely in terms of national sovereignty, but Tejera and his friends now went further, proposing a socialist transformation of the economic and social structure of Cuba as a logical second phase in Cuban emancipation. Unfortunately, this Cuban Socialist Party soon died because of changes in domestic politics. But Tejera did not give up. A year later he founded the Popular Party with a program much like that of the earlier party. Under the banner of this new party he was an unsuccessful candidate for the city council in Havana. His defeat in this election was a severe personal blow and he retired from public life.

Tejera lived the last days of his life disillusioned with Cuban politics. His personal defeat, he saw, had resulted from the special circumstances the new nation was passing through, including the effects of the Platt Amendment that limited Cuban sovereignty by giving the United States control over Cuban foreign relations and the right to intervene by force if necessary in the island. For an old and uncompromising rebel, this new imperialism was unpardonable. He died on November 6, 1903, disappointed that Cuba still lacked the full independence he had dreamed of.

During Tejera's lifetime positivist social thought prevailed in Latin America; but he saw the limitations and shortcomings of this philosophy and sociology. Like the positivists, however, he relied upon science, experimentaion, and empirical analysis to understand the economic and social problems of the nation. Nor did he accept the violence of the anarchism then prevalent in Spanish labor circles. His democratic socialism, emphasizing the regeneration of Cuban life, called for a spiritual revolution to achieve the economic, political, and social redemption of the masses. "We do not," he wrote, "seek nor would we initiate a class struggle, convinced that violence does not give triumphs as complete and durable as those achieved through reason and love."

He believed that new social forces engendered by the industrial revolution had produced economic and cultural changes that had disastrous effects upon the social and economic life of the European masses; these forces, he feared, would have similar effects in Cuba. Tejera's socialism had roots in the French Revolution and subsequent European utopian thought, but with a new focus and vitality derived from the doctrines of the Second International. Yet he saw that the European experience differed from that of America and in all of his writings insisted that, since Cuba's problems and circumstances were different from those of Europe, they required an original approach. "We will follow in our doctrine," he said, "that which is applicable and responds better to the peculiarity of our exclusive problems."

Tejera's socialism was obviously influenced by Marxian thought. Yet, it should be noted that he rejected the class struggle as a matter of party strategy. He accepted a major role for private enterprise in the economy when controlled and supervised by government, and in general his conception of socialism seems to have approximated that of the mixed social and economic system of the Scandinavian countries.

The ideas of Tejera had little impact on the first republican generation of Cubans, except as a contribution to the ideological formation of the labor movement. But with the passage of time his ideas have acquired more importance. Today some Cubans would doubtless say that Tejera's democratic socialism offers a viable alternative to present day Fidelismo.

BIBLIOGRAPHY

Max Henríquez Ureña, in his "Diego Vicente Tejera," *Cuba Contemporánea* (La Habana) Vol. 6 (October, 1914), pp. 105–126, gives a good brief summary of

Tejera's life; also see *Razón de Cuba* (La Habana: Municipio de La Habana, Oficina del Historiador de la Ciudad, 1948) for a good exposition of Tejera's ideas. Other useful works include José Rivero Múñiz, *El Primer Partido Socialista Cubano* (Cuba: Universidad Central de Las Villas, 1962); Diego Vicente Tejera y García (ed.), *Prosa literaria* (La Habana: Imprenta Ramble, Bouza y Cía, 1936); and Diego Vicente Tejera y Piloña, "Los Futuros Partidos Políticos de la República Cubana," *Revista Bimestre Cubana* (La Habana) Vol. 44, núm. 2 (Sept–Oct, 1939), pp. 192–201.

8

LUIS EMILIO RECABARREN (1876–1924)

Moisés Poblete Troncoso, a Chilean labor historian, has called Luis Recabarren the first of Chile's modern labor leaders. This characterization, emphasizing his role as a labor organizer, is well deserved. But his ideological orientation is equally important, especially because it was characteristic of the revolutionary ideology of much of the Chilean labor movement as it evolved early in this century into a powerful politicized force.

During his lifetime Recabarren founded several labor journals of a radical bent that followed this evolution of his revolutionary thought and he was regarded by the rulers of Chile as a dangerous agitator during most of his adult life. Within labor circles he also became a controversial figure as he led the radical wing of the labor movement away from its (and his) original anarcho-syndicalism, through the Marxism of the second International, and finally into the pattern of the Third (Communist) International.

Identifying himself at the opening of the twentieth century with the labor movement emerging among the nitrate miners of northern Chile, Recabarren used this base, as Poblete Troncoso has remarked, to create the first important Marxist oriented national labor movement in Latin America.[1] This achievement came in 1912 when he founded the Chilean Socialist Labor Party along lines of the Second International. Then in 1921 he led his party into the fold of the Third International and brought the national Federation of Chilean Workers (FOCH) into the Communist International labor organization. His suicide in 1924 gave a dramatic cast to his life, contributing to make him a suitable subject for poetry and for a novel. An element of mystery as to whether he was moved to take his life by the disillusionment consequent to a visit to the Soviet Union, or by ill health and approaching blindness, further increased this romantic interest in his career.

Julio César Jobet, the principal biographer of Luis Recabarren, throws little light on his family background and early life. We know he was born in Valparaiso on July 6, 1876, the son of parents of modest means and that he was christened Luis Emilio Recabarren Serrano. How he achieved his elementary education we are not told, only that at an early age he entered a printing shop where he learned the skill of typesetting. Like so many others in this trade, he was stimulated by contact with the printed word to pursue a course of self-education. He read widely, as his speeches and writing show, especially in the literature of the socialist and anarchist writers of the nineteenth century.

At the age of fifteen, his biographer tells us, he shared in the direction of a short-lived paper, *El Opositor*, opposing President José Balmaceda in the Revolution of 1891, an opposition he later regretted. He seems already to have joined the marxist oriented Democratic Party, shortly after its formation, and appears as a member of the editorial staff of the party organ, *La Democracia*, in its first issue. When the paper re-appeared after a temporary suppression, he was its Director (editor). At some early date he had joined a printers' union, for he presents himself in a national congress of Argentine workers organizations in 1907 as a representative of the "Unión Gráfica."

Recabarren's identification with more radical labor trends began when he started working with groups like the *mancomunal*, or mutual, of Iquique, founded in 1901. This was an organization of employees of the Anglo-Chilean nitrate mines. Midway in form between an anarchist syndicate devoted to revolutionary resistance and a mutual society, it embraced such activities as a welfare fund, educational programs, and a consumers' cooperative to compete with the company store. It conducted a sixty-day strike in Iquique, in December 1901 and January 1902, which is considered by labor historians to be the first major strike in Chile. In 1902 Recabarren brought these northern nitrate workers together in an organization, based in Tocopilo, that soon came to have some three thousand members. As its weekly organ he published *El Trabajo*, while in another journal, *El Proletario*, he disseminated to Chilean workers his ideas of workers' rights and of the principles of social and political action.

When the Federation of Chilean Workers was organized in Valparaiso in 1903, soon to be joined by the nitrate workers syndicates, Recabarren was elected president of its Directive Commission. But he could not attend the first congress of this new organization when it was held the following year (1903), because he was in prison in Tocopilo for alleged subversive activity. As a matter of fact, Recabarren was already losing much of his earlier commitment to the subversive anarchism of Kropotkin and Bakunin and was moving toward the concept of a labor movement organized for political action through a labor party. Thus when the anarchists in this congress of workers attacked this developing national labor movement for its lack of commitment to violent revolution, Recabarren replied from prison with a vigorous defense of the democratic political approach.

In 1906 his growing influence was shown by his election to Congress as a deputy from Tocopilo, Antofogasta, and Taltal, as a candidate of the Democratic party. The victory of this party in the municipal elections in Tocopilo of that year was also attributed to his influence. His labor oriented views at this time (1906) were expressed in the daily *La Reforma* that he published in Santiago.

The election of Recabarren frightened many Chileans who had come to regard him as a revolutionary labor leader. He was accused at this time of organizing a strike of railroad and port workers in Antofogasta that was suppressed by force. A motion to bar his admission to Congress on the grounds that he denied the existence of God was defeated, but he was later rejected on the grounds that he had not been duly elected. In the subsequent election he again defeated the Radical Party candidate, but he was again denied final confirmation by the Congress. Denied membership in Congress and condemned to prison for his role in the Antofogasta strike, he escaped to Argentina. There he spent the year 1907, becoming a member of the Socialist party of Argentina and participating in various labor activities. Early in the year 1908 he went to Spain where he made the acquaintance of the popular labor leader Pablo Iglesias, with whom he has sometimes been compared, and of the leader of the Spanish Socialist party, Francisco Largo Caballero. Before returning to Chile he also visited France and Belgium.

Upon his return to Chile he was immediately arrested and imprisoned to serve out the sentence for his role in the Antofogasta strike. His foreign travel and this imprisonment after his return to Chile increased his dissatisfaction with the Democratic Party as a voice of the labor movement—a dissatisfaction that was soon reflected in new directions that his writing and his labor leadership began to assume. Two journals that he edited in Iquique at this time, *El Grito Popular* (in 1911) and *El Despertar de los Trabajadores* (in 1912) expressed these new views. By the end of the year 1912 he had established the Socialist Labor Party (*Partido Obrero Socialista*) and was publishing the daily *La Defensa Obrera* to express the views of the new party.

The reform program of this Socialist Labor party went well beyond that of the older Democratic party. It called for improvement in the political system to guarantee the right to vote and for such other rights as freedom of association and freedom of the press. Other proposals included the abolition of the standing army, the end of budgetary appropriations for the support of the Church, the nationalization of Church wealth, a progressive income tax, free obligatory education, laws regulating the work of women and children, and insurance for workers against accidents in employment. The theoretical basis of the new party was stated in a small book, *El Socialismo*, that Recabarren published at this time.[2]

The theory of the worker's revolution and political trade unionism (*sindicalismo*) that Recabarren expressed in this book had been stated in an earlier 1910 pamphlet entitled *Ricos y Pobres*.[3] It was later elaborated in the pages of a journal that he published in Antofogasta in 1918. This theory conforms in general to the ideologies of other Second International socialist parties. The socialized society he urged, is to be achieved by a variety of means, partly on the local and national levels and partly on the international level, partly through participation in government and partly through actions outside government. As a good marxist, he found in history a basis for all the means to be employed. These means included the class struggle, the syndicate (union), the strike, cooperatives, participation in government at all levels, local, national and international, the creation of socialist education and schools, labor conferences, and the press.

The concept of the class struggle, a recurrent theme in Recabarren's writing, finds one of its sharpest expressions in his *Ricos y Pobres*. An expansion of a lecture he gave in Rengo, in 1910, on the hundredth anniversary of Chilean independence, this booklet reflects the bitterness of his rejection by the national Congress at that time, his imprisonment and flight from the country, his dissatisfaction with the Democratic party because of their support for a landowner as candidate for the presidency in 1906, and his increasingly strong conviction that he was leading a class struggle. He dedicated the book to the *proletariado estudioso* (studious proletariat) that he hoped would agree with his interpretations of one hundred years of Chilean history as a history of increasing class differences. The bourgeois class has grown rich, he wrote, while the workers are as poor as they were in 1810.

During World War I, Chilean exports of copper and nitrates expanded greatly in a wartime boom. But the collapse of the world market for nitrates immediately after the War, because of cheaper synthetic production, plunged Chile into an economic depression and created widespread labor unrest. The example of the Russian Revolution of 1917 was stimulating the establishment of Communist parties throughout Latin America at this time and was attracting the growing Latin American labor movement toward ties with the Communist International. The Chilean labor movement was fertile ground for this new tendency to take root, and Luis Recabarren soon appeared as its spokesman and leader. In 1919, backed by the syndicates of the nitrate miners, he was elected president of the National Federation of Chilean workers (FOCH); almost immediately he led FOCH into affiliation with the Communist International. Under his influence, the Socialist Labor Party then became the Communist Party of Chile in 1921. In the same year, Recabarren, who had just been elected to Congress by the Socialist Labor Party, thus became the first Communist member of the Chilean Congress.

He and his labor cohorts, incidentally, had supported Arturo Alessándri's election to the presidency in 1920; they had endorsed the program of labor legislation and other reforms advocated during the campaign by the "Lion of Tarapacá" and eventually incorporated in the Constitution of 1925. In 1922 Recabarren went to Moscow as the delegate of the Chilean FOCH and the Chilean Communist party to attend an international gathering of labor unions. He returned somewhat disillusioned by the lack of labor freedom he saw in the Soviet Union. Yet his last action in the Chilean Congress was to present a resolution calling for a message of condolence to the USSR upon the death of Lenin in 1924, a motion that was not unexpectedly voted down. On December 19 of that year he committed suicide, possibly motivated in part by his disillusionment with the Russian experience, but more likely influenced by illness and approaching blindness. In the words of his biographer, Professor Jobet, he was "exhausted by thirty years of struggle and affected by the beginning of blindness."[4]

This dramatic death, at the relatively young age of forty-eight, made him a kind of martyr to the cause of a revolutionary labor movement. His disciples like to compare him to the great Spanish labor leader, Pablo Iglesias (1850–1925) whom Recabarren met, as previously noted, on his visit to Spain in 1908. The similarities are numerous. Both men lived austere private lives. Neither drank alcohol or smoked tobacco. Both devoted their lives entirely to leading workers to form labor organizations and to improving workers' political and moral education. Both wrote extensively in a clear and simple style. Both founded socialist labor parties. They read many of the same books, including works of Darwin, Marx, and Hegel. There are two distinctive things in the aura that surrounds Recabarren, however, setting him off from most other labor leaders. A novel has been written about him by Fernando Alegría (entitled *Recabarren)*, and the Chilean poet, Antonio de Undurraga, has written a long poem about him: *Recabarren, o el líder de sudor y oro, romancero. Poesía.*

In the decade following his death Recabarren was criticized in some Communist circles for his ideological deviation from strict Leninist doctrine, and his reputation as a radical leader declined. Thus, in 1933, the Chilean Communist Party adopted a resolution citing his influence as something to be overcome, and the South American Bureau of the party later put the criticism in even stronger language, urging the Chilean party to free itself from "the ideological dead weight *(lastre)* of Recabarren." More recently, however, writers on the Chilean labor movement have tended to rehabilitate his reputation, both as a great labor leader and as a defender of the cause of socialist revolution.

NOTES

1. *El movimiento obrero latinoamericano* (México: Fondo de Cultura Económica, 1946), p. 126.
2. Iquique: Imp. "El Despertar," 1912. 124 p.
3. Imprenta New York, 1910. 47 p. This work is included in Luis Recabarren, *Obras escogidos* (Santiago, Chile: Editorial Recabarren, 1965), pp. 57–98.
4. Julio César Jobet, *Luis Recabarren. Los origenes del movimiento obrero y del socialismo chilenos* (Santiago, Chile: Prensa Latinoamericana, 1955), p. 68.

BIBLIOGRAPHY

The only biography of Recabarren the author has seen is that of Julio César Jobet mentioned in footnote (3), but the bibliography in his *Obras escogidas* (see below) refers to an unpublished manuscript on "Recabarren and the Labor Movement in Chile," by Fanny S. Simon, which it has been impossible to find in Washington. Fernando Alegría's novel, *Recabarren*, was published in Santiago by Editorial "Antares" in 1938. The Undurraga poem, a book of 70 pages, was published in Santiago Editorial Cultura in 1946. For Recabarren's most important works, see *Obras escogidas* (Santiago: Editorial Recabarren, 1965). His *Rusia obrera y campesina* was reissued separately in 1967 by Talleres de las Sociedad Impresora Horizonte in Santiago. A brief sketch appears in Apendice 8, p. 1326, of the *Enciclopedia Universal Ilustrada* (Espasa-Calpe). Passing references occur in such other works as Moisés Poblete Troncoso, *El movimiento obrero latinoamericano* (México: Fondo de Cultura Económica, 1946); Victor Alba, *Esquema histórico del movimiento obrero en América Latina* (México: B. Costa-Amic, Editor, Colección Panoramas, Vol. 8, s.f.); Guillermo Feliú Cruz, *Chile visto a través de Agustín Ross* (Santiago: Imp. y Enc. Pino, 1950), pp. 152–153; and Ricardo Donoso, *Alessandri, agitador y demoledor*, 2 v. (México: Fondo de Cultura Económica, 1953, 1954), *passim*.

9

ERNESTO "CHE" GUEVARA (1928–1967)

"Che" Guevara has been one of the most controversial as well as one of the most popular revolutionary figures of the mid-twentieth century. For Guevara revolution was a life-long career and, in a moving letter near the end of his life, he called on his children to follow in his footsteps. He played a brilliant role in the success of the July 26 Cuban Revolutionary movement led by Fidel Castro and was an important, some would say the major, intellectual influence in guiding the revolutionary program adopted by Castro and his followers after taking over the government. Yet even in Cuba, his leadership of the economic program (as head of the national bank and Minister of Industry) was a disaster, and his subsequent revolutionary activities in Africa and Bolivia ended in failure, culminating in the dramatic collapse of his plan to make Bolivia a guerrilla warfare training center for the South American continent in which he believed "many Vietnams" would soon take shape.

The circumstances of his death, the secrecy with which he was "executed" after capture, and the mystery surrounding the disposal of his body all contributed to the tragedy and to making him a martyr to the revolutionary cause. In death he has become a greater revolutionary figure than in life, symbolizing the frustrated aspirations of the Latin American masses, impatient with the obstacles to the better life they have been led to hope for. Even as far away as the island republic of Ceylon, according to news reports in April, 1971, his name has been adopted to designate Marxist peasant guerrillas. Yet in life he was also a figure of great revolutionary significance, especially as an interpreter of the July 26 Cuban Revolution.

Guevara is thus notable both as a civilian revolutionary and as a guerrilla leader of revolution. In addition to acting as a physician in Castro's army, he successfully headed one of the independently operating guerrilla "columns." He also led guerrillas in the Congo and in the abortive Bolivian rebellion of 1966–67. But his critical and theoretical writing on revolution, both in general and in particular reference to Cuba, may well be his most lasting claim to fame. In this respect he has been compared with Mao Tse-tung and Vo Nguyen Giap. It is indicative of the world character of the revolutionary movement of the twentieth century, though to some readers it may seem rather surprising, that these three should come up with comparable theories of revolution despite their differences in cultural background and despite their living thousands of miles from each other. One thing they had in common, however. All three came from a middle class, professional, and non-military background. Mao was a minor government official, a bureaucrat. Giap was a lawyer. Guevara was a physician.

Guevara never became the voice of the Cuban Revolution, a voice that spoke to the Cuban people as Castro did. In another sense, however, that of theoretical analysis, he surpassed Castro. His written, critical interpretation of the Cuban movement was intellectual, giving him a unique place in the Cuban Revolution as its theoretician. As a theoretician, he had some obvious limitations however. His most impressive work, the little book on guerrilla warfare, is more prescriptive than theoretical in a basic sense. Setting forth principles of strategy and tactics, it scarcely touches on their theoretical basis or on such fundamental theoretical questions as the nature and objectives of revolution and the application of general political principles.

During the years immediately after 1959, Guevara published in Cuba a series of articles narrating and analyzing the Cuban guerrilla campaigns. These articles would probably have become a book if death had not intervened. The major principle he seemed to deduce from the Cuban experience is the dubious and superficial generalization that guerrilla forces are superior to regular armies and can always defeat them. This interpretation would doubtless have been further refined if he had lived to rework his material, for he certainly must have learned from his later defeats in the Congo and in Bolivia that the Cuban success had been due to exceptionally favorable conditions, hardly typical of other "revolutionary" situations.

All in all, however, Guevara has had a profound influence on the character and direction of the Latin American revolutionary movements. He challenged the prevailing action theories of both the democratic left and those of the Communist parties. If we accept his account, and it seems plausible, he changed the projected course of the July 26 movement when he met with Castro and his followers during their exile in Mexico. He persuaded them, he says, to give up the idea of the traditional golpe or putsch, such as they had unsuccessfully tried against the Moncada barracks in Santiago, and to plan a more profoundly revolutionary movement along Maoist lines. After the Castro triumph at the end of 1958, his counsel also guided the movement toward a dramatically rapid and complete socialization of the economy. His influence diminished only when the growth of Soviet influence forced

Cuba, in the 1964 Conference of Latin American Communist parties, to adopt a policy of hemispheric cooperation with these parties.

Ernesto Guevara was born June 14, 1928, in Rosario, Argentina. He was the oldest of five children of Ernesto Rafael Guevara Lynch, an architect and builder, and Celia de la Serna. His paternal grandmother (Lynch), it may be interesting to note, was a U.S. citizen, born in San Francisco. The family soon moved from Rosario to Alta Gracia, in the central province of Córdoba, where Ernesto grew up. The Guevara family was known for its liberal sympathies, supporting the cause of the Spanish Republic and welcoming Republican refugees into the family circle. In the family library Ernesto read works of a leftist revolutionary character, the kind of literature for which his mother had a particular penchant. From her, also, he acquired a liking for poetry, both Spanish and French, developing a special predilection for the poems of Pablo Neruda, the Chilean Communist poet.

As a boy Ernesto also developed skill in a variety of outdoor sports. All his life he was afflicted with asthma, and on this account his father urged him to take active part in games and sports. He taught him to shoot and saw that he learned to play Rugby, soccer, and golf. The rough game of Rugby was always his special favorite.

He attended secondary school in Córdoba and while there joined a youth group of the Democratic Union Party (Partido Unión Democrática), taking part in their demonstrations against the Perón government. In 1946 the Guevaras moved to Buenos Aires. Later his parents separated, and Ernesto lived with his mother while attending the University of Buenos Aires to study medicine. This close association with his mother had a special significance, for her marxist oriented views were a major formative influence in Guevara's life, inspiring a revolutionary approach to his country's unresolved social problems and animating his opposition to Perón.

At the age of eighteen he registered for military service, as required by Argentine law, but was exempted because of his asthma. This asthma did not limit his physical activity, however, for he still liked Rugby and soccer. Probably it was his activity in these sports and his gregariousness that won for him the nickname "Che." This is a term, probably of Guarani origin, meaning something like "Hey, you."

He also liked to travel and spent school vacations in journeys around Argentina, sometimes on foot, sometimes on a bicycle equipped with a small motor. In 1951 he set out on a motorcycle with a friend, Alberto Granados, to visit the west coast countries of South America. When the motorcycle gave out in Santiago, Chile, the young men, undiscouraged, went on, earning their way by various kinds of work. They traveled through Peru, down the Ucayali river to the Amazon, then back to Colombia and Venezuela. In Caracas, a family friend offered Ernesto a ride to Miami on a plane carrying race horses. He accepted the offer, leaving Granados in Caracas to work in a leprosarium. Arriving in Miami without a cent and without a visa, Ernesto had a difficult time staying out of sight of the immigration authorities. He finally got back to Buenos Aires, where he completed his medical course in March 1953.

Despite his exemption from military service because of asthma, he was liable to induction as an army physician after graduation from medical school. To avoid serving under the Perón regime he therefore left the country, embarking on the course that was to lead ultimately to his tragic end in Bolivia. He went first to Bolivia, then undergoing a revolution under the National Revolutionary Movement (MNR). From there he journeyed through Peru, Ecuador, Panama, and Costa Rica to Guatemala, then governed by President Jacobo Arbenz. The Guatemalan government was carrying out a program of land reform involving the distribution of extensive lands expropriated from the United Fruit Company. Guevara received a job under this program. There, also, he met Hilda Gadea, an exiled Peruvian Aprista leader whom he married in 1955 but later divorced.

During the uprising against the Arbenz government, led by Colonel (later President) Carlos Castillo Armas in 1954, Guevara worked strenuously to organize a last minute unsuccessful defense of Guatemala City. After the rebellion succeeded he was a marked man. Taking refuge in the Argentine Embassy, he enjoyed diplomatic asylum there for two months until allowed to leave for Mexico. In Mexico City Hilda introduced him to Fidel Castro and his band of fellow exiles, recently pardoned by the Batista government after being imprisoned for the attack on the Moncada Barracks in Santiago, Cuba.

Guevara was thus one of the band of some eighty young men who sailed to Cuba in late 1956 on the *Granma*. He was also one of the twelve, including Fidel and Raúl Castro, who were lucky enough to escape the vigilance of Batista's army and to make their way, with the help of sympathetic peasants, to the Sierra Maestra mountains. For the next two years he shared the fortunes of the Castro guerrilla bands, first as their army physician, then as commander of one of the "columns." After the success of the rebellion, he guided the revolution toward its increasingly Communist course. He held the important posts of President of the National Bank and Minister of Industry. During these years, also, as previously noted, his articles on the history of the guerrilla campaigns gave to Cuban and other readers his theoretical explanation of the Cuban Revolutionary success.

Then, after the 1964 Latin American Communist Party Conference in Havana, Guevara disappeared from sight. The following year he seems to have spent in an unsuccessful revolutionary venture in the Congo. Early in 1966, however, he appeared in Bolivia. Apparently, he had the backing of the Castro government to establish a training center or *foco* for South American guerrillas, provided only he did not work with the Peking Communists. The Tricontinental Conference in Havana (1966) had opened the way for this support when Communist party leaders had agreed to support their radical wings in guerrilla actions. The Venezuelan party had followed this line, and Guevara's plan envisaged similar support from the Bolivian party. This support never materialized, however, for reasons that are not entirely clear. All that is clear is that the disastrous effects of the Venezuelan experiment upon Communist party strength, together with Soviet pressure for a peaceful coexistence policy, had reduced the pressure on the Bolivian party to give this support.

The Guevara project had two objectives, not entirely consistent with each other. The first, as stated, was to establish a permanent *foco* or center of revolutionary training and activity in an inaccessible location in the heart of the South American continent. The second objective was to foment a rebellion against the Barrientos regime in Bolivia. Guevara was probably right in choosing the remote center of Camiri, in Southeastern Bolivia for the *foco*. If he made an error of judgment, as this author believes he did, it was in thinking that a revolutionary potential for overturning the Barrientos regime existed among the Bolivian peasantry. For, despite the military character of the Bolivian government, it had a solid revolutionary basis in the agrarian, land distribution reform that had followed the Revolution of 1952 and in the campesino organizations that President Barrientos had been organizing on a large scale.

No peasant support for Guevara materialized. Rather, it was through reports from the peasantry that the movements of his followers were made known to Bolivian authorities. The refusal of the Communist party to support the guerrilla rebellion helps to explain the breakdown of communications through La Paz and the consequent failure of the guerrillas to receive much needed money and supplies. The guerrilla campaign itself was a series of defeats, culminating in the capture of Guevara and most of his remaining supporters on October 8, 1967, as they were trying to escape after a disastrous ambush on September 27–28 by the Bolivian forces that had been trained especially for anti-guerrilla activity by U.S. Rangers. Guevara and his comrades were transported to

La Higuera and there he was executed, along with several of his followers, presumably on orders from La Paz.

If "Che" Guevara achieves lasting fame, as he may well do, it will be as an expression of the revolutionary theory that no real revolution has occurred in Latin America except in Cuba, that only armed rebellion can effect a revolution in a Latin American country, and that this armed rebellion can best be achieved by guerrilla movements operating in the countryside with peasant support. His commitment to such a view is beyond question. To his parents he wrote on the eve of his departure to the Congo in 1965: "I believe in the armed struggle as the only solution for those people who fight to free themselves. . . . My marxism has taken root and become pure."[1] The resemblance of this theory to that of Mao Tse-tung and Vo Nguyen Giap has been pointed out. But this resemblance is much less important than the fact that Guevara's theory gained wide acceptance among Latin American radicals who saw in it little or no conflict with Marxist-Leninism even though it was rejected by the Soviet and Latin American Communist parties. Guevara broke, of course, with the basic revolutionary dictum of both Lenin and Mao that subjective conditions must be right before revolution can succeed. Thus, his very distinctive principle is that subjective conditions *can be created by determined revolutionary leaders.* He also differed from both Mao and Giap in assuming that an armed rebellion could succeed by guerrilla tactics alone.

The appeal of Guevara's theory shows, as much as anything else, the basic idealism of the Latin American revolutionaries and their rejection of the materialist determinism of traditional marxist thought and of the "bureaucratic" character that Communist parties had assumed in the half century since the Russian Revolution. There is an inescapable link between this revolutionary idealism and that which inspired the Leninist doctrine of the Russian Bolsheviki. But the impatient Latin American youth of today, in its idealism, appears to reject the Lenin corrollary that a highly disciplined and secret party is needed to carry out the dictatorship of the proletariat. In this appeal to youthful idealism, many would say Guevara reveals himself as the Latin American "romantic" revolutionist.

Guevara's revolutionary thought matured as he studied the record of successes and failures of the Cuban Revolution. The best expression of his ideas appears in a little book, *Man and Socialism in Cuba,* published in Cuba, Uruguay, Argentina, and the United States shortly before his death. It bears marks of the hurried activity he was then engaged in, but also shows some interesting new insights. Looking back over a decade of struggle in Cuba, he saw that Cuban society was still divided, indicating a lack of development of the social conscience and the continued need for dictatorship. The Cuban vanguard, he wrote, were more advanced than the masses. The former were prepared to make the sacrifices required of an elite, but the masses "see only half-way and must be submitted to stimuli and pressures of some intensity." This pressure, he said, "is the dictatorship of the proletariat being exercised not only over the defeated class but also, individually, over the conquering class." The Communist party must therefore still be a vanguard party, although eventually it is to be a mass party.

He cautioned that the Cuban road to Communism was still a long one, a road "unknown in part." "The basic clay of our work is the youth," he wrote. By the education of youth "we will make the man of the xxi century." It is indeed notable that in this last published work, within the Marxist-Leninist framework, including dictatorship under the proletarian party, Guevara returned to a rather simple affirmation of the importance of education and of youthful idealism. In his last letter to his children, he wrote in 1967: "Grow up as good revolutionaries. Study hard so that you will have command of the techniques that permit the domination of nature."[2]

NOTES

1. The letter may be found in Richard Harris, *Death of a Revolutionary* (New York: W.W. Norton, 1970), pp. 37–38.
2. *Op. cit.*, p. 200.

BIBLIOGRAPHY

The passages from *Man and Socialism in Cuba* were translated from the Spanish original, published in Montevideo by Nativa Libros in 1966. An English edition was brought out by Progressive Labor in the United States the same year. Three other books by Guevara may be mentioned: *Guerra de Guerrillas* (Havana, 1960), *Pasajes de la Guerra Revolucionaria* (Havana, 1963), and the *Bolivian Diary (Diario de Che en Bolivia)* (Havana, 1968), also available in English translations. Many of Che's other writings have also been translated into English. In excerpt they are available in the collection edited by Jay Mallin, *"Che" Guevara on Revolution* (Miami University Press, 1969) and in Rolando E. Bonachea and Nelson P. Valdes, *Che. Selected Works of Ernesto Guevara* (Cambridge: M.I.T. press, 1970). Other useful books on Guevara include Richard Harris, *Death of a Revolutionary* (New York: W.W. Norton, 1970), Luis J. Gonzaléz and Gustavo A. Sánchez Salazar, *The Great Rebel: Che Guevara in*

Bolivia, trans. by Helen R. Lane (New York: Grove Press, 1970), Andrew Sinclair, *Che Guevara* (New York: Viking Press, 1971), and *Viva Che! Contributions in Tribute to Ernesto "Che" Guevara,* edited by Marianne Alexandre (New York: E.P. Dutton, 1968). Richard Bourne has a useful chapter in his *Political Leaders of Latin America* (London and Baltimore: Penguin Books, 1969), pp. 55–94.

10

CAMILO TORRES RESTREPO (1929–1966)

Many young Latin Americans consider Camilo Torres a great martyr to the cause of social revolution—in some respects the peer of Ernesto "Che" Guevara. Because, though a priest, he engaged in violent revolution as a guerrilla, he is commonly regarded as an extraordinary, even exotic, revolutionary. But not only because he was a priest. The fact that he was primarily an intellectual, a student of sociology and theology, and a chaplain for university students, seems to many to make his revolutionary role even stranger. Yet, all this is not so strange if viewed in historical perspective. History provides a number of examples of religious leaders such as Mohammed, who turned revolutionary and resorted to force. In Latin America, the independence movements also provide examples of priests who became military leaders, notable cases being the two Mexicans, Miguel Hidalgo and José Morelos. Luis Beltrán, a Chilean Franciscan and army chaplain, manufactured bayonets, gunpowder, and cannon for San Martín; he also made machines to carry San Martín's cannon across the Andes. Numerous other examples could be added.

The nature of Camilo Torres' religious and social beliefs does give his revolutionary role a somewhat unique character, however, one distinct from those of earlier leaders. Other young priests have shared his theological concepts, his Marxist-like social philosophy, and his concepts of the problems and issues presented in present-day Latin American societies. But the distinguishing thing about Camilo Torres' theology, dramatized by his joining guerrilla forces in Colombia, was his belief that theology, as Thoreau said of philosophy, was best expressed in action.

Camilo Torres Restrepo bore the name of two old and respected Colombian families, Torres and Restrepo. Born in Bogotá on February 3, 1929, he was the son of Calixto Torres Umaña, a physician, and Isabel Restrepo. Both of these old Colombian families, according to Camilo, were Liberal and free-thinking by tradition. The most famous of Camilo's ancestors, the one for whom he was named, was a martyr of Colombian independence. This earlier Camilo Torres was executed by order of the Spanish General Pablo Morillo in 1816 for having been a leader of the 1810 revolutionary movement.

The twentieth century Camilo Torres attended a German school in Bogotá and received his baccaulaureate from the Liceo Cervantes.

75

Shortly after entering the law faculty of the Javeriana (Jesuit) University he withdrew, having decided that his vocation lay in the priesthood rather than in law. One is tempted to speculate on the motives which may have led a young man coming from this background of a free-thinking family to prefer the priesthood to law. Part of the explanation, doubtless, is the increasing social consciousness of the Church. He himself has said only that his motivation was humanistic—that he discovered Christianity as a way of living one's life for his neighbor.

In the diocesan seminary in which he enrolled, he quickly showed himself to be an exceptional student. It was a mark of this ability that his ordination was advanced to permit him to go to the University of Louvain, Belgium, in 1954, to complete his studies in that outstanding center of progressive Catholic thought. There he came under the influence of the Abbé François Houtart, director of the University's center of Socio-Religious Research, and the Belgian Roger Vekemans, S.J., later to be the founder of the School of Sociology in the Catholic University of Chile. Both Houtart and Vekemans led him to study sociology and to develop concepts of pluralism and religious ecumenism. He came to believe that it was urgently necessary to bring all Christians together and to reconcile marxism with Christian theology. In 1958, while a student at Louvain, he organized a meeting of the Colombian students attending various European universities. The purpose of the meeting was to discuss these questions. In Paris, to put his beliefs into practice, he worked for a time with the famous Abbé Pierre, collecting rags.

He returned to Colombia in 1959 after receiving the Licentiate in Sociology. There he was named chaplain of the National University in Bogotá and professor of sociology. In 1962 he was also made head of the newly established Institute of Public Administration. His previous activities as a student leader in Bogotá and at Louvain had prepared him for active participation in student life and he quickly became a popular leader among the university students. As he identified himself with student movements, however, he developed increasingly radical political ideas. Thus, in 1962 he joined a protest against the suspension of ten student leaders, a protest that became a turning point in his life when his bishop removed him from the chaplaincy because of his support of this protest.

From 1962 to 1965, as director of the Institute of Public Administration, he represented Cardinal Luis Concha Córdoba in the work of the Colombian Institute of Agrarian Reform (INCORA), organizing communities of peasants and assisting in the distribution of land expropriated from larger estates under the national agrarian law. This contact with the problems of rural poverty, and with what Camilo came to regard as official foot-dragging in carrying out the agrarian reform, led him to make some increasingly radical public statements. Like many other young priests at this time, he was moved in this direction by the Pontificate of Pope John XXVI and by the liberalizing influence of the Second Vatican Council in 1962. In 1963 he invited to his home a group of Christian Democrats and other activists to consider how they might unite "groups of opposition to the system." But his break with the Church did not come until two years later, when increasing pressure from his superiors led him to renounce the priesthood and to turn his attention exclusively to promoting a united front of leftist protest groups.

The revolutionary character of the United Front (FUN) platform he then developed appears in its declaring the need for a "change in the structure of political power so that the majorities will make the decisions," its rejection of the political parties, and its assertion of the need for a new "political apparatus." The platform proclaimed ownership of land by the cultivators, planned industrialization, a progressive income tax to limit family income to that required "to live decently" (5,000 pesos annually), and the nationalization of banks, insurance companies, hospital clinics, pharmaceutical factories, and the industries of transportation, radio, and television. It also advocated an extensive social welfare program, including socialized medicine. The armed forces, the United Front declared, would be supported in so far as they did not affect adversely the needs of health and education. Defense of national sovereignty would be the obligation of all citizens. Women should be obliged to give civic service at the age of 18. The platform also echoed an older Christian position when it called for the punishment of the fathers of abandoned children.

Torres announced this program on May 22, 1965, at a meeting of the FUN held in the National University. At the same time he proclaimed himself "a revolutionary as a Colombian, as a sociologist, as a Christian, and as a priest." Succeeding events would show that this statement meant he had now come to the conclusion that only violent revolution could bring social justice to Colombia.[1]

In June 1965 Camilo Torres asked for and received release from his priestly vows, becoming a Christian layman. For the next several months he journeyed around the country presenting the platform of FUN. Then, in October, he set out from Bogotá to join the Army of National Liberation operating in the northeastern (mountain) province of Santander. In January, 1966, his last message to the Colombian people explained that he had joined the guerrillas because he no longer believed in the possibility of achieving real social change within the Colombian political system. A few weeks later, on February 15, he was shot and killed by the Colombian army in what was officially reported as an ambush of the guerrilla band in which Torres served. His devotees, however, interpret the "ambush" as the planned murder of Camilo.

The significance of Camilo Torres in contemporary Latin American social thought lies in his identification with the trend among young liberal Catholic priests and laymen to reject the slow, peaceful (and Christian Democratic) approach to reform as ineffective and counter-productive. Such an approach, they say, really strengthens those elements in society that oppose radical change. Camilo put the reason for his own rejection of peaceful measures in quite simple terms, arguing that "the old structure could not satisfy that necessity [for a social revolution]."[2] This impossibility of Christian reconciliation within "the old structure" also moved him and his peers to reconcile Christianity with marxism. By taking this position they cease to be Christians in anything other than a nominal sense, in the view of most Christians. They insist, however, that they are moved by religious conviction more genuine than that of their critics and that a marxist revolution need not be atheist. The example of Torres' career takes on something of this deeper meaning when it is noted that groups of Catholic priests and laymen in virtually all parts of America have taken up the challenge of identifying themselves with marxist movements, however much these groups and the movements with which they identify themselves may differ.

As a martyr, Camillo Torres has become a symbol of radical violent revolution equal to, though distinct from, "Che" Guevara. Thus Gonzalo Castillo Cárdenas, of Colombia, writing on the necessity of a Christian commitment to revolution, has called Camilo Torres the precursor "in the motivation and mobilization of this new Christian current and in the definition of the content of this new social conscience."[3] Castillo Cárdenas places the messages of Torres with such other statements of the newly revolutionary Christianity as those of the Brazilian bishop Dom Helder Camara, the "Letter to the Bishops of America Assembled in Medellin from 920 priests," the Protestant documents of ISAL, and the 1968 proclamation of the Galconda movement, signed by fifty Colombian priests and Bishop Gerardo Valencia Buenaventura. In this article, Gonzalo Castillo sounds an ecumenical note characteristic of these revolutionary priests when he extends a hand to the liberal Protestants in Latin America who back the publication of *Cristianismo y Sociedad* and the documents of ISAL.

The Galconda Movement in Colombia aims to keep alive the spirit of

Camilo Torres. In the words of one of its members, Father René García, "Galconda arose from the death of Camilo Torres to continue his path. . . . It seeks the creation of a society without privileges." It advocates, he says, "a socialism that should grow out of the social structure peculiar to our people and should enrich itself from the contradictions of world socialism." It rejects theoretical and dogmatic revolutionaries that are "alienated from the popular reality" and are "obsessed with foreign schemes which they wish to impose . . . on the oppressed masses." It proposes popular organization to oppose "North American imperialism operating through the national oligarchy" and advocates radical land reform to return ownership to the agricultural worker.

History will decide whether this young priest-martyr will hold a place in Colombian history comparable to that of his great ancestor of the same name, or to other great revolutionists. For the time being all one can safely say is that his example has inspired a socially conscious and revolutionary movement among young Catholic priests and laymen. But whatever the historical judgment may be in other respects, it will have to reckon with a growing literature inspired by Torres' words and deeds.

NOTES

1. *Camilo Torres (1956–1966)* (Cuernavaca, México: CIDAC, 1966. Sondeo 5), pp. 254–264.
2. Germán Guzmán Campos, *Camilo Torres* (New York: Sheed and Ward, 1969), p. 224.
3. "La tárea política de la Iglesia: de la protesta al compromiso revolucionario," *Cristianismo y Sociedad*, Año VIII, No. 22 (1970), 51–60.

BIBLIOGRAPHY

The writings of Torres may be found in *Camilo Torres: biografía, plataformas, mensajes* (Medellín, Colombia: Ed. Carpel Antorcha, 1966), in Camilo Torres, *Revolutionary Writings* (New York: Herder and Herder, 1969), and in *Camilo Torres (1956–1966)* (Cuernavaca, México: CIDOC, 1966, Sondeos 5). Of books about him the following are useful: Germán Guzmán Campos, *Camilo Torres* (New York: Sheed and Ward, 1969), a translation by John D. Ring of Guzmán's *Camilo: Presencia y Destino* (Bogotá: Servicios Especiales de Prensa, 1967); Norberto Habegger, *Camilo Torres: el Cura guerrillero* (Buenos Aires: A. Pena Lillo, 1967); Manuel Maldonado Denís, "Ernesto Guevara y Camilo Torres: revolucionarios por convicción," *Cuadernos Americanos*, Año XXVII, No. 2 (Marzo-abril 1968), 52–68; and Carlos Enrique Pareja, *El Padre Camilo: el cura guerrillero* (México: Ed. Nuestra América, 1968).

11

HUGO BLANCO GALDOS (1933(?) —)
by Eduardo J. Tejera

Although he has received less international attention, Hugo Blanco of Peru ranks in importance with such young twentieth century revolutionary Latin American leaders as Camilo Torres and "Che" Guevara. A convert to Trotskyite marxism, he led an abortive guerrilla movement among the peasants of the province of Cuzco, Peru, that has made him a notable symbolic figure of the Peruvian agrarian revolution. Like Guevara in Bolivia, he was opposed both by government forces and by the Moscow-oriented Communist party of his country. He and his little band of guerrillas failed to rally general peasant support and were soon defeated. But the national and international attention attracted by his trial and condemnation, at first to death but then reduced to a prison term, did more to speed up agrarian reform than his rebellion had done. In the eyes of Peruvian revolutionaries he became a major martyr to the cause of breaking up the system of land monopoly in his country.

He was born in Cuzco, probably in 1933, the son of prosperous middle class parents. His father was a successful lawyer. The children of the family received the education customary among Peruvian professional families. One brother, Oscar, became an engineer; another brother Luchi, is a journalist. Hugo was studying agronomy in Argentina when he left the university and returned to Cuzco to work among the peasants. He received his secondary school education in the Colegio Nacional de Ciencias of Cuzco. So far as known, he did not take part in any radical activity during his secondary school years. It is likely, however, that the generally leftist tendencies of the Cuzco environment at this time gave him an awareness of the revolutionary ferment going on. Cuzco had long been a stronghold of the Marxist but non-Communist APRA (Alliance for American Revolution), organized by Víctor Rául Haya de la Torre, as well as of other opposition groups. It would be surprising, indeed, if young Hugo had not picked up from this environment a keen awareness of the social injustice in Peruvian society and a predilection for some of the revolutionary plans and doctrines for dealing with it.

Just why Blanco went to Argentina to pursue university study is not clear. Probably it was because of the disturbed conditions in the Peruvian universities at this time. Possibly it was the attraction of Argentina. At any rate, his enrollment in the University of La Plata was a turning point in his life. Working at various jobs there to support himself as a student, he came into contact with the radicalism of Argentine workers as well as with that of the students of agronomy with whom he came into closest contact. In 1956 he seems to have joined the Trotskyite organization, *Palabra Obrera* (Voice of Labor) led by Hugo Bressano, a professor of the university who acted as a revolutionary militant under the pseudonym of Nahuel Moreno. It was probably the influence of Bressano, more than anything else, that led Blanco to his later revolutionary activity, although it is not impossible that he came to this decision independently as he viewed the problems of Peru from the perspective of the more highly developed Argentina.

In 1958 he left the University of La Plata and returned to Peru, a virtual Trotskyite, if not completely one in theory. After a brief residence in Callao, he went back to Cuzco to undertake the task of organizing the peasants and agricultural workers of the Valle Convención. Some influence of Bressano can certainly be seen at this point, because Blanco's theoretical framework for organizing the peasant movement was that of his mentor. In this rich agricultural valley of Peru he soon had established a number of peasant unions, making them into a viable political force as well as an effective instrument for driving hard bargains with absentee landlords and their agents. Successful strikes on the estates of Paccha Grande and Chaucamayo illustrated the effectiveness of the Blanco-Bressano strategy. The plan was called the *Poder Dual* or Dual power. The objective was to break the power of the landowners by organizing a peasant power structure. Rural workers were organized to take the land from those owners who were not actively sharing with the workers. Thus, the strategy of organizing and politicizing the peasants was the ideological backbone of Blanco's (now apparent) Trotskyism. It was the first stage of the revolution that he aimed to achieve ultimately. Thus, if his philosophy at times seems to be more a kind of populist agrarianism than marxist Trotskyism it is only because this political ideology was merely the first stage, a tactical move, in the basic strategic plan.

The Convención Valley boasted six agricultural syndicates in 1956. By 1962, largely through Blanco's efforts, this number had grown to 132. A number of factors contributed to this success. One factor was that the peasant federations established schools and health clinics and worked in other ways to arouse and educate the Indian peasants. But the major factor was more closely linked to the peasant land hunger. Most of the land in the valley was owned by large landowners who subleased their lands to *arrendatorios* who in turn subleased to others, who subleased to the Indian *manipuras*. Rents were not paid in money, but in days of work. The landowner thus got the labor to produce the cash crops of cacao, coffee, and (Chinese) tea that were the major products of the area. Blanco began by organizing the *arrendatarios* to demand a fifty percent reduction in their rents. When this move succeeded, he moved on to organize all the peasants of the area and to conduct a general strike. If successful the result of this strike was that the peasants were in possession of their own small plots of land without the obligation to pay customary rent in the form of labor.

After five years, Blanco's success was striking, though it was chiefly because he had confined his activity to a small area, a rather natural community, the Convención Valley, and because he had been able to confront the agents of absentee landlords with a united peasantry. So far he had avoided confrontation at the national level; but the fact that peasants in Valle Convención possessed their lands without obligation to pay rent could not long escape national attention. His success had reached its greatest height in 1961, just as national political tension was increasing in anticipation of the upcoming elections of 1962. The success of his movement had paved the way for later legislation that would confirm the peasant occupation of lands and provide for payments to the government over a long period of time, thus permitting government reimbursement of the landowners. But the public reaction in 1961 was only a heightened fear.

The enthusiasm of his followers was too hard for Blanco to restrain. They went on to more and more violent attacks on the residences of landowners and to further occupations of lands. The leader of the radical MIR, Luis de la Puente, advised Blanco to stop the attacks of his followers on the houses of the proprietors; but Blanco replied that this was impossible. He greatly desired the backing of the MIR group at this time, but Luis de la Puente told him the MIR cadres were not sufficiently prepared to go on to the more revolutionary phase toward which Blanco seemed to be headed. At this stage, however, the Trotskyites, including Blanco, seem to have erred in overestimating their power and underestimating the capacity of the government to take action. This mistake in judgment led to their fatal error of launching a guerrilla campaign.

After 1960, the increasingly radical line of the Cuban Revolution and its policy of exporting revolution in its own model supported the more militant elements within the Trotskyite movement in Peru as elsewhere. Whether he wished it or not, Blanco was being pushed toward a more ambitious and radical program involving guerrilla action. In Peru, a further influence in this direction was another split in the leftist movements. One Peruvian group now favored an overall insurrectionist line, similar to that of the Cuban guerrilla movement; another group, however, wanted to continue the more moderate approach practiced so successfully in the Convención Valley. On a regional basis, this question was apparently settled in the meeting of the Latin-American Secretariat of Orthodox Trotskyites (SLATO) in Santiago, Chile in August, 1960. In this meeting the line of guerrilla action was approved and preparations were immediately begun to launch a guerrilla movement in the Cuzco region. In June, 1961, SLATO sent from Santiago Alberto Pereyra, an Argentine Trotskyite, and José Martorell, a Spaniard, to establish contact with Blanco in order to start this guerrilla action. Hugo Bressano, Blanco's professor at La Plata, was given charge of SLATO's operations in Peru.

In the midst of the electoral crisis of 1962 in Peru, some of the SLATO members joined the followers of Blanco in guerrilla actions, both urban and rural. Two commercial banks were robbed during the first half of the year, and other guerrilla activities were carried out at both the provincial and the national level. The Peruvian government reacted vigorously and a counter-offensive against the guerrillas quickly suppressed their activity. It seems that these advocates of guerrilla tactics had not fully analyzed the consequences and repercussions in Peru of such a program of violence, had not planned their tactics with sufficient care, and had not made sufficient provisions for supplying the guerrilla bands. For as soon as the government launched its campaign the guerrillas were thrown on the defensive. They were fugitives before they had taken any real offensive action in the field.

One cause of their failure was the disunity of the revolutionary forces, which were fighting among themselves. Thus Blanco had to meet at the same time both the attacks by the Peruvian Communist Party (PCP) and the offensive launched against his guerrillas by the government. The well known cut-throat war between the Trotskyites and the followers of the Moscow and Havana lines prevented any coalescing of the radical opposition groups in support of Blanco's activities. His Trotskyite thinking and SLATO preponderance in the direction of his activity were anathema to the Moscow-oriented Peruvian Communist Party, which called Blanco an "imperialist agent provocateur" and a "putschist." Nor could the SLATO organization that backed Blanco be expected to reach any agreement with the Movimiento Izquierdista Revolucionario (MIR), supported by China and Cuba. These differences among the Communists fatally weakened the guerrilla movement, isolating the followers of

Blanco from their potential sources of support. Even within SLATO there were divisions, especially after Bressano changed tactics at the end of 1962 and adopted a peaceful line.

In November 1962, for the first time, Blanco led his followers in a guerrilla attack against a small Civil Guard post. According to the author of the only extensive book on Blanco, Victor Villanueva, the attack came about in support of Tiburcio Bolaños, an officer of the labor syndicate in Chaupimo. Bolaños was resisting arrest for having threatened a local hacendado who had raped Bolaños's wife and daughter, and the purpose of the attack on the Civil Guard post was to support his resistence.[1] The operation was successful in its objective of capturing arms, but it left a toll of several deaths, leading the army to start a vigorous campaign against Blanco and his followers. From this time on, the government counter-insurgency operations were intensified and Blanco's small band of guerrillas was soon captured. The capture of Blanco himself, on May 29, 1963, ended this ephemeral guerrilla movement in Peru. As a guerrilla war it had never really gained significant momentum.

In a 1970 interview with a correspondent of the French journal, *Le Monde*, Blanco attributed part of the failure of his guerrilla campaign to sectarianism among the marxists. "But in Peru, as elsewhere," he said, "we have to fight the pro-imperialist bourgeoisie and the pro-Soviet Communist party both at once. Because I was a Trotskyite in Cuzco, I had to defend myself against the intrigues and the smears of the Communist party for years." In a general sense this statement is true but, as Victor Villanueva points out, Blanco should have added that other factors contributed to his defeat, including lack of funds, of a party, of a more serious plan, and of an efficient organization, together with his fatal underestimate of the strength of the government.

For the hundreds of peasants that Blanco led in his organizing efforts in Cuzco province, and for thousands of others who learned of him through the press and the radio, he has become a legend. In the Cuzco province his name has so caught the popular imagination that songs have been written about him. The peasant unions that he founded still exist to perpetuate his memory and have proved to be important instruments for reform and for achieving social justice. Blanco's call for agrarian reform, while not new in Peru, gave impetus to the adoption of an agrarian reform policy by the government of President Fernando Belaunde Terry that has been continued by the subsequent military government.

One can only lament that Blanco did not continue his initial efforts along peaceful lines in the Concepción Valley, for much of the initiative he had gained there by his peasant organizations was lost when he launched an abortive guerrilla campaign. As long as his efforts were directed to organizing peasant cooperatives, to negotiating with landowners and to organizing cooperatives, he had achieved an overwhelming success. His agrarianism had a teluric force that won the needed support of the peasantry, and therein lies the reason for his earlier success. When, however, he aimed at a confrontation with the national government in guerrilla warfare he lost touch with his peasant support and his movement ended in a fiasco.

If one asks what was Blanco's significance as a revolutionary leader, the answer appears to be that he showed an unusually clear perception of the capacity of the Indian peasantry of Peru to organize, to acquire land by cooperative action, and thus to improve their income. Whether or not he realistically appraised their capacity to effect a more fundamental social and political revolution remains an unanswered question as this sketch is being written, a few months after he was released from prison in December, 1970.

NOTES

1. *Hugo Blanco y la rebelión campesina* (Lima: Librería Ed. Juan Mejía Baca, 1967), pp. 136–137.

BIBLIOGRAPHY

The only extensive work on Hugo Blanco is by his fellow partisan, Victor Villanueva, *Hugo Blanco y la rebelión campesina* (Lima: Librería Editorial Juan Mejía Baca, 1967). Hugo Neira, *Cuzco: tierra y muerte* (Lima: Populibros Peruanos, 1964) is interesting but more superficial. Blanco published his program in *El camino de nuestra revolución* (Lima, 1964). A brief sketch of his life is found in Richard Gott, *Guerrilla Movements in Latin America* (Garden City, N.J.: Doubleday and Company, 1971), pp. 314–329. See also Adolfo Gilly, "Los sindicatos guerrilleros del Perú," *Revista Marcha* (Montevideo) Agosto de 1963; "Peru's Most Successful Reformer," *Atlas* (1970) pp. 56–57, translated from *Le Monde* of Paris; "El famoso Hugo Blanco," *Caretas* (Lima) No. 429 (Enero 18–28, 1971), pp. 16ff. (an interview); Aníbal Quijano O., "El movimiento campesino del Peru y sus lideres," *América Latina* (Rio de Janeiro) Ano 8, No. 4 (Out.–Dez. 1965), pp. 43–65; and a series of articles that appeared in *Partisans* (Paris) by Gerald Suberville, Hugo Neira, and Adolfo Gilly (Numbers 9, 13, and 26–27) between 1963 and 1966.

PART II

TRADITIONALISTS

12

LATIN AMERICAN TRADITIONALISM

Although traditionalism finds expression as a social and political force in all cultures and at all times, it acquires greater importance at certain moments in time and space when circumstances evoke particularly strong human reactions. Thus, in Latin America, at certain times both before and since independence, conditions have given traditionalism special significance. As we shall see, this Latin American traditionalism is not all of one kind, but occurs, rather, in several varieties. It also changes with the passing of time, so that the ideology of a progressive or revolutionary movement of one era tends to become the traditionalism of a subsequent age.

The most obvious, if not the most influential, variety of Latin American traditionalism derives from European sources, particularly Spanish and Portuguese, and is found most commonly among Europeans in America and their criollo descendants.[1] It is the traditionalism of the European culture, religion and socio-political structure. European society and culture have changed, of course, during the nearly five centuries since the days of Columbus, so that it is not accurate to speak of a single European traditionalism. Rather, we must note the several varieties characteristic of the historical epochs: the Conquest, the colonial period, independence, the nineteenth century (possibly distinguishing between the early and late century), and the twentieth century.

European traditionalism came to America with the Conquest, accompanying the more revolutionary ideas of the Renaissance humanism brought by missionaries such as Bartolomé de Las Casas, Bernardino de Sahagún, Motolinia (Toribio de Benavente), and Manoel da Nobrega, among many others. In Spain the discovery and conquest of America produced Francisco Vitoria's application of the doctrines of Christian natural law in defense of the equal rights of the Indians, making this defense part of his emerging structure of international law.[2] But it also brought the argument of Juan Ginés de Sepúlveda based on Aristotle, that the natives of America were by nature inferior beings, destined to be ruled over by their European conquerors.

This variety of traditionalist thought, rooted in the scholastic tradition, was expressed by Ginés de Sepúlveda in the classic debate with the missionary defender of the Indians, Bartolomé de las Casas. Las Casas was a revolutionist in the fundamental sense, professing to create a Utopia based on Christian love and justice for the converted Mayan Indians of Chiapas. The revolutionary proposal that Las Casas made had its basis in the Christian tradition, but he also sought a rationale in the philosophy of Aristotle for protecting the Indians from exploitation by their conquerors. His startling argument was that the Indian civilizations were equal to or superior to those of Christian Europe in accordance with Aristotelian criteria.[3]

The active role played in the Catholic Counter-Reform by the Spanish kings (who were also kings of Portugal from 1588 to 1640) gave a special character and direction to the traditionalism of the Spanish colonial era. The Council of Trent, in crystallizing the Counter-Reform, assigned an important role to tradition as a basis for religious truth and practice, giving Spanish culture a basis in religious traditionalism. This religious traditionalism was extended further, at about the same time, by the expulsion of the non-Christian Moors and Jews from the peninsula. The Spanish Inquisition (more than that of Portugal) actively enforced religious uniformity in America. Although generally tolerant toward Indian lapses from the true faith and religious practice, the Inquisition was unrelenting in dealing with presumably relapsed Jewish converts (conversos). Many of the most important trials of the Inquisition in Spanish America were of these conversos.[4]

The policy of the Spanish and Portuguese crowns in preventing the circulation in America of books on the Index is less clear. Professor Irving Leonard believes that the major object of Spanish authorities was to prevent such works from falling into the hands of Indian converts.[5] This policy would seem to show Spanish recognition of the fact that the Indian, in holding stubbornly to old ways and ideas, expressed another kind of traditionalism.

In the era of the independence movements traditionalism appeared most obviously in the loyalism of the colonial Church hierarchy. But, as various Latin American scholars, including the Argentine Enrique de Gandía, have shown, it also appeared in a theory of independence which found its rationale in the old Spanish legal code, the Siete Partidas and in the sixteenth century natural law theories of Vitoria and Suárez.[6] Thus monarchism was an essential ingredient of the traditionalism, both of the loyalists and of the independence leaders. The former tended to defend monarchical absolutism and the latter constitutional monarchy as the basis of their Liberalism. In fact, as Sergio Villalobos has pointed out in the case of Chile, most independence leaders seemed to have favored some kind of liberal monarchical constitution.[7] The defense of the wealth and position of the Church, of the hierarchical structure of colonial society, and of the other elements of traditionalism, were more characteristic of loyalists than of the independence leaders.

The classic pattern of Latin American traditionalism, however, was that which emerged at this time in opposition to French Revolutionary Liberalism in France, Spain, and Portugal. Its literary spokesmen were Joseph de Maistre of France (1753–1821) and two Spaniards, Jaime Balmes (1810–1848) and Juan Francisco Donoso Cortés (1809–1853). In Spain it found political expression in the forces which surrounded Ferdinand VII after the restoration and later gathered around the pretender Don Carlos. In Portugal it appeared among those who supported Dom Miguel against Dom Pedro I and his daughter María de Gloria. This classic traditionalism envisaged a society that embraced three basic elements: absolute (or traditional) monarchy, the anti-Protestant religious traditionalism of the Council of Trent, and a social structure, hierarchial in form, that gave the nobility (and the military and clergy) special responsibilities and privileges. It was class conscious, in the aristocratic sense, and rejected the emerging marxist theory of the class struggle. Latin American spokesmen of this traditionalism during the decades immediately following independence included such notable leaders as the historian, Lucas Alamán, organizer of the Conservative party in Mexico, Diego Portales, the architect of Chilean Conservatism, and Juan Manuel Rosas, the long time dictator in Argentina. During these decades the revolutionary and Liberal regimes of the independence years gave way to political systems of a generally more conservative character, and some traditionalist-oriented leaders were led to feel that the forces of anarchy and atheism were on the way to being eliminated.

During the last decades of the nineteenth century, changing conditions gave a different character to Latin American traditionalism. One major factor was the reaction of Pope Pius IX to the European revolutionary era of 1848 that ultimately resulted in the publication of his *Syllabus of Errors* (1864), condemning among other errors the socialist labor movement and the Masonic lodges. A second factor, more important on the whole, was the political triumph of Liberal parties in most Latin American countries, a triumph that tended to reduce the role of the Conservative parties to that of a reactionary and generally traditionalist opposition.

In contrast to the conservative traditionalism of the early decades of the century, however, this new conservatism was the voice of a minority. It was a voice powerless to move constructive action, able only, because of the wealth and social prestige of its members, to place obstacles in the way of the dominant Liberal majority, but not to replace it. Yet, ironically, this late nineteenth century religious traditionalism and social conservatism was the seedbed from which the more revolutionary Christian Democracy sprouted in the twentieth century. Even in the last years of the nineteenth century this religious conservatism was often the sounding board for the Christian socialism enunciated by Pope Leo XIII in his encyclical *Rerum Novarum* (1891) on the condition of the working class. Antonio Caro of Colombia and Juan Zorilla de San Martín of Uruguay provide striking examples of traditionalists of this era who were also pioneers in urging the new emphasis on social Christianity.

Twentieth century traditionalism is an even more complicated phenomenon than this late nineteenth century variety. It inherited a considerable residue of reaction from the experience of defeat by the Liberals in the politico-ecclesiastical conflicts of the nineteenth century. It is also the heir of the intellectual revolution that produced such sociological theories as those of the Italian, Vilfredo Pareto, developing the intellectual basis for the fascist doctrine of rule by an intellectual and power elite. But it also includes in a a general way the revival of Thomistic and Christian thought. In Brazil, for example, Jackson de Figueiredo (1891–1928), like Antonio Caro in Colombia, formulated the basis for social action within traditional Thomistic Christian values and concepts.

This twentieth century development leads us to note that European traditionalism has not been the only traditionalism nourished by Latin American criollos. Four and a half centuries of experience in America have given them a cultural experience of their own, imbedded in folk songs, folkways, and institutions, and expressed in the cultural values associated with them. As early as the epoch immediately following independence, this native American traditionalism found expression in the ideas of the Argentine Generation of 1837 (The Association of May). In the twentieth century this criollo traditionalism became an important ingredient of such kinds of native fascism as Mexican *Sinarquismo*, Brazilian *Integralismo*, and Argentine *Peronismo*. These were traditionalist forces or movements which also owed much in ideology to their European counterparts, and usually included elements of Hispanism, linked to the reviving concern for Hispanic culture but transmuted into such nationalist ideologies as *Argentinidad, Peruanidad,* or *Mexicanidad*.[8] Manuel Gómez Morín, founder of the Party of Nacional Action (PAN) in Mexico, presents a similar yet different variety, that of a leader of the Mexican Revolution who turned from it because he came to believe it had corrupted Mexican social, cultural, and religious values.

The Argentine historian, José Luis Romero, in a book on the political thought of the Latin American Right, has remarked that twentieth century populist movements such as those mentioned above may be considered "rightist" in the sense that they rely upon authoritarian political concepts. This was the definition, he pointed out, employed by nineteenth century Liberal opponents of authoritarian rule. But these contemporary populists are often, perhaps even usually, advocates of social change, attacking the Liberal dominated society as bourgeois. The genuine "rightists," in the somewhat marxist view of Romero, are those who defend the traditional socio-economic structure "rooted in the colonial order."[9]

Traditionalism is still a notable characteristic of the Indian peoples of Latin America and of their cultures. As remarked earlier, the Spanish Conquest made the peoples of the Aztec and Inca empires culturally reactionary, causing them to withdraw psychologically and economically from the society of the conquerors and to resist assimilation into Spanish culture. While maintaining a facade of Christianity, they kept their pagan gods and rites. Stubbornly, they retained their national languages and customs. They even withdrew physically, fleeing from the Spanish occupied valleys into more remote mountain strongholds. This indigenous traditionalism had implications of revolutionary violence that found expression in frequent native uprisings during (and after) the colonial period. That of Túpac Amaru of Peru in 1782 was the most violent and far reaching. This descendant of the last Indian emperor, as we have seen, rallied this Indian traditionalism in the chaotic uprising that nearly toppled Spanish authority in South America during the time of the (North) American Revolution.

The mestizo population of Latin America, emerging between two cultures, at first rejected the traditions of both. Slowly the mestizo developed his own traditions out of his experiences in the American environment. The gaucho pattern of life and work for example, is largely a mestizo tradition, as is much of the American tradition of the caudillo, as distinguished from the older Iberian tradition. Throughout the history of independent Latin America the rising mestizo population has often been a major force for social change. J.M. Puig Casauranc has even called it the central social process in the Mexican Revolution.[10] On the other hand, however, mestizo traditionalism, either in the form of *hispanidad* (Hispanism) or of frenetic nationalism has been a source of strength for native fascist movements of the type of Brazilian *Integralismo*, Argentine *Peronismo*, and Mexican *Sinarquismo*.

The traditionalists discussed in the following pages come from different epochs and are of different varieties. Those of the nineteenth century hold views somewhat resembling the Iberian nineteenth century traditionalism of absolute monarchy, a hierarchical society, and an authoritarian traditional church, although Latin Americans commonly lack strong addiction to the first two elements. Some twentieth century traditionalists, but not all, add a major component of populism to their political ideologies, often seeking support, as previously suggested, in the folk-traditionalism of the mestizos and poor criollos. No example of an indigenous (Amerindian) traditionalist has been included. The Uruguayan, Juan Zorilla de San Martín, might have been included as an Indianist (not an Indian) because of his romantic glorification of Uruguay's Indian past in *Tabaré*, the romance of the daughter of a Spanish colonist and a young Indian chieftan. His inclusion would have been questionable, however, because of the lack of critical studies to support it. A number of other traditionalists who might well have been included, such as Andrés Bello, José Enrique Rodó, Juan Bautista Alberdi, Manuel Gálvez, and Jackson de Figueiredo, were omitted solely because the author has written of them elsewhere.[11]

NOTES

1. The Spanish term *criollo* is used here in preference to the more common *creole* (of French origin), because of the pejorative racial and ethnic connotations often associated with the latter term.

2. The "Relecciones" of Vitoria in which these ideas are developed may be found conveniently in Volume II of *El Pensamiento Político Hispanoamericano*, edited by Guillermo A. Lousteau Heguy and Salvador M. Lozada (Buenos Aires: Depalma, 1967). A facsimile of the original Latin, with a Spanish translation, was issued by the Pan American Union in 1963.

3. Cf. Lewis Hanke, *Aristotle and the American Indians* (London: Hollis and Carter, 1959).

4. Richard E. Greenleaf, *Zumárraga and the Mexican Inquisition, 1536–1543*, note in *The Americas*, Vol. XIX, No. 3 (January 1963), 319.

5. Irving Leonard, *Books of the Brave* (Cambridge: Harvard University Press, 1949), and his various articles on the book trade in Spanish America in the *Hispanic Review* and the *Hispanic American Historical Review*.

6. Enrique de Gandía, *Las ideas políticas de la independencia americana* (Vol. 5 of his *Historia de las ideas políticas en Argentina)* (Buenos Aires: Depalma, 1968), chs. 34–36.

7. Sergio Villalobos R.. *Tradición y reforma en 1810* (Santiago, Chile: Universidad de Chile, 1961).

8. Martin S. Stabb, *In Quest of Identity* (Chapel Hill: University of North Carolina Press, 1967), pp. 146ff.; Octavio Paz, *The Labyrinth of Solitude*, trans. by Lysander Kemp (New York: Grove Press, 1961), pp. 153–155.

9. *El pensamiento político de la derecha latinoamericana* (Buenos Aires: PAIDOS, 1970), pp. 23–26.

10. *El sentido social del proceso histórico de México* (Mexico: Botas, 1936).

11. See the author's *Makers of Democracy in Latin America* (New York: H.W. Wilson, 1945 and Cooper Square Publishers, 1968), *Latin American Leaders* (New York: H.W. Wilson, 1949 and Cooper Square Publishers, 1968), *Latin American Social Thought* (The University Press of Washington, D.C., 1966).

BIBLIOGRAPHY

To the author's knowledge, no comprehensive study of Latin American traditionalism and traditionalists has been made, although the previously cited work of José Luis Romero, *El pensamiento político de la derecha latinoamericana*, is an essay in this direction. Publications referred to in the footnotes in this chapter suggest the kind of studies that cast some light on the subject. But, in general, the student must consult national histories, church histories, historical monographs on other subjects that treat the subject incidentally, biographies, and the published works of political leaders and writers whose basic orientation is traditionalist in some respect.

13

LUCAS ALAMAN (1792–1853)

Lucas Alamán, the historian of Mexican Independence and the organizer of the Mexican Conservative party, typifies in many respects the intellectual traditionalism of the years immediately following independence. Diego Portales of Chile and Juan Manuel Rosas of Argentina held traditionalist views, but are better understood as activists than as intellectuals. Andrés Bello is in many respects the most sophisticated voice of conservative moderation during these years, but Bello is better understood as a humanist of the Enlightenment. He does not reflect the thought of the European traditionalists, de Maistre and Balmes, nor does his philosophy lead him to a traditionalist political ideology of American character.

In contrast, Alamán reflects direct intellectual contact with the thought of European traditionalists and does express a traditionalist political ideology. He was active in Mexican politics, but he was also a major intellectual figure. His historical treatment of Mexican independence, one of the classics of Mexican historiography, reflects his traditionalism; he defends the Spanish Conquest and criticizes independence as a decline in Spanish culture. "I am a dry leaf," he wrote in 1834, "blown violently about by the wind of adversity."[1] In this bitter, almost cynical, exclamation at the height of his brilliant career in literature, politics, and business, Alaman compresses into a few words his pessimistic disillusionment and that of many of his contemporaries in the Hispanic world as they reacted in a kind of traditionalist framework to the violence, anarchy, and fanaticism of their times. Concluding his history of the Mexican independence movement, Alamán quoted the Latin poet, Lucan as follow: "Nothing more had remained than the shadow of a name illustrious in former times."

Lucas Alamán was born on October 18, 1792, in Guanajuato, Mexico, a major center of colonial silver mining. His parents were leading citizens of the city. Juan Vicente was his father and his mother was María Ignacio Escalada, the widow of Gabriel de Arrechederreta before her marriage to Lucas's father. Through his mother Lucas had links with the Spanish aristocracy. In Guanajuato he received the education customary for a child in a well to do family—private tutors and study in the School of Belén, where he became proficient in the natural sciences, art, and languages. There, at the age of eighteen, he encountered the Revolution when the turbulent horde of followers of Miguel Hidalgo burst upon Guanajuato in 1810, killing a number of Spaniards and sacking the city. This was a traumatic experience of violence that was never erased from his memory; he later characterized it as "a monstrous combination of religion with assassination and rapine."[2]

After the sacking of the city, many of the leading families of Guanajuato, among them the Alamáns, moved to Mexico City for greater security. There, in the spirit of the Enlightenment, young Lucas pursued studies ranging from literature and history to chemistry and botany with Vicente Cervantes, mineralogy with Andrés Manuel del Rio, and languages with Manuel del Valle. In 1811 he entered the Third Order of Penitence of San Francisco. About this time he was denounced to the Inquisition for possessing forbidden books, but was exonerated. It is quite probable that he had appropriate approval for having the books; or his exoneration may have been due to family influence. In any case, the possession of books on the Index was not too unusual at this time in Mexico. His first published work also appeared about this time. It was a defense of Copernican theories of the universe and was published in *Diario de México* in 1812. The ideas expressed in it clearly identify Alamán as a child of the Enlightenment.

For five years, beginning in 1814, young Alamán traveled and studied in Spain, France, Germany, Switzerland, Italy, Belgium, and England, gaining the cultural experience customary for a Spanish American youth of wealth. His travels brought him acquaintance with such intellectual figures as Vicomte Benjamin René de Constant, Vicomte Francois René de Chateaubriand, Baron Alexander von Humboldt, and Baron Christian Leopoldo de Buch, the geologist. In Germany he perfected a knowledge of mineralogy that later stood him in good stead in Mexico. In Paris he met and gave financial aid to the priest and independence leader, Servando Teresa de Mier.

Returning to Mexico in 1819, because of the illness of his mother, he began his public career with a viceregal appointment to the Commission on Public Health. He also attracted favorable attention at this time by publishing an article on the decadence of mining in Mexico. The following year he was named a deputy from Guanajuato to the new Cortes called to meet in Spain after the Revolution of 1820. Alamán was still a Liberal at this time, and as such collaborated with the American delegates to the Cortes in presenting plans for American autonomy. On a more practical level, he secured approval of the Cortes for a reduction in the taxes on Mexican mining. When Agustín Iturbide came to power in

Mexico, he named Alamán minister to France. This was the beginning of a career in diplomacy and of his business career also. For while in Paris as Minister he began the arrangements for financing the Compañía Unida de Minas that was to become one of his major business enterprises in Mexico.

He returned to Mexico in 1823, just as the Iturbide government was being overthrown. In the transitional regime under Nicolás Bravo, Guadelupe Victoria, and Pedro Celestino Negrete, he became minister of foreign relations. As minister he succeeded in getting British and United States recognition for Mexico, but failed to get that of Spain (to be delayed another dozen years). His scientific and intellectual interests found expression at this time in founding the National Archives and the Museum of Natural History and Antiquities. It was a premonition of his later traditionalism that as minister he interested himself in protecting the remains of Cortés from profanation in the course of the *desepañolización* of the day. He stayed on in the government of Victoria, the first president elected under the republican constitution of 1824. But his tendency to move toward a more traditional political position appeared almost at once in the form of his personal disagreement with the new constitutional system.

After serving less than two years under the republican regime he resigned. During the next several years he worked at developing the mining interests of the new Compañía Unida de Minas and at the Mexican interests of the Spanish Duke of Monteleone. He returned to public office, however, in the government of Anastasio Bustamente (supported by Santa Anna) after the overthrow of President Vicente Guerrero in December, 1829. Now a spokesman for a more traditional approach to politics, he seems to have dominated the policy making of the Bustamante government until it was overthrown, in turn, by Santa Anna in 1832. After the election of Santa Anna and Valentín Gómez Farías to the presidency and vice-presidency in that year, charges of malfeasance in office were instigated against all the ministers of the previous regime. Alamán defended himself ably in a book of 126 pages and was absolved of the charges.[3]

During the following years Alamán gave his attention largely to directing his own prospering business affairs, to encouraging national industry, and to writing his *History of Mexico*. But he was not out of touch with political currents. One of the lesser known aspects of his earlier political action was an unsuccessful effort during the Bustamente government to make a peaceful settlement of the Texas question through British mediation. This failure, the subsequent humiliating political defeat in 1832, and the subsequent attacks on his reputation had embittered his mind, reinforcing his conservative traditionalism. He now began to write in defense of monarchy in *El Universal* and to criticize the leaders of Mexican independence in ways that later appear in his *History*. By this time he was almost convinced that independence had been a mistake and that the mistake had been compounded by establishing a republic in a nation not prepared by experience to make it work. Only in the hands of its aristocratic ruling class, supported by the Church, and probably organized as a monarchy, could Mexico hope to rise to the level that her size, her resources, and her traditional culture made possible. These were the ideas motivating his organization of the Conservative party and his invitation to Santa Anna in the name of this party to return to Mexico in 1853. Whatever one may think of these traditionalist views, he can hardly view the removal by death (June 2, 1853) of this able guiding hand just when it might have led Santa Anna to avoid some of the excesses of his last regime, as anything other than one of the tragedies of Mexican history.

Alamán has been likened to Prince Metternich by two contemporary historians, José María Tornel y Mendível and Arturo Arnáiz y Freg. José Vasconcelos, in his *Breve historia de México,* compared him to Alexander Hamilton. He himself would probably have found a comparison with Edmund Burke more congenial, for he seems to have been guided in much of his thought by the latter's *Reflections on the French Revolution* and other writings. As Burke reacted against the excesses of the French Revolution, so Alamán turned against the excesses of Mexican independence. Like Burke, also, he came to conceive of history as an organic development through which the present was bound to the past and to future generations. Thus, like that of Burke, the basic pattern of Alamán's thought is historical. His ideas are best expressed in his classic *History of Mexico.* With Saint Augustine and Bishop Bossuet he saw a Divine plan, the intervention of Providence in history.

From history Alamán arrived at the basic principle guiding his policy—to act in accordance with "customs formed during three hundred years," in accordance with "established opinions," and relying for support upon "established interests."[4]

For Alamán, revolutions were not the product of a mechanistic order but the work of daring and ambitious leaders who persuaded the masses to follow them. Sometimes, however, a revolution arose from a conspiratorial agreement among powerful individuals who saw their interests threatened and sought to protect them by finding a leader of capacity and resolution to follow. In either case, the revolution tended to produce a degree of political fanaticism that led to the belief that any act of violence was permissible. He extended the cynicism of this view of revolutions to his analysis of the effects of masonry in Mexico. The concept of masonry as an evil conspiracy was doubtless due in part to his unhappy relationship to the conflict between the Scottish Rite and York Rite Masons in the turbulent politics of the Guerrero and Victoria regimes. His writings give no indication that he ever studied masonry sufficiently to understand its ideology, but he was convinced that it was a "pestilence" (*peste*). He was especially violent in his attacks on the York Rite in the defence of his actions during the years 1829–1832, calling it "the source and root of all the evils the nation experienced."

Like many other Latin Americans of his day, Alamán was an admirer of Great Britain and particularly of the role of individual enterprise in that nation's economy. There was much of British political economy in his economic theory. But he was convinced that Mexico was not prepared for a parliament of the British stamp. Nor could Mexico tolerate the British system of freedom of the press. "In the hands of factions," he wrote in 1848, "freedom of the press not only is not a means of enlightenment for nations but is, on the contrary, the most powerful instrument of fraud and deception."[5]

Racism is not a notable characteristic of Alamán, but he often seems to express rather unconsciously the racial prejudice of the Mexican aristocracy. In writing of the independence leader Morelos, for example, he insists that through both of his parents Morelos came from "one of the mixed castes of Indian and Negro, although in his statements he characterized himself as Spanish because, as I have had occasion to note elsewhere, no one in that era wanted to belong to any other class; while proposing to legitimatize independence, taking a stand on the rights of the Indians that they pretended to revindicate, [and] declaiming against the injustice of the Conquest, they all wanted to derive their descent from the conquering nation and not from the conquered people."[6]

Both in thought and in action Alamán is an outstanding example of the shift to a more conservative or traditional outlook made by a number of Latin Americans as they experienced the chaos and disorder of post-independence years. He is a particularly important representative of this change, however, because his traditionalism found expression in his classic history of Mexican independence. Indeed, his history of Mexico may well be read as a massive defense of the Conquest. As the theoretician of the Conservative and monarchist party he organized in 1853, he is one of relatively few intellectuals who raised their voices in defense of monarchy in mid-nineteenth century Spanish America. On the whole, history has not been too kind in its judgment of Alamán, however. Thus one critic speaks of him as "having lived with one foot placed in an historical era that was threatened and the other in that which was being born, without having understood either one."[7]

NOTES

1. *Defensa del Ex-ministro de Relaciones, don Lucas Alamán,* p. 107, quoted by Arturo Arnáiz y Freg in his Prólogo of *Lucas Alamán: Semblanza e ideario* (México: Ed. de Universidad Nacional Autónoma, 1939), p. ix.

2. Quoted in Manuel González Navarro, *El pensamiento político de Lucas Alamán* (México: El Colegio de México, 1952), p. 12.

3. *Defensa del Ex-ministro de Relaciones don Lucas Alamán en la causa formada contra el y contra los Ex-ministros.* . . . (Mexico: Imp. de Galvan, 1834).

4. Prólogo y selección de Arturo Arnáiz y Freg, *Lucas Alamán: semblanzas e ideario* (México: Universidad Nacional Autónoma, 1939), p. xviii.

5. *Ibid.,* p. xviii.

6. *Ibid.,* p. 82. Translated by author.

7. Manuel González Navarro, *op. cit.,* p. 137. Translated by author.

BIBLIOGRAPHY

Alamán's most important work is his *Historia de Méjico,* published in five volumes (México: Lara, 1849–52). This and other works are found in his collected *Obras,* 11 vols. (México: Jus, 1942). Arturo Arnáiz y Freg has presented an excellent selection in the *Semblanzas e ideario* cited in the text. In addition to this work and the study by Manuel González Novarro, also previously cited, important works on Alamán include Juan Bautista Alamán, *Apuntes para la biografía de don Lucas Alamán* (México: Jus, 1942); Antonio Ferrer del Río, *Lucas Alamán, su vida y escritos* (México: Jus, 1942); Jorge Gurria Lacroix, *Las ideas monárquicas de don Lucas Alamán* (México: Instituto de Historia, 1951); and José C. Valadés, *Lucas Alamán, estadista e historiador* (México: Antigua Librería Robredo de José Porrúa e Hijos, 1938).

14

BERNARDO PEREIRA DE VASCONCELLOS (1795–1850)

Vasconcellos was treated more at length in the author's *Makers of Democracy in Latin America* and so will be noted only briefly here. But his inclusion at this point is imperative, if for no other reason than to illustrate the kind of traditionalism produced by slaveholding, monarchical, Brazilian society in the early nineteenth century.

Like Lucas Alamán of Mexico, Vasconcellos received his education partly in his native country and partly in Europe—in this case in the University of Coimbra. Like Alamán also, he was at first a Liberal and later turned Conservative. Like his Mexican peer he was also an Anglophile and a monarchist. But with these elements the resemblance ceases. Unlike Alamán, Vanconcellos favored the parliamentary system of government, leading the early opposition to the Brazilian Crown in the National Assembly. Though not really a federalist he favored the decentralization of power and was the author of the *Ato Adicional*, an amendment to the Constitution that authorized provincial councils of government. During the parliamentary debate on this measure he pointed out the differences between the United States and Brazil, differences that in his judgment made federalism practical in the former, impossible in the latter.

He accepted the British political economy, especially the Utilitarianism of Jeremy Bentham. Yet he won national attention, as a member of the provincial council of Minas Gerais, by denouncing concessions the Crown had granted to two companies, both backed largely by British capital. These were the Society of Agriculture, Commerce, Mining and Navigation of Rio Dulce and the Diamond Company.

As an outstanding lawyer, Vasconcellos left his mark on Brazilian institutions. In addition to being the author of the *Ato Adicional*, he drew up the Brazilian criminal code, following Bentham's principles. This code had special importance because it influenced others adopted elsewhere in Latin America. He was also the author of the Brazilian commercial code and of a procedural code. As a minister he reformed the National Guard, revised the currency system, and introduced the law establishing the College of Pedro II, the first public secondary school of high grade in Brazil. He also established an agricultural school.

From 1838 to his death in 1850 he was the leader of Brazilian

Conservatism. This meant opposition to republicanism and defense of the interests of slave owners against the abolitionists. This was the "Deputy Vasconcellos" whom Robert Walsh, chaplain of the British Embassy in Rio de Janeiro, called the Franklin or Mirabean of Brazil. Others might think the resemblance to John C. Calhoun was closer.

BIBLIOGRAPHY

For a more complete account of Vasconcellos the reader may see the author's sketch in his *Makers of Democracy in Latin America* (H.W. Wilson Co., 1945: Reprinted Cooper Square Publishers, Inc. 1968), pp. 68–72; João Pandiá Calogeras, *A History of Brazil* (Chapel Hill: University of North Carolina Press, 1939. Reissued 1963); and Octavio Tarquinio de Sousa, *Bernardo Pereira de Vasconcellos e seu tempo* (Rio de Janeiro: José Olympio, 1937).

15

MIGUEL ANTONIO CARO (1843–1909)

Colombia is notable among the nations of Hispanic America for the traditionalist writers and philosophers she has produced, as well as for the limited success achieved there by positivist social and political doctrines. The existence of links between these two Colombian characteristics is an obvious possibility.

Utilitarianism and its philosophical sensualism gained an early foothold among such Colombian Benthamites as President Francisco de Paula Santander. The utilitarianism of Jeremy Bentham appealed to Latin Americans as an ideology and as a sociology that rejected traditionalism in favor of a theory that society could be transformed through legislation and moral education. This pattern of thinking was not unlike that of the French "ideologues" and "eclectics" of the era, who were seeking principles of universal application that could be arrived at pragmatically or determined empirically. The Bentham utilitarian criterion of ethical value, that of the greatest good to the greatest number, appealed especially to the leaders of these newly established nations as they sought a theoretical basis or rationale for reform.

Closely related to this utilitarianism, and often merging with it, was a stream of anti-clerical Liberalism that flourished among Colombian intellectual and political leaders until the late nineteenth century. Many of these Liberals, of course, were also advocates of federalism, or at least of the decentralization of political power, as a means of escaping the traditional authoritarian centralism of the political system they inherited from Spain. In addition to being linked to utilitarianism this anti-clerical Liberalism was tied as well to the French eclecticism that flourished among the political leaders who advocated federalism until the era of President Rafael Núñez.

But whereas utilitarianism and eclecticism paved the way to the positivism of Comte in other countries, positivist thought made less progress on the whole in Colombia than elsewhere in Latin America. In Colombia it yielded first place to traditionalist followers of the ideas of de Maistre, Balmes, and Donoso Cortés. Nor were the ideas of Herbert Spencer received by Colombians with the enthusiasm with which they were greeted by other Spanish Americans.

One of the notable early Colombian traditionalists was José Joaquín

Ortiz (1814–1892), author of *Las Sirenas*, a work directed specifically against utilitarianism. The priest, Francisco Margallo, was another among the first to attack the Bentham ideas in Colombia, engaging in a polemic with Vicente Azuero. Ricardo de la Parra (1815–1873) wrote his *Cartas sobre filosofía moral* (1868) to refute the ideas of Ezequiel Rojas (1803–1873), Rector of the University and one of the most brilliant Liberal philosophers of Colombia. José Eusebio Caro (1817–1853) was originally a follower of Bentham, but turned against utilitarianism, adopting a traditionalist philosophy like that of Donoso Cortés and publishing one of the first outright attacks on the regnant utilitarianism of the then Liberal party.

Miguel Antonio Caro was the son of this José Eusebio Caro. The Caro family originated in Ocaña, but Miguel Antonio was born in Bogotá, where he grew up and received his education. The Caros were related to many prominent families of Colombia, including those of such notable literary and political figures as Carlos Holguín and Rafael Núñez, the longtime president of the nation (1880–1894). Miguel Caro was himself active in Colombian politics during the last several decades of his life. He was the vice-president of Colombia under Rafael Núñez from 1892 to 1894 and was president (1894–1898) after the death of Núñez. Also a poet, he was the author of a book of verses entitled *Horas de amor*.

Many of Caro's published works have titles indicating the polemic he carried on against utilitarianism and the positivism that grew out of it. But his intellectual importance lies less in this attack on utilitarianism than in his vigorous expression of the revivified Catholic thought, social, theological, and metaphysical, that was expressed in the encyclicals *Rerum Novarum* and *Aeternis Patris* of Pope Leo XIII and brilliantly developed in Colombia by Joaquín Gómez Otero in the Colegio Mayor de Nuestra Señora del Rosario, in Antioquia. Thus, paradoxically, although Caro was a Catholic traditionalist in a fundamental philosophical sense, some persons might consider him liberal because he was also a pioneer in spreading the ideas of social Christianity expressed in *Rerum Novarum*.

In 1865, at the age of twenty-two, he began teaching the traditionalist philosophy of Cayetano San Severino in the newly established (Catholic) Colegio of Pius IX. From then until his death he was an active figure in Colombian intellectual life. Carlos Valderrama Andrade, who has written the best study of Caro's thought, places him among the three greatest philosophers of his country. He considers that Caro was more Augustinian than Thomistic, seeing this quality especially in Caro's expression of an "elevated concept of human dignity" with a sense of the "Christian mystery."[1]

In the Colombian Senate, in 1867, Ezekiel Rojas, then Rector of the University and one of Colombia's outstanding intellectual figures, proposed that the teaching of the principles of utilitarianism be required in all the public institutions of the country. An angry conservative Catholic outcry greeted the Rojas proposal, and young Professor Caro became the most effective voice of this protest.[2]

Caro's attack on the utilitarians and upon their sensualism, determinism, and positivism focused on the atheism, partial or complete, that he professed to find in the utilitarian denial of natural and revealed religion, and of Christian reason. Utilitarianism as he saw it, was not new. It was fundamentally egoistic and hence Satanic in its origin. In the history of philosophy, he argued, atheists had usually been utilitarians. The Christian, he wrote, found the basis of morality in metaphysics. "Ethics is a science of which the manifestations are practical, but of which the basis is purely metaphysical."[3]

In general, despite this opposition to utilitarianism, Caro was an eclectic and an ideologue more or less in the French model, rather than an Aristotelian scholastic. Enrique Zuleta Alvarez supports this view of Caro's thought, pointing out that Caro's reading embraced the Spanish, French, and English writers "most in vogue in his time." Although he had an obvious predilection for Catholic authors, writes Zuleta, Caro also read those who might appropriately be called "spiritualist" in the broad sense in which that term has sometimes come to be applied in the Hispanic world. Zuleta lists the following authors as among those read by Caro: Bishop Jacques Benigne Bossuet (1627–1704) and Henri Lacordaire (1802–1861), both Dominican priests; Joseph Marie de Maistre (1753–1821), the French traditionalist philosopher; Louis Gabriel Ambroise de Bonald (1754–1840), French emigré philosopher; Cesare Cantú (1804?–1895), Italian historian; Theodore Jouffroy (1796–1842), philosopher; Joseph Joubert (1754–1824), French moralist; Cardinal John Henry Newman (1801–1890), English theologian; Thomas Babbington Macaulay (1800–1859), British historian; Jaime Luciano Balmes (1810–1854), Spanish traditionalist philosopher; Juan Francisco Donoso Cortés (1809–1853), Spanish traditionalist and statesman; and Marcelino Menéndez Pelayo (1856–1912), historian of Spanish heterodoxies. The list would seem to support the general view of Caro's eclecticism, but it also shows his predilection for philosophers and historians who were concerned with a restatement and reassessment of traditional Christian thought and beliefs.[4]

Since eclecticism was the mode of the day, it is not surprising to see Caro falling into it, despite his generally traditionalist orientation. Some critics, influenced perhaps by this rather obvious eclecticism, have questioned whether Caro was really a philosopher at all. The question arises in part because Caro rarely treated such fundamental philosophical questions as the nature of being, the nature of knowledge, and the logic and relationship of various areas of philosophic inquiry. It is a legitimate question to raise, of course, whether this neglect is a product of eclecticism, or vice-versa. But those who raise the question seem unaware that the Latin American nineteenth century preoccupation with social philosophy and with questions relating to the position of Christianity and the Church in Latin American society is a more likely reason for Caro's neglect of those other philosophical matters. In general, Caro discussed ideologies rather than the abstract issues of philosophy, and his refutation of utilitarian materialism was more religious or theological than philosophical. Sometimes, indeed, as in his attack on Utilitarianism, he seemed to be following the Scottish common sense school. At other times, however, he becomes more Aristotelian or Thomistic, and this trend seems closer to the heart of his thought.

Zuleta Alvarez has pointed out that the syllabus of the course in general philosophy that Caro taught in 1867 included a concept of logic virtually identical with that of the French ideologue Antoine Louis Claude Destutt de Tracy (1754–1836) and that he used a psychology text by Amadeo Jacques, a disciple of the eclectic Victor Cousin (1792–1867), even while quarreling with the sensualism these philosophers expressed. As he matured and defined his own position more clearly, however, Caro drew closer to the scholastics, or toward a new interpretation of them. By 1870, he was referring more and more to the writings of Saint Augustine and Thomas Aquinas. He also cited with increasing frequency the Spanish traditionalist Jaime Balmes, from whom he appears to derive some of his views of other philosophers.[5]

Caro's traditionalism is marked by a continued adherence to a theory of progress and a determination to reconcile this evolutionary theory with the concept of rights and duties derived from a natural law linked to the law of God, with the Catholic concept of free will, with an Augustinian concept of order in all things, and with a providential view of history. "Order, justice, and perfection" were the definition of the *good* in his attack on Utilitarianism; and this definition of the good, which he identified with the classical concept of "the good, the beautiful and the true," also became his definition of God. Thus, the major mark of Caro's traditionalism is its defense of Catholicism. For him this is "the complete moral law." Unlike the European traditionalists, he did not become involved in defending the social and political status quo ante; he defended neither monarchy nor aristocracy. It was his retention of the idea of progress and perfectibility, rather than the elements of traditionalism, that opened the way to his full acceptance of the emerging papal doctrines of social Christianity, making him one of the earliest and most earnest defenders of the *Rerum Novarum* and of the socially conscious Catholicism it advocated.

NOTES

1. *Pensamiento filosófico de Miguel Antonio Caro* (Bogotá: Instituto Caro y Cuervo, 1961) p. 240. See also Enrique Zuleta Álvarez, "La iniciación filosófica de Miguel Antonio Caro," in *Libro de homenaje a Luis Alberto Sánchez en los 40 años de su docencia universitaria* (Lima: Universidad Mayor de San Marcos, 1967).
2. Enrique Zuleta Alvarez, *op. cit.*, pp. 539–563.
3. *Ensayo sobre el catolicismo, el liberalismo y el socialismo*, quoted in Valderrama Andrade, *op. cit.*, p. 230. For the background of philosophy in Colombia, Valderrama seems to have relied greatly on Francisco M. Renjifo, "La filosofía en Colombia," *Revista del Colegio Mayor de Nuestra Señora del Rosario*, vol. XXVI, Núm. 256 (julio de 1931), pp. 337–343, and on various writings of the Colombian philosopher, Jaime Jaramillo Uribe.
4. Zuleta, *op. cit.*, 551.
5. *Op. cit.*, pp. 555–557.

BIBLIOGRAPHY

The collected *Obras* of Caro have been published (1962) by the Instituto Caro y Cuervo of Bogotá, with a preliminary study by Carlos Valdarama Andrade. In addition to the Caro works cited in footnotes, the student may find it useful to consult his *Estudio sobre el utilitarismo* (Bogotá: Imp. de Foción Mantilla, 1869) and "Informe sobre los 'Elementos de Ideología' de Tracy," *Anales de la Universidad de los estados Unidos de Colombia*, t. iv, núm. 22 (Sept. 1870); *Autoridad es razón* (1871); *La filosofía sensualista* (1871), *Bastiat y Bentham* (1872), and *Galileo* (1888). These works are in the collected *Obras*. See also Carlos Valdarrama Andrade, *El pensamiento filosófico de Miguel Antonio Caro* (Bogota: Instituto Caro y Cuevo, 1961) and Enrique Zuleta Alvarez, "La iniciación filosófica de Miguel Antonio Caro," in *Libro de homenaje a Luis Alberto Sánchez en los 40 años de su docencia universitaria* (Lima: Universidad Mayor de San Marcos, 1967).

16

JOSE MANUEL ESTRADA (1842–1894)

José Estrada of Argentina, born in Buenos Aires in 1842, illustrates the process that a number of intellectuals went through as they moved from their earlier Liberalism, through positivism, to a new traditionalism in the late decades of the century. Salvador M. Dana Montaño has remarked that Estrada was a dogmatic Liberal in his youth and that he became an "orthodox Catholic" in maturity.[1] In his *Liberal Policy Under the Tyranny*, written in 1873,[2] Estrada is still the Liberal, studying with some sympathy, if not agreement, the Generation of 1837, that opposed Rosas. Subsequently he became a critic of both Liberalism and of the positivism of his day; eventually he moved to a traditionalist position with strikingly Argentine characteristics.

Though pointing out what he thinks are Estrada's errors, Dana Montaño considers him the founder of political science in Argentina and the third most important Argentine writer on political themes, following in the footsteps of Juan B. Alberdi, author of the famous *Bases*, and of Florentino González, known for his *Lessons on Constitutional Law (Lecciones de derecho constitucional)*. Dana Montaño is referring in this context to the course on constitutional law inaugurated by Estrada in the Colegio Nacional in 1877, a course based on Joseph Story's classic *Commentaries on the Constitution of the United States*.[3]

In large measure Estrada was self-taught. Dana Montaño correctly calls him a genuine and talented autodidactic *(un genuino y genial autodidacta)*. He never attended a university and consequently lacked the degree of "doctor," the essential symbol of intellectual and professional prestige in Argentine society. His formal education terminated in the secondary school but he continued his self-education informally in his career as teacher, first at the elementary level and then in the normal school. It was in a normal school, at the age of twenty-four, that he began his real intellectual career with a notable series of lectures on Argentine history, anticipating in some respects the work of later "revisionist" and "institutional" historians.

Two years later he inaugurated the study of constitutional law in Argentina from this historical standpoint, lecturing now from a professorial chair *(cátedra)* created in the Colegio Nacional for instruction in "history and civics" *(instrucción cívica)*. The governmental decree establishing this professorship, it may be noted, was signed by two of Argentina's greatest Liberal statesmen and scholars, reflecting the pro-United States bias of the Sarmiento era: Nicolás Avellaneda and Domingo F. Sarmiento. The decree provided for instruction based upon the classic work of the Harvard Professor of Law, Joseph Story, *Commentaries on the Constitution of the United States*. But Estrada, drawing upon his already notable interpretation of Argentine history, soon changed the basis of his constitutional interpretation to that of Argentine political history. As early as 1866–68 he had presented in historical lectures the importance of tradition as a means to counteract anarchic trends. He had also presented the danger of tyranny that arose when tradition was too narrowly interpreted, as in the case of Rosas.

Soon after his appointment to the Colegio Nacional, Estrada was named to the chair of constitutional law in the Faculty of Law of the University of Buenos Aires, succeeding Joaquín V. González. Thereafter his influence came to be felt on a whole generation of legal and historical scholars. In some cases it was their notes on his lectures in the Law Faculty that first made his ideas known. One of his objectives was to rid the study of constitutional law of the formal and exotic character it had acquired as a result of studying theoretical, constitutional systems without relation to Argentine political reality. Thus he brought the study into the stream of historical realism earlier initiated by Juan B. Alberdi. For Estrada, national history and national constitutional structure were two aspects of a single reality. Hence the "political science" that he created was not only closely akin to Alberdi's view of the historical philosophy of law, but it also resembled the later "institutional" history that appeared in Spain and Spanish America in the early twentieth century. It is in this sense, largely, that his thought may be properly described as traditional.

In his *Liberal Policy Under the Tyranny of Rosas*, Estrada criticized the *Dogma Socialista* of Echeverría as doctrinaire, saying that its failure was due to this doctrinaire quality. In his later *Catholicism and Democracy*[4] he defended the record of the Church, refuting the revolutionary Liberalism and anti-clericalism of Francisco Bilbao's *America in Danger (La América en peligro)*. He also rejected the positivism of his day, including that of Herbert Spencer because, as he said, it culminated in a theory of sovereignty of the state, based on social determinism, that leaves the human spirit unsatisfied, a spirit that demands individual freedom in the exercise of free will.

Positivism, he said, errs in rejecting a dialectical analysis in favor of a too simple empiricism. In his own historical and dialectical method

Estrada also rejected a simple "historical" explanation, such as that of Aberdi, one that merely showed what he called the derivation *(filiación)* of institutions and did not justify them. The sources of institutions and of constitutional law, as he saw it, were fourfold, including (1) written law, (2) tradition, (3) history, and (4) principles. By the latter he meant principles of natural law in the scholastic sense. His insistence on "spiritualizing" history, constitutional law, and political science made him a forerunner of such twentieth century idealist-traditionalists as Manuel Gálvez. Even more significant, however, was the renewed emphasis he brought to the natural law basis of institutions and to religious aspects of social thought.[5]

NOTES

1. *Las ideas políticas de Jose Manuel Estrada* (Santa Fe, Argentina: Imp. de la Universidad, 1944), p. 23.
2. *La política Liberal bajo la tiranía de Rosas* (Buenos Aires: La Cultura Argentina, 1927). Cited in Dana Montaño, *op. cit.*, pp. 26–27.
3. Estrada's lectures were published the same year, *Curso de derecho constitucional,* from notes of his students, according to Dana Montaño. *op. cit.*, p. 20, citing Rodolfo Rivarola, *El Maestro José Manuel Estrada,* p. 60.
4. *Catolicismo y la democracia.*
5. This discussion of Estrada is drawn largely from the work of Dana Montaño referred to above. The latter, in turn has relied upon Rodolfo Rivarola, *El maestro J.M. Estrada en la ciencia política argentina* (Buenos Aires: Imprenta de Coni Hermanos, 1913). Other works treating the thought of Estrada include Rodrigo Octavio, *Noçoẽs de direito federal professadas na Universidad de Buenos Ayres por D. José Manuel Estrada* (Rio de Janeiro: Livraria de Alves & Co. 1897). Major works of Estrada in addition to those mentioned, are *La libertad y el liberalismo* (Buenos Aires, 1878) and the earlier two volume *Lecciones sobre la historia de la República Argentina* (1866–1868). His *Obras completas* were published in four volumes in 1899 by the Librería del Colegio.

17

MANUEL GOMEZ MORIN (1897–   )
by Donald J. Mabry

Manuel Gómez Morín has been an important figure in the history of the Mexican Revolution and in the governments which emerged from it. He is a former revolutionary who created the current major opposition party in Mexico. His importance comes not only from his activity as the founder and leader of the anti-Revolutionary, or National Action Party (*Partido de Nacional*, or PAN), but also from his work in finance and education. As a young member of what Frank Brandenburg has called the "Revolutionary Family," he wrote some of the important early financial laws of the Revolutionary regime. He is an educator who has taught for twenty years in the law school of the National University and has served as rector of the University. In his private career he has been one of the most successful corporation lawyers and financiers in the country.

The intellectual ability of Manuel Gómez Morín has been the key to his success. He started life unspectacularly in the small mining town of Batopilas, Chihuahua, where he was born in 1897. He was the child of a Mexican mother from Parral, Chihuahua, and a Spanish immigrant father who had come to Mexico from Santander, Spain, in 1887 and who died less than two years after the birth of Manuel. Little is known of the family social position, other than that Manuel's mother was left with sufficient means to hire servants and to educate her son. He began school in Chihuahua and continued his education in León, Guanajuato, and Mexico City as the family moved southwards. In the law school of the National University he made a brilliant record as a student and, soon after receiving his law degree in 1918, became a professor of law in the University. He had attracted attention among his fellow students as one of the "Seven Sages," an informal group of bright young men who met to discuss philosophy and politics and who taught in the Popular University created by leaders of the student movement during the Revolution. As a student of Antonio Caso, the great humanist philosopher, Gómez Morín showed an early interest in marxism and the Russian Revolution. This knowledge of marxism came into use later in his service to the Soviet Legation as consulting attorney. But, unlike his fellow "sage," Vicente Lombardo Toledano, who went on to become a marxist labor leader and the founder of the Popular Socialist Party, Gómez Morín became more conservative as the Revolution progressed.

Through his university reputation and connections he was able to begin his governmental career close to the center of power. In 1919 he became Under-secretary of Finance. Although he flirted with the de la Huerta rebellion a few years later, he quickly rejoined the ranks of the Sonora Dynasty of Alvaro Obregón and Plutarco Calles, preserving and extending his position within the Mexican government. He remained in the Finance Ministry for several years and after he left continued to serve the ministry as a semi-official adviser. Thus, he was the co-author of the first Mexican income tax law, of the organic law of the Banco de México, and of the first agrarian credit law. From 1925 to 1929 he was a director of the Banco de México. Although he has not held a Mexican governmental post since 1929, when he joined the government's opposition, he has served on a United States Monetary Commission to Ecuador in 1937 and has continued to serve the Mexican government informally as a financial advisor.

His private, professional career as a lawyer has been aided by his governmental service and by his university connections. His political influence, as much as his reputation as an excellent lawyer, brought him influential and well-paying clients. His legal speciality has been the creation of joint Mexican-foreign capital enterprises such as Euzkadi-Goodrich. He has also held important positions in banking circles, serving as vice-president of the Banco de Londres y México, one of the larger private Mexican banks. While still in his 'twenties Gómez Morín served as secretary to the Law School Faculty and he became rector of the University in 1933–34. As university rector, he fought for the autonomy of the University and against what he and his followers believed to be a marxist takeover of the institution in accordance with a constitutional amendment requiring socialist education.

There were several reasons why in 1929 Gómez Morín left the revolutionary camp, where he would have been assured an important position in Mexican life, in order to join the political opposition which offered little, if any, chance of affecting public policy. The magnetism of José Vasconcelos, the opposition presidential candidate in 1929, was certainly one key factor in this decision. Vasconcelos enjoyed a political prestige and following uncommon to United States intellectuals and Gómez Morín was one of his disciples. Gómez Morín also believed that his generation was destined to create the new Mexico and that he could be one of its leaders. Moreover, it had become apparent to him that he lacked the power base necessary to exercise great influence within the circle of the revolutionary elite.

The Vasconcelos movement gave some indications of having the capability of taking power. By joining it early, Gómez Morín hoped to become an important member in the new government, assuring the destiny that he seems to have marked out for himself. He served as the unofficial treasurer of the Vasconcelos movement. After Vasconcelos' defeat, he joined his mentor in exile, urging him to call for a Madero style uprising against the government. When it became clear, however, that the population acquiesced in the election results, he pleaded with Vasconcelos for the creation of a permanent opposition party.

While political opportunism and personal ambition partly explain this action, Gómez Morín was also moved by his evolving traditionalist view of Mexico. He had accepted the Revolution as a necessary and irreversible event. But when he became convinced that the Revolution was not only becoming a more sophisticated dictatorship than that of Porfirio Díaz, but also that is was molding Mexico into a secular and marxist state, he joined the opposition. Gómez Morín was not a traditionalist in any reactionary sense however. He did not believe that it was possible or desirable to return to the past. But while he accepted the Mexican Revolution as a fact, his acceptance of the necessity of revolutionary change did not extend to countenancing the Revolution's anticlericalism, its collectivization of property, or its continuance of an authoritarian political system.

The political ideology of Gómez Morín has to be examined within the context of Mexican history because his ideas have evolved largely as reactions to events. Thus, most of his political statements began to appear with the founding of PAN in 1939, a party created initially to oppose such measures of the Lázaro Cárdenas regime (1934–40) as appeared to be a marxist assault on Catholicism, private property, and Mexican traditions. Had the Cárdenas regime not occurred when it did, the men of PAN would not have been so likely to turn to Gómez Morín for leadership. But it was a period in world history when men were despairing of the effectiveness of liberal democracy, when Communism appeared to be rapidly gaining converts and influence, and when Nazism and Fascism had come to power in a number of countries. To many men in 1938–39 the world appeared to be adrift and to offer few palatable alternatives.

Through its "socialist education" program and its class struggle rhetoric and actions the Cárdenas regime seemed to be making Mexico into a marxist state. Nazism, Franco's *falangismo,* and Italian Fascism were rejected by Gómez Morín. Nazism seemed bizarre, anti-Christian, a dictatorial movement alien to Mexico. *Falangismo* and Italian Fascism had certain attractive aspects. Their Christian emphasis, their anti-communism, their respect for traditions, and their call for decisive action were more appealing to him than Cárdenas' disorderly left-wing government. But their authoritarian-dictatorial character was a disadvantage that far outweighed these attractions. In his reactions to these movements, Gómez Morín's early political statements reflected a radical fear of world and domestic events not unusual at the time. But his ideology moderated in later years as tensions were reduced. Although he never became completely reconciled to Mexico's "directed democracy," preferring a more truly democratic state, he came to concede that the Revolution had made important improvements in the lives of ordinary Mexicans.

An objective analysis of the writings and speeches of Gómez Morín leads the thoughtful student to reject the reactionary and fascist labels sometimes attached to him by critics. A more balanced judgment goes something like this. Gómez Morín rejected the authoritarian state in favor of a pluralistic, federal, democratic state that actively intervenes in human affairs to create and encourage social justice. In his view the state, by strengthening and protecting such natural communities as the family, workers associations, religious groups, avocational interest groups, and the political entities of government, should encourage and allow individuals and these natural communities to work for social justice. It was important, however, as he believed, that the national state should work for social justice within its peculiar sphere of action, acting quickly and decisively to correct abuses.

Many of the problems of creating a just state, Gómez Morín said, could be solved by democratic planning conducted by public and private sectors. One prerequisite for the achievement of this social justice, he believed, was the recognition that the right of private property was the right to use it for the common good. Hence, Gómez Morín agreed with the need for land reform and the end of *latifundios* (large holdings) in Mexico; but he rejected the *ejido*, the community based collective farm nurtured by the Revolution. He found the *ejido* objectionable on two counts. Since the peasants did not receive clear title to property under this system, he argued, they felt insecure. Moreover, the ejidal system lent itself to being used as an instrument of political control. Gómez Morín preferred the idea of an agricultural society of family farms, organized in voluntary cooperatives that should be encouraged by government.

He agreed that it was important to have independent labor unions, capable of protecting the workers' interests. But, as in the case of the *ejidos*, he objected to their use by government as part of the political system. During the first years of his leadership of PAN he appeared to be arguing for compulsory arbitration of labor disputes, but he later dropped that stance. In this, as in other matters, he has generally rejected governmental paternalism. But he believes that citizens and government have a joint responsibility for providing comprehensive social security benefits, schools, and other social services.

His position on education has been quite clear; he wants the anti-clerical provisions of the Constitution changed so that Church sponsored schools may operate freely. His ideas of the proper role of the state in the economy are less clear. Basically, he has urged that the government should guide but not own economic enterprises. How much economic guidance the state should give he has not clearly defined, although he appears in recent years to have accepted a somewhat larger economic role for the state in accord with contemporary Christian democratic thought. He has argued that private enterprise, not the government, should be the creator of jobs in the economy; but he has also advocated joint capital-labor ownership and management of industries.

Essentially, then, Gómez Morín has been advocating what is a Catholic social position—an alternative between Marxism and classical liberalism. He has found his inspiration in the papal encyclicals and in Catholic writers, combining their thoughts with those of Antonio Caso and José Vasconcelos. Thus, as might be expected, his writings through the years have shown a marked similarity to the evolution of the thought of Christian Democrats in Europe and America. In the crisis years from 1934 to 1945 he was attracted to the ideas of *falangismo* and to the example of Antonio Oliveira Salazar of Portugal, in whose image he saw himself. But he has been more moderate and democratic than they, principally because his experience with Mexican political regimes had taught him to fear authoritarianism.

His whole political framework is based upon the democratic belief that the citizens of a country should make the decisions in society. Sometimes they should make them as individuals, at other times as members of interest groups. This latter position is reminiscent of Catholic corporativism of the 1920's and 1930's. But, on the whole, Gómez Morín has asserted that the most effective mechanism of a political democracy is the free operation of permanent political parties. By conducting his own party democratically he has shown that he believes in this system, one which he fails to see operating in the government of Mexico.

Part of the confusion surrounding Gómez Morín has resulted from misunderstanding his pronouncements on Hispanidad, Franco, and Pan-American relations. In World War II years he spoke frequently of the necessity of recognizing Mexico's Hispanic heritage and her common ties with other Hispanic-American nations. Accordingly, he rejected Pan-Americanism when it meant that Hispanic-American nations had to imitate the United States. These attitudes need to be understood, of course, in the context of the times. His seeming sympathy for the Franco regime, for example, is best understood as a reaction against some of the leftist trends in the Cárdenas regime. His hispanicism is also understandable, in part, as a reaction against the emphasis the Revolution was giving to the indigenous elements in Mexican culture and its deprecation of the Spanish heritage. He professed to believe that Mexico was a mestizo nation and that a mestizo culture had a hispanic basis. The Indianism of the Revolutionary thus appeared to be a denial of Mexican reality. Opposition to Pan-Americanism was not uncommon among Mexican nationalists of all kinds who feared the power and influence of their northern neighbor. Viewed in this perspective, Gómez Morín's anti-Pan-Americanism was rather superficial. Thus, it is not surprising that he called for full support of the Mexican war effort once Mexico entered the war on the side of the United States, even though he had argued for neutrality prior to the war.

Gómez Morín's contributions to the development of modern Mexico may be summed up as those of a leader of the loyal opposition who has also been an author of consequence, an adviser on financial laws, and a leading private entrepreneur. Under his guidance PAN has become a democratic, loyal opposition party, despite his occasional lapses into demagoguery. He has made it a party that has contributed to the growth of a stable political system, one that uses arguments instead of arms to resolve public problems. Although the party has held only minor posts of power, it has served an important purpose as a critic of the ruling power structure and as a generator of political ideas. Gómez Morín's business and professional success have given added weight in some quarters to his political comments. Sometimes, indeed, the effect of this latter factor has been to suggest that he is the major spokesman for the interests of Mexican private enterprise.

BIBLIOGRAPHY

The writings and speeches of Gómez Morín are found in scattered sources. His admiration for Spain is best seen in *España fiel* (1928). Early opinions on agricultural credit were expressed in *El crédito agrícola en México* (1928). His belief that his generation was destined to build the new Mexico is stated in *1915*

(1927). Most significant for his later views are the reports to PAN when he was its president, collected in *Diez Años de México* (1950). His views on the important aspects of social security are collected in *Seguridad Social* (1966), while his most recent thought is found in the interviews reported in *México Visto en el Sigle XX*, edited by James W. Wilkie and Edna Monzón de Wilkie (México: Instituto Mexicano de Investigaciones Económicas, 1969), pp. x, 770. Vicente Fuentes Díaz, *Los partidos políticos en México*, 2nd ed. (México, 1969) offers a substantial but hostile view. Donald J. Mabry, "Acción Nacional: The Institutionalization of an Opposition Party," (Ph.D. Dissertation, Syracuse University, 1970) adds important data on the founder of the party.

PART III

DICTATORS

18

DICTATORS

Next in importance to the concept of the revolutionary, in Latin American political history, perhaps even exceeding it in prevalence, is that of the dictator. A loose and pejorative use of this term has been common in modern times in many parts of the world. But no where has it been used more loosely than in Latin America to cover so wide a variety of authoritarian regimes, or so generally in a pejorative sense. The literature on dictatorship in Latin America has tended to treat authoritarian regimes as a unique characteristic of the Latin American political experience, presenting most of the presidents of the nations of the area as little more than dictators, products of political anarchy produced by political incompetence. For example, George S. Wise, in his *Caudillismo, A Study of Dictatorship in Latin America*, includes as dictators rulers as different as Juan Manuel Rosas of Argentina and José Balmaceda of Chile. In a symposium edited by A. Curtis Wilgus, the leaders treated covered an equally wide range, from José Artigas of Uruguay and Dr. Francia of Paraguay to the Emperor Pedro I of Brazil, who is called a "Constitutional Dictator." [1]

This tendency to reduce all authoritarian presidents to a single type results partly from the simplistic assumption that authoritarianism is a constant. Sometimes, however, the tendency seems to reflect a kind of parochialism in scholarship that insists on viewing these phenomena through United States eyes and in judging them by United States norms. Unconsciously, this tendency appears even in the recent work of as discriminating a scholar as Hugh M. Hamill, Jr. The latter's otherwise excellent "Introduction" to the collection of essays he has brought together on the subject quotes with approval the damning half-praise of John J. Johnson that "the chief executives, the caudillos, and the colonels who shoot their way into the presidential chacr are no longer the effective agents of all political change." Hamill then goes on to remark that comparisons of Latin American dictators with those elsewhere are "only incidentally useful," because the "pressing question" is "the unique quality of the strong man in Latin America."[2]

Authoritarian regimes have abounded in all parts of the world throughout the course of history. Whether or not they have been more frequent than "legitimate" constitutional or customary regimes is

121

arguable, but this author is inclined to think that authoritarian regimes have been the more common. If this is so, it may well be that the "strongman" in Latin America is not unique after all, and that dictators have been no more characteristic of nineteenth and twentieth century Latin America than of other parts of the world during these years. This would certainly appear to be the case if the comparison is made to include Spain and Portugal, whose political experience of the past two centuries has been strikingly similar to that of their former American colonies in respect to authoritarian regimes.

Few writers have gone to the heart of the matter of authoritarianism in Latin America as directly and realistically as did Juan Bautista Alberdi of Argentina (1810–1884). Alberdi interpreted the Rosas dictatorship and the dictatorships of the provincial caudillos of the Plata region as a product of the social conditions and the political changes of the times. He explained them more explicitly as part of the problem of effecting a transition from absolute and hereditary monarchy to a presidential system in which power was shared with a ruling elite and in which that class could make and unmake their rulers.

Alberdi's view of dictatorship is historical, in accordance with the emerging historical philosophy of law which he embraced. With this historical insight, he discerned two successful types of institutional adaptations in Spanish America in the mid-nineteenth century when he wrote. One was the type of Argentina and Paraguay, in which supreme power was placed in the hands of a despot. The second was the type of Chile, in which "a constitution gave to the executive power the means for making itself respected with the efficacy of which dictatorship itself is capable."[3] At this point, this analysis led Alberdi to remark that the problem of achieving constitutional government in Spanish America was simply that of maintaining the power and position of the viceroy while moving toward the new constitutional form of the presidency. The political history of the republics in the nineteenth century seemed to bear out his interpretation, oversimplified as it may at first appear.

Authoritarian regimes arise in differing circumstances, but one of the common denominators of the situations that produce them is the lack of an adequate power structure and of institutions strong enough to deal effectively with the problems confronted by government. In early nineteenth century Spanish America the elements of this weakness were the lack of "legitimacy" consequent to the rejection of monarchy, the divisions among the criollo elite that were assuming power, and their inability to agree upon either the form or the reality of a constitutional structure based upon real power. They often thought they were agreeing

upon the necessary political institutions when their seeming consensus
wa an illusion since it was not backed up by an agreed power structure.

In such a vacuum dictators of various types took over, and it is this
dictator-inducing power vacuum that makes intelligible the remark of Dr.
Francia of Paraguay to be referred to again later, that it would be forty
years before his country would have leaders like Benjamin Franklin and
so be ready for democratic government. In the twentieth century this
weakness of power structure that has produced past dictators appears in
another form, that of a political polarization or schism preventing the
achievement of the consensus essential to the true operation of political
power in any society. In contemporary Argentina, for example, this
political schism is the chasm between the *Peronistas*, on the one hand,
and the right wing of the old Radical party leadership on the other.

Dictatorships, it should be noted, have come from both the left and
from the right. Sometimes they come from regimes established by radical
reforming groups and at other times from those of conservatives and
reactionaries. A century and a half of Latin American political experience
since independence seems to provide more examples of dictators coming
from the political left than from the right. But such a judgment of course,
depends in part upon definition; both reformist and traditionalist regimes
have at times utilized or depended upon extraordinary use of the armed
forces. Both have collaborated with the armed forces leadership at times
in driving their political opponents from office. On the whole, however,
governments established by Conservative parties seem to have been
more likely to govern within the established constitutional system than
regimes of Liberal or other reforming parties that have tried to effect
substantial change in the social, economic, or political order.

One of the fascinating aspects of Latin American political thought has
been the attention given to the theoretical explanation and occasionally to
the justification of authoritarian regimes. As one would expect in light of
the realities of political experience, as well as from the nature of the
continuous debate carried on by Latin Americans over the nature and
problem of social identity and stability, the theories are rather more likely
to be revolutionary than traditionalist. These theories appear in a number
of different forms.

The first theory is that appearing in the persistent stream of idealist and
utopian philosophy that sees dictatorship as evil in its very nature,
whatever its origin, and also considers it unnecessary. This is the view
popularized by krausist though in the hispanic world and is linked to its
fundamental belief that the right of suffrage was the essential of any

system of freedom. The Radical party of Argentina, and particularly its leader, Hipólito Irigoyen, expressed this view, as did President Francisco Madero (not a Krausist but a Spiritualist), in his book so central to the Mexican Revolution, *The Presidential Succession in 1910*. Both believed that authoritarian regimes were an unnecessary evil because a political system based upon free suffrage would lead to a solution of all other problems. Both also believed the solution to political problems lay in strengthening the national congress in relation to the presidency.

The second rationale is one that may be called Bolivarian. Taking their cue from Rousseau (and others), many independence leaders assumed that it was desirable to provide constitutionally for authoritarian political regimes in time of crisis, especially because of the long continued refusal of Spain to make peace with her former colonies, and even more specifically because of the American lack of experience with anything other than authoritarian political regimes. They cited the classic Greek and Roman examples. This concept of constitutional dictatorship was linked to, but distinguishable from, the concept of the lifetime presidency, for which Bolívar found a model in the Haitian presidency of Alesandre Sabès Petion. Underlying this Bolivarian concept was the basic rationale that Spanish America could not stand the stress of periodical political crises surrounding the election of presidents. One may see in this theory a resemblance, if not a derivation from, the Montesquieu theory of the British constitution—that its stability was due to the role of a nobility that stood between absolute monarchy and levelism or mobocracy. In accordance with these concepts the Bolivarian type of dictatorship relied for its legitimization upon bringing together an assembly of notables in time of crisis, while its normal constitutional structure aimed to create stability around a kind of aristocracy of the criollo independence leaders.

A third concept of dictatorship appears in the thought of Francisco Bilbao of Chile, Domingo F. Sarmiento of Argentina, and other Liberals of their time. For these militant Liberals of the post-independence era, dictatorship was evil in its very nature, but they saw it as an evil derived from their past history and as part of the hispanic heritage. As such it was an evil to be eradicated, by violent revolution if necessary, and possibly only in this violent manner. Bilbao saw this historical heritage as that of authoritarian Spain and a tradition-ridden Church. Sarmiento found its roots at least partly in the American experience that had produced the barbarism of the Argentine gaucho and partly in the geography of the pampa. Yet, he too, attributed part of the evil to the Spanish heritage. Both were rebels in spirit; both advocated violent revolution and supported movements of a revolutionary character to overthrow authoritarian regimes.

Fourthly, Latin Americans have often accepted dictatorship as a necessary instrumentality for carrying out the revolutions they have so frequently experienced. This concept of dictatorship is a part of the revolutionary tradition. It derives in some measure from the Spanish and Portuguese experience in opposing the Napoleonic conquest of the Peninsula and in part from the comparable experiences in Hispanic America. The expected form is that of a revolutionary junta composed of the leaders of an armed uprising or of a *golpe de estado*. If the junta is not dominated by some "strong man" it soon produces one. This concept of dictatorship has usually been expressed in action and has rarely found theoretical expression, but the model is probably the one most commonly seen in Latin American political history. The most notable recent exceptions, or variations in the model, have appeared in the speeches of Fidel Castro and in the writing of "Che" Guevara. The latter's idea, however, resembles the Lenin concept of the necessary dictatorship of the proletariat, to be mentioned later. Castro's less doctrinaire expressions seem somehow to be more in accord with the Latin American tradition than those of Guevara.

A fifth view of dictatorship is one that evolved in nineteenth century positivist thought and evolutionary and institutional social thought. The *científicos* of Mexico, for example, justified the Díaz dictatorship as a necessary step in Mexico's evolution toward political stability. For them the question was not one of how to abolish dictatorship (with which they disagreed), but rather how to take advantage of the social and political stability the Díaz regime had produced in order to move toward the system of freedom they desired. Francisco García Calderón, the Peruvian diplomat and historian, saw Latin American political history as essentially the institutional evolution of *caudillismo*. He saw it advancing from the barbarous military caudillos of the early years to those of late nineteenth and early twentieth century who provided the social stability for economic and cultural development.

The rationale of the Francia and Rosas dictatorships, in Paraguay and Argentina respectively, may be taken as a sixth theory, although it resembles both the Bolivarian and the positivist concepts in some respects. Dr. Francia was concerned with carrying out a revolution for independence and Rosas was more concerned with maintaining the traditional culture. But they were alike in their view that an authoritarian regime was necessary until new leadership and institutions were produced to make a free regime possible. Francia, as has already been mentioned, believed it would take forty years.

The Lenin or Bolshevist theory of dictatorship, that of an authoritarian power structure based upon a highly disciplined Communist party acting for the proletariat to carry out the worker's revolution, has not yet found clear expression in a Latin American political regime, although the Castro regime in Cuba suggests it in many respects. This theory of the necessity of dictatorship to effect the worker's revolution finds much lip service among Latin American Communists, however, and one may presume that it will yet find concrete expression. The difference from the Lenin model in the Cuban case is that the dictatorship could not be based upon the old Communist party, but has required the creation of a new revolutionary party.

Finally, an eighth theory of dictatorship in Latin America is that stated by the former president of the Dominican Republic, Juan Bosch, in his sensational diatribe against United States militarism and imperialism, entitled *Pentagonism: a Substitute for Imperialism.*[4] This concept, more in line with the Latin American tradition, is a populist concept of "the dictatorship with popular support" *(la dictadura con respaldo popular)*. The essence of the Bosch theory is the rejection of the idea that popular elections and elected congresses can provide regimes of both freedom and social development. Bosch is of course expressing the pessimism and disillusionment born of his unhappy experience with the Aprista-like Dominican Revolutionary Party (PRD) and with his short presidency that was terminated by a military intervention. But he is also giving expression to diverse but widespread currents of populism in Latin America. Indeed, his view is not too unlike that of Fidel Castro with whom he had feuded politically. Probably, what most gives vitality to this Bosch theory is that it echoes so much of the history of dictatorship in the area.

These concepts and rationales of dictatorship suggest that dictators are not just one but of many kinds. The most rudimentary kind of typology we find in the kind of historical literature expressing the theory that all dictators in a sense are "bad." Some dictators, it must be admitted, have been much less "bad," in the sense that they have made lasting contributions to a nation's welfare, while others have been "worse" in the sense that their overall influence has been destructive. But all, in the most fundamental sense, are bad in some way. A more sophisticated or critical view would be that while no dictator has been entirely "good" in the sense of being the best possible answer to the problem of political leadership in the times and circumstances, few dictators have been entirely "bad." Produced in large measure by historical conditions, they have almost always, if not always, served some social purpose, if only that of inducing the reaction against themselves. In line with this essentially pragmatic view, the following outline of essentially historical types is suggested. Some, but not all, of these types are represented in the biographical sketches that follow.

The first is that of independence leaders who became dictators. An outstanding example is Simón Bolívar, who became dictator of Colombia during his last years as president of the country that he had brought into being. Another quite different example is that of Dr. Francia of Paraguay. Both thought of dictatorship as a constitutional arrangement, however much they differed in their ideas as to what this arrangement should be. For Bolívar, while always an eventuality, it was a last recourse to be used when the Congress was unable to resolve national problems. For Francia, as noted, dictatorship was a necessary condition precedent to the development of representative government.[5]

The second type of dictator, closely related to the first, is that of the early caudillos who had been lieutenants of Bolívar or San Martín in the armies of independence. This is the type of Andrés Santa Cruz in Peru and Bolivia, of Juan José Flores in Ecuador, and of José Antonio Páez in Venezuela. While they were authoritarian in temperament, with power deriving from their control of what were virtually their private armies, these leaders were generally loyal to the reform objectives of the Liberal program and to the constitutional republicanism of the independence leadership. They tried to work through congresses, in accordance with the constitutions they helped to establish, however arbitrary their interpretations of these constitutions may sometimes have been.

Another group of early caudillo-dictators are cast in a somewhat different mold. This group includes such figures as Manuel Rosas of Argentina, Rafael Carrera of Guatemala, Diego Portales of Chile, and Antonio López de Santa Anna of Mexico. Disparate in many respects, they reveal two common denominators. The first is that they had participated in the movement for independence. The second is that they were disillusioned with the Liberal reforming tendencies of the early independent governments and had accepted more traditionalist ideas, perhaps partly in response to some influence of the clergy who at this time were swinging away away from their earlier Liberalism of the independence era and toward ultramontane traditionalism.

The Indian population had an importance in the careers of both Rosas and Carrera, but the importance was quite different in the two cases. Rosas fought the wild Indians of the *pampa*, Carrera built his power on control of the peasant Indian population of Guatemala. Both Rosas and Portales left their nations more united than when they took them over.

But their politics differed. Whereas Rosas drove the Liberal Unitarists into exile, Portales wisely brought Chilean Liberals into the Conservative party regime he established. Carrera missed the opportunity to do what Rosas did in Argentina—to create a de facto national unity in Central America that could later be translated into organizing the Central American republic earlier broken up. Of the four, only Portales did not rise to power as a leader of armed forces. But he relied upon military power, meeting his death, in fact, in a mutiny inspired in part by his having built up an army to prevent the impending union of Bolivia and Peru under President Santa Cruz.

Santa Anna is the hardest of this group to categorize. Meteoric and chameleon, a charismatic professional soldier and amateur politician, he always lost his battles, both political and military; yet he always rose, phoenix-like, to renew the struggle. Eventually he emerged as the head of a political regime dedicated to monarchism and a centralist political system supported by "notables" and the Church. But ideologies and principles meant less to him than political power. In only one respect does he seem to express in his actions a significant constitutional principle. This principle is the Bolivarian concept that the president should be above political factions, a political figure to replace the viceroy as a representative of monarchy, one who would allow the government to be exercised by ambitious political leaders who would change as political conditions changed.

Mariano Melgarejo (1818–1871) is a different type, that of a number of dictators that arose in some of the largely indigenous countries, produced by service in the revolutionary armies and by the conditions of political anarchy engendered by factional civil strife. An illegitimate mestizo, he expressed the rising importance of this amorphous ethnic class. He was virtually illiterate, his only education being that received in the army. It was through the army that he rose to political power by the destruction of his enemies, with some of whom he previously cooperated. His power has a vaguely populist basis, but in the main his regime rested on a primitive and personal power structure that lasted only as long as he could hold his rivals at bay by fear of reprisal. Except for an obvious hostility toward the old families of Bolivia, it is hard to see any ideological basis to his regime.

Gabriel García Moreno (1821–1875) may be described in many respects as a unique type of dictator in Latin America. The contrast with his contemporary in Bolivia, Mariano Melgarejo, is striking. Melgarejo was an illegitmate child, whose only education came from the army. García Moreno was well educated and highly intelligent, the scion of a prominent Ecuadoran family and the son-in-law of the former (Conservative) president and independence leader, Juan José Flores. García Moreno gave Latin America its clearest example of the application of the traditionalist principles in a national political regime dedicated to his own concepts of reform of the Church and of other aspects of national life. He believed that the nations of Spanish America could best achieve a peaceful social and political order by restoring as much of the Spanish colonial culture and political system as possible. But he was also a reformer, bent on making the Church an instrument of the state and on reforming the clergy by purifying their lives and making them dedicated servants of society as well as of God. Not many early Latin American dictators met death by assassination; García Moreno stands out as one of these.

About the middle of the nineteenth century a new type of dictator began to appear. Sometimes he came from obscure social origins, rising to power through the army. Sometimes he came from one of the older political families. Often he was identified with a Liberal reform movement. He built power by mobilizing military and popular support from the emerging urban middle class and by courting the backing of some of the new economic interests of his country. Porfirio Díaz of Mexico is an outstanding example, but similar types also appeared in other countries.

The twentieth century has produced a number of authoritarian rulers who may be roughly classed together as being inspired by principles similar to, if not identical with, those of Italian fascism, German National Socialism, and the regimes of Franco in Spain and Salazar in Portugal. This type includes such varied leaders as Juan Perón of Argentina, Getulio Vargas of Brazil, Jorge Ubico of Guatemala, Anastasio Somoza of Nicaragua, Rafael Trujillo of the Dominican Republic, Gustavo Rojas Pinilla of Colombia, Marcos Pérez Jiménez of Venezuela, and Alfredo Stroessner of Paraguay. The pattern of the regimes they sponsored has varied from one country to another. The most highly developed and successful pattern was that of Peronismo. Organized around a populist, army-labor party, it supported a vigorous, if not always successful, program for economic development through industrialization. It also aimed to lessen the economic differences that separated workers from middle and upper class sectors of society. Sometimes, as in Spain and Portugal, these regimes worked to strengthen the position of the Church. More often their motives were more purely secular.

Finally, we have the newest type of Latin American dictator, that of Fidel Castro, the type described by Juan Bosch as the dictator with popular support, the populist dictator. But this Castro populist type is not all new by any means. Both Juan Perón and Getulio Vargas were populists. Like them, Castro came to power as the leader of a rebellion, taking over power with the support of his armed followers. Even the ideology and program he had advanced after the failure of his original putsch in 1954 had a familiar ring. His objective, he said, was to overthrow the dictator, Fulgencio Batista, restore the Constitution of 1940, and reestablish legitimate government through free elections. Once in power, however, Castro moved in more Lenin-like style to gather all the power structures of the nation into his hands—the army, the labor unions, the banks, the universities and student organizations, private schools, and the mining, sugar, and cattle industries—everything indeed except the Church!

Castro had led a popular uprising, both among the peasants who supported him in the countryside and among students, professional people, and workers of the city. Nor was the dictatorship he imposed one that was based on the Communist party, which at first gave only lukewarm support. Once in office Castro set about organizing his own Communist party but this party, it must be noted, came after rather than before the fact of dictatorship. Nor was it originally a party, in the Soviet model, based upon the organizations of urban workers. Only in the years after he took over, in January 1959, did Castro's dependence upon the Soviet Union for economic and military aid lead him to tighten the links with labor unions, thus giving his party a political orientation more like that of the party of the Soviet Union. In some respects, the Castro type of dictatorship seems to be closer both to Maoist models, and to the theoretical model advanced by Juan Bosch, than to the Leninist type. Whatever its theoretical basis, after nearly thirteen years in power, as of this writing, the Castro dictatorship stands out as one of the of the longest lasting authoritarian regimes of Latin America and has become part of the Latin American establishment.

NOTES

1. The Wise study, a Ph.D. dissertation, was issued in mimeograph, Columbia University, 1946. The volume edited by A. Curtis Wilgus, is *South American Dictators During the First Century of Independence* (Washington, D.C.: The George Washington University, 1937. Reissued by Russell and Russell, New York, 1963).
2. *Dictatorship in Spanish America* (New York: Knopf, 1965), pp. 4, 7.
3. *Bases y puntos de partida para la organización política de la República Argentina*, Edition by Francisco Cruz (Buenos Aires: L.J. Rosso, 1933), pp. 166–7, 215. Original

edition, 1852.

4. Translated by Helen R. Lane (New York: Grove Press, 1969).

5. Bolívar is not among the dictators sketched in this book, chiefly because the author has already written of him in *Makers of Democracy in Latin America*. Moreover, there is a voluminous literature in English on Bolívar.

BIBLIOGRAPHY

The literature on dictatorship in Latin America is, as suggested, quite extensive, and only a few of the more important works are here listed: Juan Bosch, *Pentagonism, A Substitute For Imperialism*. Trans. by Helen R. Lane (New York: Grove Press, 1969); James Bryce, *South America, Observations and Impressions* (New York: Macmillan Co. 1913) ch. XV, "The Conditions of Political Life in Spanish American Republics"; Guy Stanton Ford, ed., *Dictatorship in the Modern World* (Minneapolis: University of Minnesota, 1935), ch. 4 by J. Fred Rippy, "Dictatorship in Spanish America"; Hugh M. Hamill, Jr., Ed. *Dictatorship in Spanish America* (New York: Knopf, 1965); Cecil Jane, *Liberty and Despotism in Spanish America* (Oxford University Press, 1929); Ariel Peralta Pizarro, *El cesarismo en América Latina* (Santiago, Chile: Ed. Oribe [1966]; Norman L. Stamps, *Why Democracies Fail* (Notre Dame, Indiana: University of Notre Dame Press, 1957); Laureano Vallenilla Lanz, *Cesarismo democrático* (Caracas, 1919); A. Curtis Wilgus, ed. *South American Dictators During the First Century of Independence* (Washington: George Washington University, 1937. New York: Russell and Russell, 1963); George S. Wise, Caudillismo. *A Study of Dictatorship in Latin America* (Mimeograph: Columbia University, 1946). The reader may also wish to consult the author's *Government and Politics of Latin America*, especially Ch. 1, "The Political Experience of Latin America" and Ch. 10, "The Presidency" (New York: Ronald Press, 1958) and his *Latin American Leaders*, "Introduction" (New York: H.W. Wilson Co., 1949 and Cooper Square Publishers, 1968).

19

DR. FRANCIA, "EL SUPREMO" (1766–1840)

José Gaspar Rodriguez Francia ruled Paraguay from 1811 until his death in 1840. He is one of the earliest, as well as one of the most dramatic, examples of a Latin American revolutionary turned dictator. A century and a half after his death he remains a paradoxical enigma, even for Paraguayan historians. It would be difficult to find a Latin American ruler who has been painted blacker, at least by non-Paraguayans. Thomas Carlyle, in his classic essay on Francia, characterized the writing by Europeans, especially the Robertson brothers of Scotland who produced some seven volumes on the Paraguay of Francia, as "a running shriek of constitutional denunciation, 'sanguinary tyrant' and so forth."[1]

In the novel, *El Supremo*, Edward Lucas White pictured Francia as an enigmatic sadist who built his tyrannical power on the ignorance and superstition of the Paraguayan masses by the indiscriminate use of violence and terror against personal and political enemies. It is a matter of record that after Francia's election with virtually absolute power in 1814, a maternal uncle called him "a bilious hypochondriac, [with] a heart filled with bitterness and ice, an egotistic spirit . . . tortuous ideas, unexampled pride, insufferable audacity . . . Machiavellian methods." Some later historians agree with Carlyle, however, in giving Francia a more favorable, or at least a more understanding analysis, describing him as a ruler who was a legitimate expression of the revolutionary independence movement. Carlyle portrays him as a populist who followed the ideas of Rousseau and who saw dictatorship as a necessary stage in the process of creating the kind of democratic regime he professed. Some writers have seen in Francia's later career a complete reversal of his youthful Liberalism. The mystery with which he surrounded himself and his secretiveness support this view. More probably, however, as we shall see, his later authoritarianism is a natural evolution from his revolutionary theory.

His father was of uncertain ancestry, and consequently, there is much speculation over the origin of the family name, Francia. The father had come to Paraguay as an immigrant from Brazil with the purpose of growing, processing, and exporting tobacco. To the closed society of Asunción, he always remained a foreigner, even after his alliance by marriage with the aristocratic Velasco and Yegros families. Because he was a Brazilian, he was assumed to be a half-breed and was variously referred to as *mameluco* or *mulato*. As the years went by he prospered and by the time of independence had become wealthy through his tobacco and other export business. He held positions of responsibility, both as a provincial government official and as a captain in the militia.

His son, José Gaspar, was the third of five children. There were two older sisters, Lorenza and Petrona, and two younger brothers, Pedro and Juan José. José's early education was acquired in Asunción, in the school of the Convent of San Francisco. Either there, or in another school conducted by Dominicans, he studied Latin and, probably, philosophy and theology as well, before going at the age of fifteen to the University of Córdoba, in present day Argentina. After the expulsion of the Jesuits from the Spanish empire in 1767, this University had passed into the hands of the Franciscans. Two of José's maternal uncles, both Franciscans and one of them his godfather, taught there; they would help to guide his studies and his conduct. The family objective in sending him to the university was to qualify him for a benefice established in the will of his pious maternal grandmother, Francisca de Yegros, of which his father was administrator. But José never went beyond taking minor orders, rejecting the security of the theological career to prepare himself in civil law.

In the Royal College of Monserrat, where he was lodged in Córdoba, he lived with students from other parts of Spanish South America, many of whom were soon to be leaders of independence. As a brilliant student, he attracted attention for excellence in both speech and writing. But he was nervous, excitable, and quarrelsome, reputedly threatening those who opposed him in any way with a dagger which he always carried. Some such incident may have been the cause of his having to give up residence in the college. It was a portentous omen that his companions at this time called him "the dictator."

Despite living outside the college, he completed the course quickly. Shortly thereafter he graduated from the University as Licenciado (in law) and as Master of Arts. Within another year he had also qualified for a doctorate in sacred theology. What was equally important, he had absorbed the ideas of such Enlightenment authors as Voltaire, Rousseau, and Montesquieu, whose works were tolerated under the liberal Franciscan university regime.

A few years after his return to Asunción, José Gaspar quarreled with his father, possibly over the latter's taking a mistress after the death of his wife (José's mother). José left the family home at this time and for the next decade engaged in youthful roistering, drinking and sexual license, until a serious illness brought this phase of his life to an abrupt close. After this illness he retired to the family plantation Ibiray, outside Asunción, and began to live as an ascetic valetudinarian. Devoting himself to a law practice, he acquired a reputation of astuteness, rectitude, and concern for justice for poor petitioners. For his studies he accumulated the best library in Asunción.

Spanish and criollo society continued to reject him as they had rejected his father. Not only was he referred to as "that mulatto," but his enemies now circulated the rumor that he had not really received a doctorate at Córdoba! In 1798 his election to the municipal council was blocked by the syndic-procurator, who had been a fellow student at the university. He was also rejected at first for the post of professor of theology in the College of San Carlos. Seemingly, this rejection was an act of revenge against his father, because José was clearly the best qualified of the applicants for the post. Only after two years was he grudgingly allowed to assume this position. In 1804 his resentment further increased, especially against two of the families that dominated the social life of Asunción, when he was rejected as a suitor by the father of his would-be bride. Petrona Zavala was the only real love of his life, but her father scornfully rejected "the mulatto" as a son-in-law, giving his daughter, instead, to Juan José Machaín. Francia never forgave the Zavala and Machaín families. It was a grudge ominous for the future, an ill will that was destined to give a color of vengeance to many of his later actions.

Paraguayan independence found Francia well established in Asunción as a successful lawyer though largely cut off from Asunción society. He was known on the one hand for his arrogance toward clients among the old criollo families and, on the other hand, for his disinterested defense of causes of the humble poor. He had also begun to satisfy in some degree his ambition for political activity. In 1804, he had helped to dislodge from office Governor Lázaro de Ribera, who was refusing to carry out the royal decree abolishing the remaining encomiendas in Paraguay and was at the same time proposing to abolish the long established exemption of tobacco producers from military service and from certain other public obligations.

Francia's chief contribution to this action consisted of attacks, both written and verbal, upon the criollo favorite and lieutenant of the governor, José Espinola y Pena, for abuses of his office. These attacks won Francia the emnity of another powerful family of Asunción at the very time, as it happened, that he was rejected as a suitor by the Zavalas. One notes, also, that in this case Francia was defending his family interest in tobacco. The legal counselor of the new governor turned out to be another companion of Córdoba days, Pedro Alcántara Somellera, and through this friendship, contrasting with the hostility of the other fellow student who had blocked his election to the municipal council, Francia's political influence grew further.

Political conditions in Paraguay began to change after the British expeditions were expelled from Buenos Aires and Montevideo in 1806 and 1807. Paraguayan militia had taken part in these actions, and Francia did not fail to take political advantage of the feverish patriotic spirit that had developed from them. In 1808, "the paulista mulatto" was elected to the membership in the municipal council (cabildo) that he had vainly sought ten years earlier. Thereafter he continued to find a major source of support in the cabildo, even when not a member. His participation in the independence movement thereafter was astute and cautious. News of the May 1810 Revolution in Buenos Aires reached Asunción in June and found Francia at his *chacra*, Ibiray, where he had gone to live after finishing his term as syndic-procurator in the cabildo. Having now reached the age of forty-four, he had learned to measure his steps carefully and to await the development of events patiently. How important his political influence had become by this time, however, appeared when he was nominated by the cabildo of Asunción to represent the viceroyalty in the Cortes summoned by the opponents of Napoleon to meet in Spain. He was not chosen, however, in the final election held in Buenos Aires.

The movement for Paraguayan independence, culminating in the revolutionary actions of May 14–15, 1811, developed in three main stages. In the first stage the municipal cabildo turned down the invitation of the Buenos Aires revolutionary junta, established after the May 25, 1810 revolution, to join in rejecting the authority of the regency that had just been set up in Spain. Governor Velasco assembled some two hundred leading citizens of Paraguay who voted to oppose the Buenos Aires action, to support the Spanish regency, and to put the province in a state of defense, presumably against invasion from Brazil. Francia attended this meeting but seems to have left in disgust; his signature does not appear on the resolutions adopted.

In the second stage, the governor used the armed forces he had raised to turn back an army sent by Buenos Aires under the command of Manuel Belgrano to force Paraguay to join them. In the battles of Paraguarí and Tacuarí the criollo leaders snatched victory from defeat after Governor Velasco had fled, believing he had lost the battle. This victory gave the Paraguayan leaders confidence to go further, as appears in the third stage. When they learned that the governor was planning to restore his command of the situation, and to nip independence in the bud by stationing Brazilian troops in the province of Misiones, they forced him on May 14–15, 1811, to turn over to them the military forces of the province. Thus began the independence of Paraguay, an independence from both Buenos Aires and from the Spanish Bourbon claimant in Brazil, Queen Carlota.

Francia was the guiding genius of this revolution of May 1811, working with the criollo militia leaders, Fulgencio Yegros, Vicente Ignacio Iturbe, and Pedro Juan Cavallero. Shrewdly, he avoided overly radical action, so as not to alienate either the militia leaders or the supporters of the governor. Thus, at first the governor was merely forced to accept two deputies, one of whom was Francia. The other was a highly respected Spaniard, Juan Baleriano Zevallos. This arrangement lasted less than a month; the governor was then forced out of office and was replaced by a junta of which Francia was secretary. From this post, directing the Paraguayan course during the next six years, Francia began a meteoric, uninterrupted rise to power that eventually made him *el supremo dictador* for life. As secretary of the junta he managed affairs until 1814. In that year, a new congress which he assembled granted him dictatorial powers for three years. In 1816 he was made dictator for life by the last congress he assembled. Thereafter, until his death in 1840, he ruled unchallenged except for one conspiracy against his life; this he suppressed with great vigor and cruelty.

"A revolutionary of law" is what one biographer, Julio César Chávez, has called him, saying that "he advocates the necessity of working with a hand of iron to achieve radical reforms and a transformation of the political, social, and economic order."[2] This amazing career was the result of his unerring exploitation of the external dangers that beset Paraguay, then living under constant threat of conquest by both Argentina and Brazil, and of the internal dissension in Paraguay. The internal division was partly the product of the external threats and partly the result of deep seated anti-Spanish feeling among the criollos and of jealousies among these criollo families.

Late in 1811 he withdrew from participation in the governing Junta to indicate his displeasure with some of its actions. He did not resign from the Junta, however, and kept his influence alive through the cabildo. In September he again acted as a member of the governing Junta to prevent the execution of a group of Spanish sympathizers who had conspired against the revolutionary government. Ironically, one of those he saved was Juan José Machaín, the husband of his once beloved Petrona Zavalla.

This act of clemency, together with previous actions, gained him the reputation of being overly-friendly to the *pytaguas*, as the Spaniards were

called. *(Pytagua* is the Guarani name for a kind of giant flycatcher.)
Working through the cabildo, also, as well as through militia officers who
were not supporters of the popular criollo militia leader, Vicente Ignacio
Iturbe, and who were in some cases his rivals for power, Francia arranged
to be recalled to active service in the Junta. This he achieved by pitting
these new military elements against the old. He agreed to resume his
place in the Junta on condition that he be given his own batallion of
troops. From this point on Francia was firmly in control of the armed
forces, pushing aside his military rivals by assigning them and their troops
to outlying posts.

His fine shrewd hand appeared in the negotiations that the Junta
carried on with Buenos Aires. Like Artigas in Uruguay, and like Mariano
Moreno in Buenos Aires, Francia urged decentralization of power in the
viceroyalty in some form of federalism. He showed himself wiser than
Artigas, however, when he kept Paraguay from sending representatives
to a constitutional assembly in Buenos Aires in which Porteño interests,
he was sure, would prevail.

Francia proposed, instead, to submit to a popular assembly the
question of Paraguayan participation in the Buenos Aires meeting. This
congress met in 1812, and the astute planning of Francia was seen clearly
in the large size of the congress (1000 members were called for, one for
each 50 to 100 families). His purpose was to check the power of the criollo
families by giving predominance to small farmers and herdsmen of the
countryside. By carefully soliciting the support of these rural members he
gained a clear victory for his policy. The congress not only rejected the
Buenos Aires invitation, but also decided that Paraguay should go her
own independent way. Francia was elected as one of two Consuls, the
other being his kinsman and prominent military leader Fulgencio Yegros.
As president of the Junta, Yegros had been following Francia's advice and
seemed content to allow Francia to continue to dictate policy.

This executive of two consuls obviously suggests the Napoleonic
example. But just as clearly it shows Francia's realistic political insight.
He saw that he and Yegros were the only two possible candidates for the
unipersonal executive he was convinced was necessary, because they had
become the two nuclei of power in the revolutionary situation—he as the
spokesman of the small farmers and herdsmen, Yegros as the leader of
the criollo militia. But Francia also saw that he could control the criollo
aristocracy through Yegros. Two years later Yegros had ceased to be a
serious rival, and Francia could again use the system of 1812. A large
congress dominated by rural members, as noted, made him a dictator for
three years, with the title of *El Supremo Dictador*. Again, in 1816, as the

Argentines were finally declaring their national independence and formalizing a government, another such congress made him dictator for life.

It seems clear that Francia's rapid rise to absolute power resulted largely from his shrewd Machiavellian strategy of playing off against each other the potentially divisive forces in Paraguayan society. As we have seen, these forces embraced the newly confident criollo military leadership, the old criollo landowning families (including a newly aggressive group of tobacco cultivaters and exporters), the Spanish officials and clergy (pytaguas), the small farmers and herdsmen of the countryside, and the largely illiterate indigenous masses. Within this revolutionary strategy, the device of the large congress with one representative for each fifty to one hundred families was a well conceived instrument for creating a dictatorship.

Another factor in the strategy that brought his rapid rise was the refusal in 1811 to reassume his place in the Junta until he was given a battalion of troops under his direct command. In this action he struck at the heart of the criollo power structure, and showed the criollo militia leaders that he was not a man to be trifled with. But this action was only one of many through which he gathered all the reins of power into his hands. In a comparable move he took control of the Church and thus of education. He also seized economic power when he assumed control of all foreign commerce, essentially stopping it in the subsequent trade war with Buenos Aires.

The most amazing aspect of his political intuition, and the source of much of the air of mystery that surrounds his career, is his instinctive grasp of the emerging ethnic basis of power in Paraguay. Whether or not he speeded up the mesticization process, and a good argument can be made to show that he did, he saw in the mestizo and the Indian a sure basis for building his personal power and for creating a kind of primitive sense of nationality around this personal loyalty. Thus, one of his most revolutionary decrees forbade the marriage of Spaniards with Spaniards, in effect requiring that the Spanish families be assimilated into the mestizo masses. His effective system for gathering information, one through which he imposed his will and warded off rebellion, utilized the ambitions for leadership then emerging among the poor Indian peasants. He played upon these ambitions in selecting the members of his congresses of a thousand members.

Like Bolívar, it is interesting to note, Francia was a dedicated revolutionary who believed that republican Spanish America required a lifetime, unipersonal executive. Like Bolívar, also, he believed in the necessity of dictatorship under certain conditions. It should be added, of course, that Bolívar never accepted the need for the kind of perpetual dictatorship Francia believed necessary.

This devotion of Francia to the principle of perpetual, as opposed to temporary, dictatorship is one of the more difficult elements of his political thought to understand. As late as the Congress of 1814 he continued to believe in the necessity of periodic congresses. Only in 1816 did he arrive at the authoritarian principle that a congress should assemble at his call alone. At this stage his reasoning, as expressed to the Argentine Esteban Echevarría, was that Paraguay would not really be ready for democracy for forty years! Speaking of Benjamin Franklin as "the model democrat, that we should imitate," he added: "Within forty years these countries may have men who resemble him, and only then may we enjoy the freedom for which we are not prepared today."[3] In this statement one cannot avoid seeing the class-conscious sense of *noblesse oblige* that permeates and gives the major tone to his populism and his authoritarianism. The secret of constitutional government for Francia was to create a responsible and unified political elite that could stand between autocracy and mobocracy. Meanwhile he played the thinly disguised role of an absolute monarch.

This explanation of Francia's amazing success in forging a new nation from the Guarani masses of Paraguay would be incomplete if it did not underline three major policies that contributed to this success. The first is the policy of economic isolation that caused the nation to live largely within its own economic resources. The second is the policy of political non-intervention that saved Paraguay from the devastating civil conflicts of the Plata region during the first decades of independence. The third, a kind of corrollary to the second, was the policy of playing off Brazil against Argentina, while avoiding an open break with either.

As we have seen, Francia avoided participation in Argentine constitutional assemblies, even while asserting his belief in federalism for the former viceroyalty. Though he supported Artigas in the alliance against Rosas that included several interior Argentine provinces, he refused to follow Artigas in the consequent civil war. In this policy of non-intervention he was also moved by the necessity of avoiding conflict with expansionist, monarchical Brazil. A conflict with Brazil might well have been the result of his coming to the aid of Artigas, for the latter was simultaneously fighting off a Brazilian invasion.

The basis of the third policy was Francia's intuitive understanding that Brazilian policy called for preventing the organization of an Argentina that would include all the former viceroyalty (Bolivia, Uruguay, and

Paraguay, as well as present day Argentina). He used this knowledge of the Brazilian interest to keep clear of Argentina, while threatening Brazil with the possibility of throwing his support to Buenos Aires. Pursuing this policy, he gave an amazingly successful demonstration of tightrope walking for three decades, keeping his country free of both civil and foreign war.

NOTES

1. "Dr. Francia," in *Critical and Miscellaneous Essays* (New York: John B. Alden, 1885), 7–65, at p. 26.
2. *El supremo dictador* (Buenos Aires: Ed. Nizza, 3d. ed. 1958), p. 125.
3. Quoted from Barolomé Mitre, *Historia de Belgrano*, I, 402, in Chaves, *op. cit.*, 183–184.

BIBLIOGRAPHY

The author has relied very largely upon the previously cited *El supremo dictador* by the Paraguayan historian, Julio César Chaves (Buenos Aires: Ed. Nizza, 3d. ed, 1958). Other useful works include the classic essay of Thomas Carlyle; Chaves, *La revolución del 14 y 15 de mayo* (Asunción and Buenos Aires: Biblioteca Histórica Paraguaya, 1957); Arturo Bray, *Hombres y épocas del Paraguay* (Buenos Aires: Nizza, 3d. ed. 1957); Justo Pastor Benítez, *Formación social del pueblo paraguayo* (Asunción and Buenos Aires: Ed. América-Sapucai, 1955); H.G. Warren, *Paraguay: An Informal History* (Norman, Okla.: University of Oklahoma, 1949); and Philip Raine, *Paraguay* (New Brunswick, N.J.: Rutgers University, 1956). An excellent article by Jerry W. Cooney, "Paraguayan Independence and Doctor Francia," *The Americas*, XXVII, No. 4 (April 1972), 407-28, unfortunately appeared too late to be used in the preparation of this book.

20

JUAN MANUEL DE ROSAS (1793–1877)

Few dictators in Latin American history have been more violently excoriated by their triumphant opponents than Juan Manuel de Rosas. Nor have many been more the subject of controversy among historians attempting to treat them with some degree of objectivity. The black legend of Rosas is that of a fiendish, sadistic, cruel fanatic, ruling Argentina by calculated terror. In recent years this legend has given way at the hands of revisionist historians sometimes to that of an enlightened "strongman"; more often to that of a less sinister though still Machiavellian ruler, traditionalist in his view of society, religion, and politics, puritanical in his ethics, and committed to the employment of force to impose unity on his newly born country. What is more significant, however, is that he is also seen as the leader who forged a nation out of the anarchy that prevailed in the Plate river area after independence.

Rosas was born March 30, 1793, in the home of his mother and his wealthy maternal grandfather, Clemente López de Osornio. The house was located on what is today Calle Sarmiento in Buenos Aires. His mother was Agustina López de Osornio; his father, León Ortiz de Rosas, was a lieutenant in the Infantry Regiment of Buenos Aires. An air of tragedy still reigned in the large López home because of the violent death ten years earlier of the rich landowner Clemente López and his oldest son, Andrés, in an Indian attack on the López *estancia* in the south of Buenos Aires province, where the Rio Salada enters the sea. This tragic death of his grandfather and uncle was a portent of the Indian warfare in which the newly born child was to gain his reputation as a leader of men. Another significant portent was his baptism (on the very day of his birth) by a military chaplain, hastily brought in by the young soldier father. It was an omen of double meaning, since Rosas was to become a defender of the Church, but was also to make his fortune by raising cattle and salting meat, while extending his ownership of lands, in the course of his wars against the Indians of the pampa.

As a boy he attended one of the best schools in Buenos Aires. Then, at the age of 13, he enlisted under General Santiago Antonio María de Liniers to drive the British from Buenos Aires in 1806. Nine years later, in 1815, he established at Quilmes the first meat salting business in the province of Buenos Aires. Still later he acquired extensive cattle lands in the Rio Salado area where Buenos Aires was expanding into Indian territory, and where his grandfather and uncle had met death. There, as a kind of lord of the manor, he exercised undisputed sway, severely punishing drunkenness, idleness, and theft. His discipline made of his gauchos not only an army that ensured safety of these frontier areas from Indian raids but also one that could be used effectively in the civil wars.

Thus, in 1820, Governor Martín Rodríguez called upon Rosas to put down an uprising against his rule. Eight years later Governor Manuel Dorrego was on his way to seek the protection of Rosas troops when he was captured and executed by the Unitarist General Juan Lavalle. After the execution of Dorrego, Rosas defeated Lavalle with the aid of Governor Estanislao López of Santa Fe, but even more specifically by the guerrilla tactics of his gaucho cavalry. In a dramatic gesture of surrender, General Lavalle went with a small guard to the Rosas' headquarters. For a time after his surrender, joining forces with Rosas, Lavalle was allowed to remain at the head of a government supported by both unitarists and federalists. But Rosas soon forced him to return to Uruguay.

This was the Rosas summoned by the provincial legislature in 1829 to become governor of the province of Buenos Aires in the midst of the anarchy that followed the death of Governor Dorrego. A born leader of men, hardened by years of frontier life, idolized by his gauchos, fearless in time of danger, and accustomed to violence, Rosas seemed to be ideally qualified to restore peace and order. Keenly intelligent, he had an intuitive understanding of political forces and strategy. His popularity among the gauchos of the countryside and among the Negro and mestizo masses of the city was a major source of his influence.[1] But unlike his predecessors in the government, and unlike other contemporary leaders, his experience of life and culture was provincial. His personal experience had never extended beyond the confines of his province and his successes had been won in the savage life of the pampas. Yet his letters, as his biographers attest, reveal a high level of culture and acquaintance with the ideas of his times.

Rosas' first task was to confront an uprising supported by eight interior provinces and led by the Unitarist General José M. Paz, a confederate of Lavalle, who had installed himself in Córdoba. The campaign came to an unexpected end when General Paz was captured in 1831, after being felled from his horse by a boleadora. The forces supporting him then disintegrated.

Rosas refused re-election as governor in 1832, but assured instead the election of a friend and confidant. He himself assumed command of a force to suppress an Indian uprising in the south. He returned to the office of governor in 1835, after declining several times, when the legislature placed all the powers of government in his hands. His personal power was so great by this time, and he seems already to have inspired such fear, that no other leader in Buenos Aires would accept the office. For the next seventeen years he ruled as a dictator.

Argentina had not succeeded in adopting a national constitution and Rosas gave it none, except in a de facto sense. As governor of Buenos Aires he conducted foreign relations for the nation and led the nation in war. When provincial governors opposed him, he eliminated them remorselessly by force or intrigue. But he appears to have been satisfied to hold the provinces together as a loose league of caudillo dominated

The Rosas dictatorship was a product of the anarchy of the day and of the divisions in the ranks of the political oligarchy. Rosas himself was'one of the provincial *estancieros*, cattlemen who were taking over public lands for their increasing herds. With them he had opposed the Law of Emphyteusis adopted under the government of Bernardino Rivadavia. This law permitted only the leasing of public lands, thus retaining for the state the increase in their value. Rosas also had opposed the banking and other centralizing policies of Rivadavia's administration. He promptly reversed these measures after coming to power.[2]

Rosas' rule was a reign of terror. Proclaiming "death to the filthy, loathsome, savage Unitarians," he used a secret organization called the *Mazorca* (ear of maize) to impose his rule by terror and violence. The *Mazorca* included many good and peaceful citizens, but it also included ruffians recruited from the rabble of Buenos Aires who were ready to perform acts of violence at the bidding of the dictator. In its ranks were household servants, some of them ex-slaves, who informed against their "aristocratic" masters. Dedicated to the cult of Rosas, the *Mazorca* also appears to have arranged those public ceremonies, emphasized so such by his critics, in which the portrait of the dictator was paraded and even placed on the altars of churches. Thus, in many ways, the harshness of the system seems to have been directed mainly against political opponents in the criollo elite, while the dictatorship had a popular basis among the gauchos and especially among the mestizos and emancipated Negroes of Buenos Aires. These, of course, were the groups that disliked the "aristocratic" unitarists.

Terrorism is never justified, although it has been cogently argued by one of the best Argentine students of the Rosas regime that "it was not possible to think of constituting the country on any different basis in those blind moments."[3] Rule by terror was not alien to the Spanish tradition, and resort to violence had actually increased during the wars for independence, as the "war to the death" proclaimed by Bolívar. In the Plate river area both the war for independence, and the civil wars that followed provided other antecedents. In 1810 the leaders of the Córdoba uprising were summarily executed. A conspiracy of the Regiment of Nobles against Manuel Belgrano had been punished with the wholesale execution of sergeants, corporals, and soldiers. In 1812 Martín Alzaga and thirty-eight fellow conspirators were shot. Their corpses were publicly displayed in Buenos Aires, where young Rosas saw them.

The heads of executed political rivals were displayed publicly during the political anarchy and strife of 1820, and this violence culminated, as we have seen, in the shooting of Dorrego, the constitutional governor of the province of Buenos Aires, after his capture by Lavalle.

Rosas understood this heritage and was no more addicted to violence than many others of his contemporaries. Other regimes, both before and since, have exacted a greater toll of human lives. He was scrupulously honest in handling financial affairs and never accepted a salary as governor. When he retired to exile, accompanied by his devoted daughter, Manuela, it was to a life of comparative poverty, although he had been one of the wealthiest landowners of Buenos Aires. Only a pension from the Urquiza government supported him in his last years in England. But, to his lasting infamy, he made a system of rule by terror. His Unitarist opponent, General José María Paz, writing of the Mazorca in his memoirs observed that "posterity will have trouble persuading itself that what we have seen is possible."[4]

Yet however this reign of terror is judged, it had the effect of welding Argentina into a nation. The political system Rosas presided over was an oligarchy of *estancieros*. By rejecting the aristocratic porteño reformers he was able to base his control to a considerable degree on popular acceptance. Yet his rule was essentially a triumph of the forces of social conservatism similar to that which occurred in Chile and Colombia at this time. In its reliance on terror it was closer to that of Francia in Paraguay. But, much more significantly, it was a triumph of the localism represented in the provincial caudillos upon whom Rosas' power rested. Either from fear or self-interest, the caudillos accepted his rule and supported him for more than two decades.[5]

One of his biographers, Carlos Ibarguren, has given notable insight into this populist basis of Rosas' power, citing his remarks to Santiago Vázquez, representative of the government in Montevideo, on the day of his first election as governor. As reported by Vázquez to his government, the remarks of Rosas also suggest the traditionalist basis of his theory of government:

> . . . Rivadavia, Aguero and others . . . made a great error: they conducted themselves well with the *clase ilustrada,* but they looked down on the men of the lower classes, those of the countryside (campaña), who are the people of action. I noted this from the beginning . . . . Thus it seemed to me very important to achieve a great influence over this people in order to control them, or to direct them, and I proposed to acquire that influence at all cost; for that I had to work with great constance, with many sacrifices, to make myself a gaucho like them, to speak like them, and to do whatever they did, to protect them to make myself their agent. . . .[6]

The young intellectuals of the Association of May shared this understanding of the popular basis of Rosas' power. Juan B. Alberdi wrote in one of his earliest works that Rosas "is not a despot who sleeps on hired bayonets. He is a representative who rests on the good faith, on the heart of the people. And by people we do not mean the intelligent, landowning class alone, but also the universality, the majority, the plebe."[7]

In 1852, one of the oldest of Rosas' supporters, Governor Justo José Urquiza of Entre Rios, led an army of Argentines, Brazilians, and Uruguayans against the dictator, defeating him in the Battle of Caseros and driving him from power in the name of the restored nation. Foreign relations partially explain Rosas' fall, as they explain his long hold on power. From his access to absolute authority in 1835 until an agreement with France and Britain in 1850, Argentina was engaged in conflicts with these two foreign powers. The difficulties grew largely out of Argentine intervention in the civil war then going on in Uruguay and in the war of Chile against the union of Peru and Bolivia that occurred at this time. British and French intervention followed, and this external threat strengthened the loyalty of the provincial caudillos. When the threat ended, Brazilian and Uruguayan forces joined with Urquiza and other provincial caudillos to drive Rosas from power.

Opposition to the Rosas regime had centered in Montevideo, where exiled leaders of the Association of May (enemies of Rosas) were welcomed and supported in their campaign against the dictator by the Uruguayan Colorados (Reds) led by Fructuoso Rivera. Rivera had supported Rosas' enemies, including Paraguay, in the campaigns of General Lavalle, and Rosas retaliated by supporting Rivera's opponent, Manuel Oribe, in the long siege of Montevideo, which began in 1842 and continued until settled by an agreement in 1850. The raising of the siege at this time opened the way for Rosas' enemies to unite against him.

One of the notable things about Rosas is that he and his record have been preserved, in the form of violent literary attacks, by the brilliant generation of Argentine intellectuals known as the Generation of 1837. The leader of this group, Esteban Echeverría, romantic poet and author of the *Dogma Socialista*, in a short story entitled *El Matador* (the Killer), wrote of the mass support for Rosas' execution of his enemies. In his novel *Amalia*, José Marmol depicts the atrocities and episodes of 1840, portraying Rosas and his family as cruel and pitiless. The same author's *Rosas*, a poem full of invective but regarded as a classic, has been widely read as such in Argentine schools.

The most telling indictment of Rosas, all the more so for being indirect, came from the pen of Domingo F. Sarmiento. His *Facundo*, although it was the story of the caudillo of San Juan, Facundo Quiroga, was also a sharp attack on Rosas who, like Quiroga, represented to Sarmiento the "barbarism" which civilization had vainly sought to overcome. In his later *Conflict and Harmony of the Races in America*, Sarmiento returned to the theme, although now he argued in more positivist terms that the root of the barbarism was racial—a Spanish and mestizo heritage.

In general, Sarmiento considered Rosas a product of American forces, understandable though evil. But he misunderstood or misrepresented the political nature and effect of Rosas' rule when he spoke of it as the triumph of "the idea of the unitarists."[8] For the union Rosas effected and the political principles he held were really federalist, however much he may have been guided in his action by practical political considerations. In this respect Rosas would have understood the Uruguayan independence leader, José Artigas, if they had happened to act in the same epoch. But he was convinced that what he called "the present state of the Republic" was not appropriate for deciding upon a constitution. Thus, he wrote to the governor of Santiago, Felipe Ibarra (1831?), answering the latter's suggestion that the time was ripe for a constitutional assembly, that it was impossible to believe that the political anarchy which reigned could be eliminated by drawing up a written constitution. In this letter Rosas also reveals that his political theory had a revolutionary character. He believed, he said, that it was necessary "first to destroy with energy, and by the union and uniform action of the peoples, all the resources which might be used by the party we have combatted."[9]

Rosas has often been depicted as a traditionalist, and some aspects of his policy fit the American pattern of traditionalism, as distinct from that of Europe. That he was an authoritarian is obvious. But he seems never to have suggested monarchy as the political solution to Argentine anarchy. He was a conservative in defending the interests of the landowners, but did not see that a nobility, least of all the unitarian "aristocracy," could be the basis for stability. He did not advocate the pre-French Revolutionary monopoly economics, even though he destroyed the physiocratic land system of Rivadavia.

His traditionalism, such as it is, appears most clearly in his Church policy, his general approach to religion, and in a fanatical puritanism shown in his ordering the execution of a priest and his young lover. One of his first acts to carry out the mandate of the legislature that granted him the plenitude of power was to restore to the rural priests the parish industries that had been taken from them by the anticlerical government of Bernardino Rivadavia.[10] But Rosas was not in any sense controlled by the Church leaders. He seems, rather, to have thought of and used the Church and religion as instruments to achieve political ends.

NOTES

1. Manuel Gálvez, *Vida de Don Manuel de Rosas*, 5th ed. (Buenos Aires: Tor, 1963), 92–95.

2. Miron Burgin, *The Economic Aspects of Argentine Federalism, 1820–1852 (Cambridge, Mass.: Harvard University Press, 1946).

3. *Ernesto Quesada, De Caseros al 11 de septiembre*, quoted in Ricardo Levene *History of Argentina*, W.S. Robertson trans. (New York: Russell and Russell, 1963), p. 415.

4. Quoted in Ernest Quesada, *La época de Rosas* (Buenos Aires: Facultad de Filosofía y Letras, 1923), p. 42. This citation was suggested by A.F. Boni, a graduate student in my seminar.

5. José Luis Romero, *History of Argentine Political Thought*, trans. by Thomas F. McGann (Stanford University, 1963), p. 123.

6. *Juan Manuel de Rosas* (Santiago, Chile: Ediciones Ultra, 1936), p. 178. Author's translation.

7. *Fragmento preliminar al estudio del derecho* (Buenos Aires: Libreria Hachette, 1955), p. 72. Published originally in 1837. Author's translation.

8. *Facundo* (Buenos Aires: Losada, 1963), p. 230.

9. Original document in Museo Mitre, quoted by Ibarguren, *op. cit.*, p. 196–199.

10. Manuel Gálvez, *Vida de D. Juan Manuel de Rosas*, 5th ed. (Buenos Aires: Tor, 1958?), p. 12.

BIBLIOGRAPHY

The literature on Rosas is extensive and much of it, as we have seen, tends to be polemical. Since some of the more important works have been mentioned in footnotes, a few only will be mentioned here. Two of Argentina's most notable historians of this century have written on Rosas. Emilio Ravignani has given us *Inferencias sobre Juan Manuel de Rosas y otros ensayos* (Buenos Aires: Ed. Huarpes, 1945) and Ricardo Levene wrote *Iniciación de la vida política de Rosas* (Buenos Aires: Imprenta López, 1933). José María Ramos Mejía, in his *Rosas y su tiempo* 3v. (Buenos Aires: Ed. Científica y Literaria Argentina, 1927) explained Rosas in a positivist evolutionary context. *La política liberal bajo la tiranía de Rosas* (Buenos Aires: Ed. Claridad, 1942) by José Manuel Estrada, on the other hand, is the discriminating work of one of Argentina's most notable traditionalist intellectuals, criticizing the band of young intellectuals organized in the Association of May who became Rosas' major opponents. Because Carlos Pereyra is Mexican, his excellent *Rosas y Thiers* (Buenos Aires: Ed. Forjador, 1952) is especially welcome as a non-Argentine appraisal by a historical scholar. Ernesto H. Celesia, *Rosas: Aportes para su historia*, 2v. (2d. ed. Buenos Aires: Editorial y Librería Goncourt, 1968–69) is a well documented work by an Argentine historian with an anti-Rosas slant.

21

RAFAEL CARRERA (1814–1865)
By Keith L. Miceli

The Merriam Webster *Biographical Dictionary* concludes its brief summary of the life of Rafael Carrera by saying that "illiterate and conservative, [he] favored the Church." The *Encyclopedia of Latin American History* ends its short article on Carrera with almost identical words. These phrases are a striking illustration of a persistent prejudice that links illiteracy with political conservatism and loyalty to the Catholic Church. That Carrera had no schooling and was virtually illiterate seems clear. That he was guided by churchmen in his career, probably from the beginning of his guerrilla activities against the Liberal regime of Mariano Gálvez and Francisco Morazán, also seems reasonably clear. In this sense he was a Conservative, guided by traditionalist social and political views. But neither of these elements was as decisive in shaping the career of Rafael Carrera as his primitive lust for power, his intuitive grasp of the nature and uses of power, and particularly his understanding of how to control and command the support of the Indian and mestizo or *ladino* masses of Guatemala.

Rafael Carrera is an example of the *caudillos* who dominated the histories of various Latin American nations following independence from Spain. Even more particularly he illustrates the kind of caudillo that was identified with the forces of social conservatism in the early nineteenth century struggles between proponents of colonial traditionalism and those of Liberal innovation. As subsequent revolutions and counter-revolutions ensued, this caudillo militarism set the pattern of national politics. The caudillo who had the most powerful army, organized or irregular, controlled the nation, either as president or as the power behind the throne.

Like Juan Manuel Rosas of Argentina, Carrera owed his power to certain traditionalist forces and to the support of conservative leaders, rather than to the kind of Liberal reforming forces that produced Francia in Paraguay. But there the similarity to Rosas ceases. Carrera was not a federalist, but an opponent of federalism in Central America, helping to destroy the Federal Republic of Central America. His popularity among the Indian and ladino (mestizo) masses suggests a certain resemblance to Francia. But this similarity, too, is largely superficial. For Francia, as we have seen, used his influence over the Indians *against* the Spanish and criollo elite; Carrera seems to have controlled the Indians of Guatemala to protect the interests of the criollos.

In spite of the confusion and anarchy of his rule, Rosas forged an Argentine nation. Was Carrera's failure to do the same in Central America the result of his shortcomings as a statesman? Did it stem from his lack of political sophistication? Or was it due simply to the fact that the basis for Central American nationality did not exist? The student will search in vain in the writings of historians of this period for a satisfying answer to these questions; Carrera is still an intriguing enigma.

Like Moreno of Ecuador, Carrera defended and in some respects restored the authority of the Church under attack by the Liberals. Like Benito Juárez of Mexico he defended the interests of the Indians from which he rose. He also demonstrated the political shrewdness of Mexico's Santa Anna and the cruelty of Bolivia's Mariano Melgarejo. But he lacks the authoritarian theory of a Moreno or a Santa Anna or the moral authority of a Juárez. Although he resembles Melgarejo, he can not be charged with the latter's lack of a sense of responsibility in the exercise of power.

He was born in a poor section of Guatemala City on October 25, 1814, the son of Simón Carrera and Juana Turcios. Both parents were probably of ladino derivation. His education was gained in the streets of this ghetto area in Guatemala and in the army of the Federal Republic in which he enlisted as a boy and served until 1829. Upon leaving the army he became an itinerant farmhand, one of the nameless landless proletariat who had furnished the labor supply during colonial days and continued to do so after independence.

When the rebellion against the Guatemalan government broke out in the midst of the catastrophic cholera epidemic in 1837, Carrera was employed as a swineherd in Mataquescuintla, one of the centers of the rebellion. This insurrection was instigated by the rural clergy and held together by Carrera who immediately appeared as a leader. The objective of the clergy was to regain the political and economic preeminance they held during the colonial period. Hence they took advantage of the chaotic circumstances created by the cholera epidemic to incite the ignorant and religiously fanatical masses to open rebellion against the Liberal reforms of the administration of Governor Mariano Gálvez. It was a popular rebellion, Carrera and his followers fighting to restore religious and social customs that had a strong hold on the popular mentality.

Carrera's military experience, a well as his audacity and shrewdness, pushed him to the forefront of leadership almost immediately. Within a few months the leader under whom he originally enlisted withdrew in his favor. At the end of three years of civil war the rebels had ousted the Liberals from office and established a Conservative government dominated by Carrera. The adulation of his parish priest-advisors, the adoration of his followers, and his military success had by this time given him an exaggerated sense of self-importance. He had convinced himself that he alone had delivered the Guatemalan people from the Gálvez regime.

Retaining military control, Carrera collaborated with the Conservative leaders of the government to restore much of the paternalistic order of colonial times; but neither Conservative nor Liberal politicians were able to control him. He arbitrarily invaded every branch of public administration, demanding to have his own way. Governors, ministers, and assemblies in Guatemala rose and fell at his bidding. By December, 1844, the Assembly, realizing that Carrera was the only real and effective power in the state, elected him governor.

In this way he completely dominated the country from 1839 to 1848, surviving military uprisings, political intrigues, and attempted assassinations. Through brute force, through mock revolts that he seems to have staged, and through threats of resignation he usually achieved whatever he wished. But in 1848 a popular uprising similar to that which brought him to power caused his temporary overthrow. As occurred in 1837, a natural calamity precipitated this insurrection. Excessive rains in 1846 and 1847 had ruined most of the wheat and corn crops and monopolists had cornered the grain markets, accentuating the grain shortage and raising grain prices.

Carrera tried unsuccessfully to alleviate the grain shortage and to curtail the monopolists' activities. He issued circulars to the departments, ordering the *corregidores* and *alcaldes* to take adequate measures to stop the plunder and to promote planting. He decreed a six month suspension of taxes on all domestic and imported flour, and his government bought grain to sell to the most needy municipalities at the purchase price.

These measures were not enough, however. The rains, grain shortages, and monopolists' practices continued, while abuses by local officials in carrying out the government measures created further resentment among the peasants. They complained that they were being forced to plant community fields and rebuild washed-out roads, leaving their own fields unattended.

The first signs of insurrection occurred in Mita, Carrera's old stronghold; among its leaders were some who had fought with Carrera ten years earlier. Some of the rebels may have been seeking revenge against

Carrera for not having given them expected favors. Liberal party leaders, aroused by the success of the French Revolution of 1848, also extended their support to the insurgents, although they did not have the same grievances as the Mita rebels. They joined them, however, in wishing the downfall of Carrera.

Bewildered by the growing strength and success of the rebels, Carrera resigned in August, 1848, and sought sanctuary in Mexico. This self-imposed exile was only temporary, however. Representatives of the clerical and aristocratic oligarchy, fearing the mutiny of the troops and the consequences of anarchy, soon persuaded him to return to Guatemala.

Taking command of the armed forces he quelled the insurrection, though it persisted until 1851. A new constitution was then drafted under which he was chosen chief executive. Before this term expired he was proclaimed president for life (1854), with an unusual provision that granted legal exemption from responsibility for his public acts (1855). Until his death ten years later he governed Guatemala without serious challenge to his dictatorial power. He steadily extended his country's hegemony throughout Central America, but made no effort to restore the federation.

Upon reassuming power after the Revolution of 1848 Carrera abandoned his earlier policy of playing one political party against the other. Instead, he established an informal alliance with the Conservatives that lasted until his death. Members of this Conservative clique who monopolized the most important government positions came chiefly from such prominent colonial families as Pavón, Batres, and Aycinena. Carrera's system was that of a government administered by the Conservatives, protected by an Indian army, Catholic indoctrinated, and dominated personally by Carrera.

Under this system the Catholic Church reclaimed many of its old colonial privileges. Priests often occupied government posts and the Jesuit order was allowed to return in 1851. The following year Carrera concluded a concordat with the Vatican, stipulating that public and private education should conform to Catholic doctrines. It committed the government to pay four thousand pesos annually to the Archbishop and to provide subsidies to individual parishes.

The most important source of Carrera's power lay in the Indian and ladino followers who made up his armies. The humble circumstances of his own ladino background gave him a natural sympathy for them and their grievances, and despite his alliance with the forces of social conservatism, he gave the Indian peasants more protection and attention than they had received since the close of the colonial era. Through letters, meetings, and proclamations, Carrera responded to the Indians' petitions, gaining their respect and loyalty because he personally received their complaints and attempted to redress their grievances. Some of the most onerous taxes were repealed. Many of the provisions of the Spanish Laws of the Indies that had protected the indigenous population during the colonial period were restored. The president called attention to abuses in the judicial system that exploited the peasants and demanded that the unfair quota assignments of the church tax (the tithe) be redressed. During his last days, as he lay dying, Indian pilgrims from throughout Guatemala came to the capital to pay their respects to the man they called "Our Lord."

His influence over the huge Indian population, the army, and the oligarchy brought political stability to a country which had known only chaos since independence. Upon the basis of this stability Guatemala prospered. During his tenure the Guatemalan one-crop export economy was diversified; roads and port facilities were improved to aid commerce. Since independence, the exports of cochineal had been the principal source of foreign exchange. In the 1850's, however, new chemical dyes that were developed in Europe began to replace cochineal on the world market. Fortunately, Carrera's government had already undertaken to lessen this reliance on one export crop. Subsidies and tax incentives stimulated the growing of coffee, sugar, and cotton; the success of these measures subsequently saved Guatemala from economic ruin.

This political stability enabled Carrera to strengthen Guatemalan influence elsewhere in Central America and to safeguard Guatemalan sovereignty against foreign intervention. He overturned the Liberal-controlled governments of El Salvador and Honduras in 1853 and 1854, respectively, establishing Conservative regimes in their place. His last war was against El Salvador, early in 1863. Like other interventions, this one was undertaken to preserve the hegemony of Guatemala and of the Conservatives in Central America. He thwarted Mexico's attempts to annex Central America, helped the other Central American countries to expel from Nicaragua the North American filibuster, William Walker, and stopped the territorial expansion of British Honduras by a treaty with Great Britain.

As we have seen, Carrera was adored by his peasant followers and adulated by the criollos. He was also celebrated by foreign governments. Indians deified him and students compared him with Napoleon. Priests dedicated hymns to him. France, Mexico, Belgium, Spain, and the Vatican decorated him. His death in 1865 marked the passing of Central

America's most enigmatic, important, and powerful caudillo of the post-independence type. It was also the end of the effective control of Guatemala by Conservative party forces.

BIBLIOGRAPHY

The two major nineteenth century histories treating the Carrera period express the bias of Liberal political beliefs. See Hubert Howe Bancroft, *History of Central America*, Vol. III (New York, 1887) and Lorenzo Montúfar, *Reseña histórica de Centro-América*, 7 vols. (Guatemala, 1878–1888). Recent and more objective accounts are Keith L. Miceli, "Rafael Carrera: Defender and Promoter of Rural Interests in Guatemala, 1837–1848" (M.A. thesis, Tulane University, 1968) and Mac Leon Moorhead, "Rafael Carrera of Guatemala: His Life and Times" (Ph.D. dissertation, University of California, 1942). The observations of foreign travelers and residents may be read in Robert G. Dunlop, *Travels in Central America* (London, 1847), Chevalier A. Morelet, *Travels in Central America, Including Accounts of Some Regions Unexplored Since the Conquest*. Trans. by Mrs. M.F. Squier (New York, 1871); and John L. Stephens, *Incidents of Travel in Central America, Chiapas and Yucatan*, 2 vols. (New York, 1853). Thomas L. Karnes, *The Failure of Union: Central America, 1824–1960* (Gainesville, Florida: University of Florida, 1960) presents Carrera's policies on the union of Central America. See also Mary Holleran, *Church and State in Guatemala* (New York, 1949).

22

MARIANO MELGAREJO (1820–1871)

Many Bolivians have passed through the presidential office of their nation, leaving little in the way of an impression. This certainly cannot be said of Melgarejo, although the nature of the impression he left is somewhat mixed. He has challenged the imagination of the French writer, Max Daireaux, to present him in a novelized biography as a "romantic tyrant." For Daireaux, Melgarejo was "the grandiose man, extravagant and fatal, who pushes to the extreme the virtues and vices of his times: bravery and cruelty, ignorance and vanity, audacity, arrogance, contempt for death, contempt for men, a kind of burlesque and sanguinary demi-god, a monstrous aberration of the genius of history."[1]

The Bolivian historian, Alcides Argüedas, describes him less lyrically as a born tyrant, a product of the violence and disorder of the times in Bolivia, to which he was also a major contributor. In some respects he must be seen as a product of the Liberal rebellion against the dying traditionalist order, and of the violence and despotism to which that rebellion often led. Thus he was the political heir of the aristocratic Liberalism of President José Ballivián and also of the populism of the demagogic Manuel Isidoro Belzú ("the Arab") credited by Argüedas with initiating an era of "barbarism" in Bolivian politics.

Because he first saw light on an Easter Sunday (April 13, 1820) Melgarejo, in sacrilegious arrogance, celebrated his birthday on that changeable date. He was born in Tarata, between Cochabamba and Sucre, Bolivia. An illegitimate child, he was the son of a criollo landowner, Justo Valencia, and Ignacia Melgarejo, a fifteen-year-old mestiza. The father refused to give his name to Mariano, who consequently bore his mother's name as a permanent mark of his illegitimate birth. This consciousness of illegitimacy may well have been an element in his romantic insistence upon celebrating his birthday on the movable feast day of the Resurrection of Christ, saying that if God chose to give him birth on the day of His own rebirth, it was because "He wished me to share with Him the madness of mortals and that I should withdraw myself, I alone, from the rigors of the calendar."[2]

These were troublous times in which the boy Mariano grew to manhood. The movement for independence in Spanish America was approaching its denouement as the Revolution of 1820 in Spain prevented any further effective military move of the mother country to suppress the American rebellion. Bolivia had experienced several invasions by the independence armies of Argentina during the preceding decade, but all of them were eventually repulsed. Guerrillas committed to independence had continued to operate on the eastern slope of the Andes, but Bolivia was not destined to be liberated by them. She was to be finally liberated, not so much by her own forces, as by an army of Colombians, Venezuelans, and Peruvians led by Antonio Sucre.

Thus, as Melgarejo grew to manhood, Bolivia was suffering the pangs of a nation trying to be born but not even certain that it should be born. For, like himself, Bolivia was not the child of an entirely free and legitimate union, but was forced into being by Bolívar to balance the rival claims of Peru and Argentina. If Bolivia was not illegitimate, she was at least incompletely legitimatized, as her subsequent chaotic history would indicate. Clashes of rival political factions and conservative reactions against the constitution imposed by Simón Bolívar brought the government of President Antonio José de Sucre crashing down. The subsequent regime under the independence leader, General Andrés Santa Cruz, who had served in the armies of both Bolivar and San Martín, also came to a tragic end. Santa Cruz intervened in Peru to create a federal union of Peru and Bolivia. Chile, seeing in this union a threat to her independence, went to war with Argentine support to prevent the union. The war not only forced a breakup of the union but also overthrew President Santa Cruz in Bolivia. At this point, Bolivia plunged into a sea of political anarchy. Out of this "time of troubles" came the tyrant Melgarejo.

Pedro Blanco had been Sucre's immediate successor as president. Fifteen days later Blanco had been overthrown in an uprising led by two army colonels, one of whom was the "aristocratic" future president and protector of Melgarejo, José Ballivián. Santa Cruz had seized power from these two leaders, and its was during his ten year rule that Melgarejo grew to manhood. How Mariano acquired even the rudiments of an education, even the ability to read, during these turbulent years is something of a mystery. There is no record of his having attended a school; most Bolivian schools were closed for that matter. Rejected by his father and abandoned by his mother he had no one to see to his education. Somehow he learned to play the guitar, to dance, to drink chicha, the native beer, and to make love to women immoderately. There is some suggestion that he may have acquired more education later, as a youthful exile living in Puno, Peru, in the household of Ballivián. He frequented army barracks at an early age, seeking admission to the army before his age justified it; the barracks was thus his school. Rejected as too young for military service at the age of fifteen, he continued to besiege the authorities until he was allowed to enlist the following year. This occurred during the war previously mentioned, in which Chile, with Argentine support, broke up the confederation of Bolivia and Peru.

His strength and daring spirit soon won him the respect of older colleagues in the army. He showed his courage in a battle in which an invading Argentine army was defeated, winning the rank of sargeant at an early age. Under Santa Cruz and General Isidoro Belzú, "the Arab," he experienced the disastrous defeat of Peruvian and Bolivian arms at Yungay by the invading Chilean force under General Manuel Bulnes. When Santa Cruz took the road to exile, José Ballivián, Miguel de Velasco, and José María Linares, with their armies, overthrew the government and called for a constitutional assembly. Melgarejo had joined the forces of Ballivián, who assigned him several dangerous tasks. Later, he supported Ballivián in an unsuccessful rebellion against this new government; when the uprising failed, Melgarejo was assigned (exiled) to outlying Oruro. There, a short while afterward (1840?), he led an uprising of his own, presumably in support of Ballivián. The rebels he led were defeated and captured by loyal troops and sentenced to be *quintado*, meaning that one out of each five was to be shot. Melgarejo escaped at night in disguise, carrying a captured rifle, and joined Ballivián in exile in Peru.

Between June 20 and October, 1841, fourteen abortive uprisings occurred in Bolivia. Four of them favored Santa Cruz, seven favored Ballivián, and three favored Miguel de Velasco, who was deposed on June 15 and fled to Argentina. Civil strife was rampant, in a political situation confused by rival militarist demagogs and by outside influences from Argentina, Chile, and Peru. When President Augustín Gamarra of Peru decided to invade Bolivia, Ballivián saw his opportunity to return in order to lead his nation in opposing the invasion. Melgarejo returned with him, serving under his command in the Battle of Ingaví in which the invading Peruvians were defeated with great loss. In this battle Gamarra was killed along with some seven hundred of his five thousand man army. Three thousand Peruvians were captured.

Ballivián ruled Bolivia for the next five years, giving the country one of its rare periods of relative peace during these early years of independence. Melgarejo was stationed in mountainous Tarija, in southern Bolivia, not far from the Argentine border. There he made love to and eloped with the belle of the town, Simone Cuenca, "the pearl of Tarija." She was the most romantic and probably the most serious love of his turbulent life, a more serious devotion than the infatuation with Juana Sánchez during his later years.

In 1848 Belzú overthrew Ballivián but yielded the presidency to Velasco. The next year, with an army of Indians and mestizos, he overthrew Velasco. He captured and sacked Chuquisaca (Sucre), burning priceless archives of colonial days in the process. Belzú was the first of a series of *caudillos barbaros,* as the historian Alcides Argüedas has called them, of which Melgarejo was to become the most notorious example. The former dictators had been negligent, vengeful, and often cruel; but they had been great landowners from distinguished families. The new breed, like Melgarejo, arose from the lower levels of society.

During the presidency of Belzú, Melgarejo passed his longest period of exile in Peru, with Ballivián. He returned to Bolivia, supporting Linares to whom he transferred his allegiance after the death of Ballivián in 1857. Stationed in Cochabamba, he then led an abortive rebellion in support of José María de Achá. He was condemned to death, but by pleading drunkenness won a commutation of sentence to exile in fever infested San Matías, in the Bolivian Amazon country. In 1861, Linares was overthrown by a golpe in Potosí led by Achá and a favorite of Linares named Fernández. Achá then betrayed Fernández, assumed the presidency, and called Melgarejo, his friend, to be commander of his guard. Melgarejo defeated Fernández when he rebelled, and for this victory was made governor of his home province of Cochabamba. In 1862 he gave a striking example of his courage and capacity for leadership when, despite the advice of the generals, he led an attack on the greatly superior forces of rebellious General Pérez, defeating him. Achá then made Melgarejo a general, and the Congress, after long debate, confirmed this nomination of the illegitimate orphan from Tarija.

In 1864, in the midst of the international crisis provoked by the attack of Spain on Peru and Chile, Melgarejo overthrew his friend and supporter, Achá. He was proclaimed president (dictator) the following year. When Belzú came back in 1866 and gained temporary control of the capital in the new president's absence, Melgarejo returned at the head of his army, entered personally into the national palace and killed Belzú with his own hand. For the next five years Melgarejo defeated every challenge to his power, surprising his enemies and defeating them with vigor and cruelty.

As a soldier, Melgarejo had led a life which frequently caused public scandal, carousing in barracks in drunken orgies with his troops, and disturbing the peace in drunken rioting. As president, his personal life continued in this scandalous pattern, although his public life took on more decorum. This was true at least in his meetings with foreign diplomats. Yet more than one of these, for example the Chilean minister who exercised great influence over him, had to leave the country at last rather than face the humiliation of participating in one of the orgies in which Melgarejo publicly insulted his ministers.

Melgarejo learned to refrain from participating publicly in the Carnival, for example. But, in private he continued what was virtually a daily orgy of drunkenness, in which he specialized in sadistic humiliations of his ministers. The society women of La Paz refused invitations to the presidential palace, and his soirees became almost exclusively male. But, this did not prevent the president's insisting upon lively dancing without the benefit of female partners. Particularly scandalous to Bolivian mores, if one is to believe Alcides Argüedas, were the stories that he exhibited his mistress in a kind of pagan rite, lying nude before his drunken companions, punishing them sadistically if they gave the least sign of being sexually excited.

The source of Melgarejo's power is not hard to discover. Basically it lay in the social forces released by a chaotic and anarchic social rebellion against control by the little aristocracy of power inherited by Bolivia from colonial days. During his long exile in Peru, while achieving political sophistication in the household of Ballivián, Melgarejo had lost whatever instinctive elements of romantic loyalty he may have had earlier to these "aristocratic" leaders. A simple but true political instinct had thereupon shown him how to conquer both Achá and Belzú, betraying them while using against them their own populism. Like the "Arab" Belzú, he rose to power by opposing the "aristocracy" represented in Ballivián. In his simplistic fashion he indiscriminately labeled as "demagogs" the followers of Achá, Belzú, and Ballivián! But this name calling serves chiefly to illustrate his sensitivity to this aspect of their power.

The anarchic conditions of Bolivia, in which what political power the traditional ruling class had was being dissipated in factional strife, together with the interventionist politics of Chile, Argentina, and Peru, had created a political vacuum that favored the rise of such leaders as Melgarejo. His military prowess was a major factor in his success, but equally important was his unscrupulous betrayal of those to whom he had been loyal. And he built his power by rewarding his followers generously with land, much of which was wrested from the Indian communities.

In the final analysis, the most significant element of Melgarejo's extraordinary power, and what gives his regime significance, is his largely unconscious populist appeal. Unscrupulous as he was, he was not a secretive, calculating Machiavellian. Rather, he was something more earthy, as Manuel Rogoberto Paredes has pointed out, something much more intimately connected with the telluric concepts that twentieth century Bolivian writers say are characteristic of Bolivian mentality. This meaning is what one may see in his drinking bouts, his riotous barracks room fraternizing with his troops, and his participation in the Carnival street processions.

He was overthrown by the same forces and the same devices that had brought him to power. His return to Bolivia with Ballivián, to oppose and defeat a Peruvian invasion, had helped to project him into power. Similarly, treaties he negotiated with Brazil and Chile helped his enemies to bring him down. By a treaty of 1866, he ceded Atacama to Chile, fixing the international boundary at 24° south latitude, but with the unusual provision that mineral resources between 23° and 25° belonged to both countries. In return, Melgarejo received the insignia and uniform of a Chilean General of Division. The following year a treaty with Brazil ceded to that country much of the Amazon territory claimed by Bolivia (Mamoré and Bení). It was probably more than coincidence that he spent three months of this same year of 1867 leading an army into the interior to suppress rebellion in Oruro, Cochabamba, and Chuquisaca (Sucre).

Much of his effort at legislation by decree was whimsical and arbitrary, alienating the support of Bolivians of intelligence. Yet one of his decrees of an international character was a kind of stroke of genius that elicited praise from South American colleagues. This was the decree of March 16, 1866, declaring that national frontiers were merely mathematical lines which would no longer exist in respect to economic and certain political matters. Anyone entering Bolivia, he decreed, would have all the rights of Bolivians, except that of becoming president. This echo of the Bolivarian dream of a single Spanish American nationality was the occasion of his receiving the rank of general at the hands of the Chilean minister who had negotiated the cession of Atacama.

The year 1870 was the fatal year for Melgarejo. It began with an ill-advised attack that he directed against Indians near the Peruvian border who were resisting the loss of their lands. The general that Melgarejo sent to suppress the revolt acted with great cruelty; but what was worse, he pursued the fleeing Indians into Peru, killing Peruvian officials who tried to stop him. Peru demanded and received damages, apologies, and the punishment of the Bolivian general.

In July, 1870 the national congress which Melgarejo assembled in Oruro approved all his proposals unanimously. But then occurred one of the unbelievably naive and romantic incidents of his rule. He had often spoken of his admiration for France and especially for Napoleon. In the vocabulary of invective that he directed against his enemies, "Girondin" and demagogue were more or less synonymous terms. So when word arrived of the outbreak of war between France and Prussia, he ordered his army to go to the support of his beloved France. Probably drunk, as was his custom, he assembled his forces during a rainy night, leading them out of Oruro toward the plain and the Ocean, stopping only when he came to an impassably flooded river.

Shortly thereafter the rebellion that was to prove his undoing began. General Rondón, the loyal comrade in arms whom he had put in charge of Potosí, deserted him, taking advantage of the fact that Melgarejo, excellent horseman though he was, had broken a leg one day when his horse brushed against a stone wall. He was carried back to La Paz in a litter. Despite this broken leg, however, Melgarejo put himself again on horseback at the head of his troops, led them by forced marches to Potosí, and defeated the rebels in one of his usual slashing attacks. It was his last great victory. Soon word came that his enemies in La Paz had gained the support of Hilarión Daza, the military governor, and that La Paz was in full revolt. Melgarejo's courage failed him at last. Either because of his failing strength, because he realized the strength of the combination against him, or more probably because his mistress, Juana Sánchez, had been captured and was held as a hostage, he resigned his command and fled the country, hoping his mistress would be released to join him.

Chile, grateful for the cession of Atacama, gave him asylum and a general's pay. He could have lived there quietly in exile, but he used the money instead to purchase arms to equip an invasion force. When the arms he was gathering were seized in Tacna, his last chance to recover power disappeared.

His thoughts now turned to his beloved mistress, Juana Sánchez, who had been allowed to leave Bolivia and was in Arequipa with her mother and brother, both of whom had benefitted greatly from Melgarejo's generosity. But Juana and her family refused even to see him. He lived alone in Arequipa, attended by his two youngest daughters, until one day he decided upon the final romantic gesture that ended his life. "Invading" the home of his former mistress, to claim her, he was shot by Juana's brother José. It is superb irony that José had long been Melgarejo's favorite and was the husband of Melgarejo's daughter.

NOTES

1. *Melgarejo, un tyran romantique* (Paris: Calmann Lévy, Editeurs, 1945), p. 14. Translation by author.
2. *Ibid.*, p. 15.

BIBLIOGRAPHY

The Bolivian historian, Alcides Argüedas, in *Los caudillos bárbaros, historia, resurrección. La tragedia de un pueblo* (Barcelona: Viuda de L. Tasso, 1929) gives a hostile account of Melgarejo and of his confederate and successor, Augustín Morales. Max Daireaux, *Melgarejo, un tyran romantique* (Paris: Calmann Lévy, 1945; also in Spanish translation by Pilar Lage de Gancedo, Santiago, Chile: Ed. Oribe, 1963) adds an air of romance in a novelized biography. Tomas O'Connor d'Arlach has expressed his admiration of Melgarejo in two works: *Rozas, Francia y Melgarejo* (La Paz: González y Medina, 1914) and *El General Melgarejo. Dichos y hechos de este hombre* (La Paz: Librería "La Universitaria," Gisbert y Cía, 1947). The Chilean diplomat, R. Sotomayor Valdes, has published documents from the Chilean legation in La Paz during the Melgarejo years: *La legación de Chile en Bolivia desde setiembre de 1867 hasta principios de 1871* (Santiago, Chile: Imprenta de San José, 1912). Manuel Rigoberto Paredes, in *Melgarejo y su tiempo y otros estudios históricos* (La Paz: Ediciones "Isla", 1962) presents Melgarejo as a symbol of Bolivian telluric thought. Alcibíades Guzmán, in *Libertad o despotism en Bolivia* . . . (La Paz: González y Medina 1918) attempts a revision of the "anti-Melgarejismo."

23

PORFIRIO DIAZ (1830–1915)

Porfirio Díaz of Mexico exemplifies a number of aspects of authoritarian rulers of Latin America. He rose to political prominence as a revolutionary and as a largely self-taught leader of irregular revolutionary forces. A mestizo, of predominantly Mixtecan Indian family background, he illustrates the rise of the mestizo through politics and the army. Although a lawyer by training, his political power came to rest largely on his military career and on his influence in and control over the army that defeated the monarchist and conservative forces which supported the Maximilian empire. Finally, while his power rested in this fundamental sense upon the army, he governed in accordance with the procedures set down in the Liberal constitution of 1857, even while prostituting the constitutional forms to his authoritarian rule.

If long continuance in power is taken as the criterion, he may well be judged one of the outstandingly successful dictators of nineteenth century Latin America. With the exception of four years (1880–1884) during which his lieutenant, Manuel González, held the presidency of the country, Díaz ruled Mexico from 1876 to 1911. Leandro J. Canizares, in a book that is more an encomium than a critical biography, has described him as "the ruler of keen mind, patriotic heart, and iron hand."[1] Fifty to sixty years ago the leaders of the Mexican Revolution usually gave a much less favorable view of Díaz than this, picturing him as a tyrant who suppressed all freedom and governed Mexico with his army and rural police for the benefit of the privileged classes and the foreign investors in railroads, mines, and public utilities. Carleton Beals, expressing this Mexican Revolutionary viewpoint, has written of Díaz's career as "the tragedy of all power embodied in one human being . . . who perforce must compromise with the strong at the expense of the weak. . . ."[2] The truth, as we shall see, lies somewhere between these extremes.

José de la Cruz Porfirio Díaz Mori was born in the city of Oaxaca, in southern Mexico, in the year 1830. Parish records show that he was baptized on September 15 of that year. Since the baptismal or "saint's" day is commonly celebrated as the birth anniversary, he was able to celebrate his birthday on the Mexican national holiday, the day of the Grito de Dolores with which the priest Miguel Hidalgo had initiated the move for Mexican independence twenty years before. Porfirio's parents were mestizos, both culturally and racially. His mother, Petrona Mori, came from the Tilantongo district of the almost purely Indian region of the Mixteca Alta. His father, José de la Cruz Díaz, came from a *ranchero* (small farmer) family of largely Mixtecan origin. The father was a "jack of all trades." At the time of independence he was employed by a British mining company to transport silver ore by burro to Oaxaca. He then settled on the south coast of the present-day state of Guerrero, where he cleared lands for the cultivation of sugar and built a press and refinery. Soon he joined the Guerrero forces in the struggle for independence, serving as a veterinarian.

At a time when goats were dying in large numbers on the open range, he bought up the goatskins and taught himself tanning. To sell the hides he was soon engaged in contraband trade. After eighteen years of this unsettled life, and shortly before the birth of Porfirio, he moved his family, consisting of his wife Petrona and five children, to Oaxaca. There he rented an inn, the Mesón de la Soledad, opposite the church and convent of the same name. Porfirio was born in the Mesón and spent his early years there. The father also established a tannery and a blacksmith shop, and set himself up as a veterinarian. At this time in his life he became devoutly religious, as did his wife. Shortly before his death in 1833 he was stirred to oppose the Gómez Farías anti-clerical reforms. He and two sons, Cayetano and Pablo, older brothers of Porfirio, died in the cholera epidemic which swept Mexico in that fateful year of 1833, a national catastrophe that helped to turn the superstitious against the Gómez Farías reforms.

Petrona, Porfirio's mother, was left with five children to bring up. These included three daughters older than Porfirio, Desidera, Manuela, Nicolosa, and a younger son named Félix. She struggled for a short while to maintain the Mesón and hired men to run the blacksmith shop. But the unsettled political conditions and the general spirit of unrest, combined with the loss of her husband's driving energy and skill, made it increasingly difficult to make both ends meet. Soon she moved to a more modest house on the outskirts of the city, *La Toronja*, so named for its large grapefruit tree. Here, with occasional help from relatives, Petrona raised her family. It was this house that young Porfirio remembered as home. A serious and industrious boy, he quickly learned the rudiments of carpentry and shoemaking and soon was able to help eke out the family income by his boyish labor.

At the age of seven he began to attend the public elementary school. Quick to learn, he made an excellent record as a student. At fourteen he entered the Conciliar Seminary, taking preparatory courses to study for the priesthood. His sponsor was his godfather and cousin, José Augustín Domínguez, the parish priest of Nochixtlán and later bishop of Oaxaca. Another cousin-priest, Ramón Prado, tutored him in Latin. His mother and these clerical relatives hoped that as a priest, assured of a good parish by these family connections, Porfirio would be a support for his mother, his sisters, and his brother.

These were troublesome times in which to grow up and many family plans for children went awry. The disorder, anarchy, factionalism, and civil strife during the early years of Mexican independence almost pass belief. The climax came when this internal dissension made it impossible for Mexico to unite nationally, even when confronted with an invasion by the armies of the United States. As a nation Mexico seemed to be breaking up. Central America had separated after the overthrow of Iturbide. Texas had rebelled and defeated the Mexican army sent against her. The war with the United States would take away the large territory of California and New Mexico. Yucatán was in revolt, and in 1846 Oaxaca "resumed its sovereignty" under a triumvirate of which Benito Juárez, the future president, was a member. The triumvirate was overturned in 1847, but subsequently Juárez ruled as governor until 1852. It was even rumored that Mexican priests counseled supporting the United States invaders against the Liberals in the Oaxaca government. In the midst of all these uncertainties, however, Porfirio enlisted in the Oaxaca militia at the age of sixteen or seventeen, at the time of the war with the United States, getting his first acquaintance with the rudiments of military training.

This first contact with the stark realities of Mexican political life and the acquaintance he made with other young volunteers at this time brought him to a critical turn in his life. He now decided to leave the seminary and to enter the Liberal-dominated Institute of Arts and Sciences of Oaxaca to study law. One reason for this decision was a friendship that had developed with Marcos Pérez, a close friend and collaborator of Juárez and like Juárez a professor in the Institute. Both Juárez and Pérez were Zapotec Indians. Pérez was also the father of a boy whom Porfirio was instructing in Latin. Through this family acquaintance Porfirio met Juárez, and the future president encouraged him to pursue studies in the Institute.

This change in Porfirio's career plans produced a serious family crisis, both emotional and financial. His mother's objections were so serious that Porfirio decided at first to give up his plan. But Petrona reluctantly gave her consent later on, even though it meant losing her best hope for financial security. It was a decision that took great courage on her part, one worthy of the great spirit she was. She said she did not want Porfirio to act contrary to his principles on her account. The godfather's reaction was less generous; he exploded in a towering rage. Because the Institute represented the anti-clerical Liberalism he abhorred, he withdrew all his support from the young student.

During the next five years of study in the law school in Oaxaca, young Díaz earned part of his living as a clerk for a merchant. He also worked as an assistant to the librarian of the Institute. His ability was recognized during the year 1853–54 when he was invited to teach natural law and international law as a substitute for a professor who was forced to flee to escape imprisonment at the order of the Santa Anna government. About this time Porfirio passed his examinations in law; but he never received the official license to practice law, probably because the Santa Anna forces crushed the Liberals in Oaxaca at this time. Juárez was sent to prison in San Juan de Ulúa. Marcos Pérez, in whose law office Porfirio was employed at this time, was also thrown in jail in Oaxaca. In an effort to secure his release, Porfirio engaged in a feat worthy of Alexandre Dumas' Count of Monte Cristo. With the help of his younger brother Félix, he lowered himself by rope from the roof of the monastery prison to talk with Pérez and to provide him with paper and pencil to communicate with the outside world. Pérez believed that this daring action probably saved his life; in any case it established an unbreakable personal tie between the older man and his young assistant.

In the plebiscite then ordered by Santa Anna to confirm his election to the presidency Porfirio dared to record a vote, in the open and oral voting of the day, for the revolutionary (Liberal) Juan Alvarez. This defiant act made him a marked man. To avoid arrest he fled into the Mixtecan mountains, accompanied by the fugitive "bandit" patriot, Esteban Aragón. There he joined a guerrilla band led by the Indian Francisco Herrera. Thus Díaz began his political career as an outlaw and a guerrilla in the company of Indians of largely Zapotec and Mixtec origin, in the very region from which his parents came.

When the Liberal revolt of 1855 gained ground, Díaz returned to Oaxaca, at first in disguise. Soon he was named *jefe político* (local governor) of the Ixtlán District in the mountainous Villa Alta Department where his father had once worked among the Zapotecs. There, under the authority of the revolutionary government, Porfirio raised and trained a volunteer militia regiment of Zapotecs. He was so pleased with this military venture that when Juarez, as governor of the state, ordered the separation of the offices of military commander and *jefe político*, offering

Porfirio his choice, he passed up the office of *jefe político*, although it paid
a higher salary, in order to retain command of his militia unit. It was the
beginning of the military career that gained him national fame and
eventually was to give him the army support that enabled him to seize the
presidency by force.

Díaz rose to power in the wake of this Liberal Revolution of 1855. The
uprising had been headed by the old Liberal and Indian revolutionary,
Juan Alvarez, and by Ignacio Comonfort. Following in the footsteps of his
fellow Oaxaqueños, Benito Juárez, Marcos Pérez, and Justo Benítez,
Díaz occupied the city of Oaxaca in 1856 with his militia unit to ensure
Juárez taking over as the newly appointed governor. During the War of
Reform (1858–61) that resulted from the Liberal anti-clerical reforms and
the changes embodied in the Constitution of 1857, he had many
opportunities to show his military prowess in the campaign that finally
brought Juárez back to Mexico City victoriously in 1861.

In 1861 he entered Congress as one of the delegates elected from
Ixtlán, but he took little part in the proceedings. When the Conservative
General Leonardo Márquez was at the gates of the capital, Díaz took
leave to resume command of his Oaxaca unit. Operating under the
command of General Jesús González Ortega he captured the entire force
of General Márquez in a surprise nocturnal assault at Jalatlaco. He then
returned briefly to the Congress, but soon departed in disgust with a
group of delegates whose departure left the Congress without a quorum.
Resuming his military command, he gained more laurels in the decisive
defeat of enemy troops near Pachuca in late 1861.

These events took place on the eve of the British-French-Spanish
intervention that led to the French occupation of Mexico and the
establishment of Maximilian as the French puppet emperor. Díaz played
a decisive role in the initial defeat of the French occupying forces at
Puebla, on May 5, 1862, leading a successful calvary charge. Later, when
the reinforced French army occupied Puebla, Díaz was captured and was
imprisoned because he refused to give his word not to engage in further
combat. But he managed to escape, making his way to Mexico City to join
Juárez who was having to abandon the capital to the French invaders at
this time. Impressed by Díaz's loyalty, Juárez offered him the post of
commander in chief. Díaz refused, however, saying he was too young.
But he recruited and organized his own division of troops to cover
Juárez's retreat to Queretaro. Juárez then commissioned him to organize
a new Army of the East. With this army, Díaz fought his way through
Taxco and the state of Guerrero to his native Oaxaca. There, at the nadir
of Liberal fortunes, he rejected an offer to join the cause of Maximilian,

an offer brought by a friend, Manuel Dublán, who was a former head of the Oaxaca Institute and a relative of Juárez. Few Mexicans showed greater loyalty to the cause of Juárez and the Liberals in these dark days when Juárez suffered defeat after defeat in Chihuahua. Still fewer contributed to the later defeat of Maximilian with greater daring and courage.

Deserted by colleagues and by most of his forces, Díaz finally surrendered personally to French Marshall Achille Bazaine in February, 1865. Refusing, as earlier at Puebla, the pledge not to take up arms that would have brought his release, he was again imprisoned. He started to dig an underground tunnel from this prison to effect an escape, but was transferred to the Caroline Convent prison before completing it. From there he made another Count of Monte Cristo kind of escape. Climbing by a rope to the roof of the Convent, he passed over the roof and let himself down, also by rope, into a sty of squealing pigs from which he made his way to the horse that a faithful servant held for him. Galloping away in the night, he evaded sentinels and Imperial forces to regain his native Oaxaca. There he fought as a guerrilla during the following months, gradually building up an army of rebels among his loyal Oaxaqueños. With them he eventually occupied Mexico City in 1867 as the war against Maximilian came to a close.

Could one predict from this twelve year record of loyalty to the Liberal revolution and this success as a guerrilla and militia leader that Díaz would become a "dictator"? Perhaps one clue lies in the disgust he showed with the pusillanimous behavior of the national congress in 1861. Although not trained as a professional soldier, he seems to have derived from his experience in arms something of the distrust and suspicion of civilian leaders that professionals have sometimes displayed. Yet, in all fairness, we must note that his later record does not show a rejection of the two things most fundamental in the Liberal Revolution of 1855, the Constitution of 1857 and the subsequent opposition to the French Intervention and the Empire of Maximilian. In some respects, therefore, he may be even truer to the Mexican heritage in his Liberalism than some of his enemies and critics, both contemporary and later.

In 1871 Díaz was a candidate for the presidency, opposing Juárez's reelection. Since none of the three candidates received a majority in the initial (indirect) balloting, the Congress had to make the election. Juárez was chosen president and Sebastiano Lerdo de Tejada, as the second choice, was elected to head the Supreme Court (in effect becoming vice president). Juárez died suddenly a few months later and Lerdo succeeded him as president. When the Congress, on Lerdo's urging, adopted laws carrying out the anti-clerical reforms, Díaz began to cultivate elements of support among pro-Church elements that had been quiescent since the days of Maximilian. In 1876 he ran against Lerdo for the presidency, appealing to the Juárez Liberals and proposing an amendment to the Constitution that would prohibit presidential reelection. When the Congress confirmed the election of Lerdo, despite Díaz's charges of fraud, he rebelled, subsequently capturing the office by forcing a purged congress to confirm his election.

Díaz was a popular leader, however, among the Mexicans who had supported the Liberal cause. As Napoleon was a "son" of the French Revolution, so Porfirio Díaz was a "son" or heir of the Mexican Liberal Revolution. Within his view of the realities of Mexican politics, he remained loyal to the Constitution of 1857 and its reform features. He worked within the power structure of landowners created by Juárez largely on the basis of the forced sale of Church lands. In his inaugural address he announced a policy that the Juárez Liberals would have endorsed. It was a policy of encouraging immigration, constructing railroads, and establishing new industries, all to be accomplished in cooperation with "farmers, miners, and merchants of the country." This policy of development was soon extended to enlist the cooperation of foreign capitalists.

Díaz eliminated the banditry that had plagued Mexico since independence by enrolling the bandits as rural police. He reformed the army, balanced the budget, paid army and government officials promptly, and met payments on the domestic and national debt when they fell due. The credit rating of the Mexican government rose suddenly to equal that of the most stable nations. Long outstanding claims of United States citizens against Mexico were settled under a mixed claims commission. Contracts for the construction of railroads were signed with companies from the United States and Great Britain, giving Mexico one of the two best rail systems in Latin America.

True to his campaign pledge of no reelection, Díaz supported a constitutional amendment to this effect and stood aside in 1880 to permit the election to the presidency of his faithful lieutenant, General Manuel González. But Díaz kept the power structure in his own hands through control of the army. He was elected president again in 1884, and his control was never challenged seriously thereafter. The constitution was again changed to *permit* reelection, and he was successively chosen for the office in 1888, 1892, 1896, 1900, 1904 (for a six year term), and 1910.

The Díaz system was not unlike that of other strongmen of Latin America, except that he managed the "constitutional" apparatus more successfully than most did. Some of the landowning families that had supported Juárez withdrew their support, but Díaz kept that of many others. He added the support of army leaders, high Church officials (some of them enemies of Juárez), and the new criollo group who gained wealth and power through railroad building, mining, commerce, and the distribution of public lands under the generous program promoted by Díaz. It was rule with a gloved hand of steel. Constitutional forms were carefully observed. Elections were regularly held. But they were carefully supervised in ways permitted by the lax system of controls then in effect. It was not a system adequate to ensure a free ballot to all adult males who were enfranchised under the Juárez system.

Though the rule of Díaz brought national stability and prosperity, it bore heavily on the peons of the haciendas, on the Indians (still a majority of the population), and on the increasingly restless urban workers who were beginning to form labor unions. But his power base became increasingly narrow while the population of Mexico, particularly the urban population, grew rapidly. In many respects, the fall of Díaz was a case of the rejection of an earlier popular revolutionary leader by a new political generation of leaders of a new popular movement. It is possible that if Díaz had pursued his original intention, as stated to the reporter James Creelman in 1908, to sponsor a completely free presidential election, he might have gone down in history as a great and successful president of his country. Instead, he was persuaded to be a candidate again in 1910 when the popularity of the Francisco Madero and Bernardo Reyes campaigns appeared to threaten the success of his own choice for the presidential office.

Thus the end of the public career of Porfirio Díaz was a tragic anti-climax. He won the election of 1910, but only after ordering the arrest of his more popular rival, Francisco Madero, and at the cost of provoking a violent revolution. When confronted with an almost general national uprising after the election he resigned, leaving the future of the country to Madero and his followers. Understandably, the leaders of the Mexican Revolution almost universally blackened the record of the Díaz years. But such historians as Daniel Cosío Villegas have now restored a balance in the evaluation of the Díaz record. Today we see that he did not so much reverse the current of the Liberal (Juárez) reforms as bring them to terms with Mexican reality; furthermore, that his years of rule gave Mexico the opportunity to realize her destiny as a nation, while providing the social and economic basis upon which the Mexican Revolution would later build.

NOTES

1. *Don Porfirio. El gobernante de mente lucida, corazón de patriota y mano de hierro* (La Habana: Editorial Lex, 1946).
2. *Porfirio Díaz* (Philadelphia and London: J.B. Lippincott Company, 1932), p. 25.

BIBLIOGRAPHY

The published *Memoirs* of Díaz, unfortunately, reveal little of his personal life or politics. The *Archivo del General Porfirio Díaz; Selección y notas de Alberto María Carreño*, 27v. (México: Editorial Elede, 1947–1960) provides basic documentation. Carleton Beals, *Porfirio Díaz* (Philadelphia: J.B. Lippincott Co., 1932) is biased against Díaz and contains errors of detail, but is very readable. Francisco Bulnes, *El verdadero Díaz y la Revolución* (México: Editora Nacional, 1967. Original ed. 1920?) has a pro-Díaz bias, as does Leandro Canizares, *Don Porfirio* (La Habana: Ed. Lux, 1946). Daniel Cosío Villegas, *La república restaurada: la vida política 1867–1876* (México, 1955) is an impartial account by an outstanding historian, as is Moisés González Navarro, *El porfiriato. La vida social* (México: El Colegio de México, 1957). Other useful works among many that might be named, include James Creelman, *Díaz, Master of México* (New York and London: D. Appleton & Co., 1911); Charles C. Cumberland, *Mexican Revolution, Genesis Under Madero* (Westport: Greenwood, 1969. Original edition, 1952); Jorge Fernando Iturribarria, *Benito Juárez—Porfirio Díaz* (México: Populibros "La Prensa", 1960); Francisco Madero, *La Succesión Presidencial en 1910* (3rd ed. México: Librería de la Vda. de Ch. Bouret, 1911); and Angel Taracena, *Porfirio Díaz* (México: Ed. Jus, 1960)—an interesting treatment of Díaz as caudillo, revolutionary, and dictator.

24

GETULIO DORNELLES VARGAS (1883–1954)

Getulio Vargas introduced a new style of dictatorship in the Latin American scene. The change was particularly notable for Brazil, because she had previously escaped the types of dictatorship so common in Spanish America. In its ideological base, the Vargas dictatorship had characteristics that suggest those of Benito Mussolini in Italy and Antonio de Oliveira Salazar in Portugal. As a power structure, his dictatorship was built around Brazilian economic and military interests that wished to turn the country away from its coffee and export trade orientation and toward a more nationalist policy of economic development, including agricultural, diversification and industrialization. Thus, it had a revolutionary basis.

These characteristics of his rule, plus its long duration, would have been enough to give the political leadership of Vargas a distinctive stamp and an important place in Brazilian political history. But another dramatic aspect of his career gave him even more notoriety and historical importance. This was a politically motivated suicide, not during his dictatorship, but near the end of the constitutional presidency to which he was subsequently elected in 1950. The suicide occurred when he was confronted in 1954 with an ultimatum from his military leaders. Hence, in the eyes of many Brazilians, he was a martyr to the cause of social justice and a symbol of the political and social aspirations of the Brazilian masses. The authenticity of his suicide notes that are the basis of this symbolism has been the subject of controversy among scholars.[1] But certainly in the popular mind Getulio Vargas has joined the illustrious and highly select company of President José Balmaceda of Chile (1891), President Baltasar Brum of Uruguay (1933), and President Germán Busch of Bolivia (1939), all three of whom succeeded in making of their suicides a call for programs and principles of social justice and political freedom:

Getulio Vargas was born April 19, 1883 in São Borja, in the southern Brazilian state of Rio Grande do Sul. His father was General Manoel do Nascimento Vargas, who six years after the birth of Getulio was to be one of the leaders in the revolution that transformed Brazil from a monarchy to a republic. His mother, Cándida Dornelles, came from one of the province's wealthiest families. Getulio first studied in Ouro Preto, in the state of Minas Gerais, where his father was stationed. His education was continued in the (military) Escola Preparatoria e de Tática in Rio Pardo, in the state of Rio Grande do Sul. There he received his *bacalaureato* in 1902.

In 1907 he completed the course in law in the University of Porto Alegre. But before entering the university he had experimented briefly with a military career, intending to follow in the footsteps of his father. This brief military career terminated after one year when he reached the age of twenty and withdrew from the military academy of Rio Pardo mentioned above, to enter the university. For twenty three years following his graduation in law, and until his presidential candidacy in 1930, he combined the practice of law in Porto Alegre with politics, both state and national. During these years he was a district attorney and member of the state legislature. He also organized a military unit that he commanded with the rank of lieutenant colonel to defend the state government against rebellion in 1923. In that year, too, he was elected a deputy to the national Congress.

In the federal congress in Rio de Janeiro he quickly became the leader of a group of southern deputies who were committed to a program of national reform. His leadership of this group made him a political figure of national importance. In 1926 his support of the presidential candidacy of the Paulista, Washington Luiz, won him a place in the president's cabinet. In 1928 he was elected president of his home state of Rio Grande do Sul and for the next two years he gave his state a vigorous and progressive administration. He established an agricultural bank, increased dramatically the number of schools, sponsored highway construction, and in other ways evinced a lively interest in making government an innovator in social development.

In 1929 Brazil was facing a serious crisis in her coffee-oriented international trade, a crisis that was part of the more general collapse of world commerce. To protect the system of coffee subsidies (*valorização*) President Washington Luiz (a Paulista) endorsed the presidential candidacy of Julio Prestes, president of the state of São Paulo, thus violating the gentleman's agreement under which leaders from the two powerful states of São Paulo and Minas Gerais had previously rotated in the presidential office. Reacting to this Paulista action, the president of Minas Gerais stirred up leaders in the other states to oppose the Prestes candidacy. The result was the formation of the *Aliança Liberal* that supported Getulio Vargas as a presidential candidate against Julio Prestes in the election of 1930.

Vargas's campaign program was indicative in many ways of the revolutionary changes he would later inaugurate as president, but it gave only the vaguest hint of his future authoritarianism. He proposed a broad program of social welfare and health measures, the creation of a ministry of labor, economy in government, the elimination of political corruption, diversification in agricultural production, and the gradual extinction of large landholdings by transfering ownership to agricultural workers. Surprisingly, he gave no hint of what came to be the most notable aspect of his economic policy, the encouragement of industrialization.

His political campaign for the presidency was aggressive and in a sense demagogic. It was conducted in a manner suggestive of the populism of Mussolini. On January 2, 1930, for example, he spoke to a crowd in Rio de Janeiro estimated at 100,000. Yet when the votes were counted two months later, Julio Prestes was declared the winner. Vargas charged that the election was fraudulent, a charge not unfamiliar in Brazilian politics, and called upon his supporters to join in taking by force the office he claimed he had really won in the election. At this point he got the support of most of a group of dissident younger army officers, committed to political and social change, who had earlier rebelled against the government. These were the already famous *tenentes*.[2]

Oswaldo Aranha, a civilian, became the effective organizer of the rebellion. But a professional soldier, Colonel Pedro Aurelio de Goes Monteiro, was the chief of staff of the revolutionary forces supporting it. Under the efficient direction of these two loyal collaborators a revolutionary army moved northward from Rio Grande do Sul, gathering reinforcements as it went. Soon the national armed forces as a body went over to the Vargas side. In Rio de Janeiro, a junta of generals then took over the government, forcing the resignation of President Washington Luiz.

A new era of the intervention of the military in Brazilian politics had begun with this Vargas revolution. It should be noted, however, that military intervention at this time was fundamentally the product of civilian leadership. One month after proclaiming the rebellion Vargas took over the presidency in Rio de Janeiro. It was not long until it appeared that he had taken over the whole government·as well.

Vargas had come to power with the support of the army and the *Aliança Liberal* in an essentially bloodless revolution. But his subsequent actions were those customarily associated with the successful leader of an armed revolutionary movement that had triumphed by force. Moving rapidly, in a way that alarmed conservative Brazilians, he replaced state presidents with federal interventors and installed army officers in many public offices. As the months went by, this public alarm increased and he was criticized for not calling elections of a congress to draw up the promised constitutional changes. As might be expected, opposition to his rule centered in the state of São Paulo, the richest state and the state most closely identified with the coffee economy. There a rebellion broke out in 1932, organized by Vargas' rival in the elections, Julio Prestes, and supported by an armed force led by General Bertholdo Klinger. In contrast to the relatively peaceful rebellion by Vargas in 1930, this São Paulo uprising was violent and bloody. Armies fought against armies. The revolutionary forces advanced on Rio de Janeiro, but were defeated by loyal troops commanded by General Goes Monteiro and reinforced by troops called from the northern provinces. General Klinger surrendered before reaching Rio and the civil war was over.

Meanwhile the economic crisis arising from the collapse of world trade became worse. Obviously, only a revival of international trade or a revolutionary change in the economic system of the country could bring permanent relief. But world trade could not be expected to revive quickly, and Vargas had alienated important economic interests in the country to such an extent that he could not rally the political support to carry out broad economic changes. National production of sugar and coffee was restricted with some success, and barter agreements with Germany increased exports to that country by fifty percent, bringing some economic relief. But the German agreements also brought troublesome political and economic complications.

A new national constitution was adopted in 1934. While retaining the federal system, it gave the central government increased power, especially power to legislate on social and economic matters. Women were given the right to vote and to hold political office. Although the constitution provided for the direct election of the president (with no reelection), the assembly that drew up the constitution proceeded to elect Vargas as president for a term of four years.

Prosperity slowly returned to Brazil, but the increased political polarization of national politics brought severe challenges to Vargas's authority. The Communist party was growing rapidly under the aggressive leadership of Carlos Prestes, one of the *tenentes*. Soon it claimed several hundred thousand adherents or followers. At the opposite end of the political spectrum was the party of Integralist Action, organized by Plinio Salgado. This was a fascist-like movement whose members were distinguished by the green shirts they wore. It resembled the party of Antonio de Oliveira Salazar in Portugal. Both of these groups came from elements that had originally supported Vargas. Hence, when street fighting broke out between the two in 1935, he faced the possibility of losing some of his strongest support. Turning first against the Communists, he suppressed the party and imprisoned its leaders. Among these leaders was the popular Carlos Prestes, who was thus destined to spend most of Vargas's remaining period of rule in prison. The following year he suppressed the Integralistas. As the next presidential election neared, Vargas was governing with little or no party support, relying almost entirely upon the army for the support of his government. Despite this political weakness, however, he allowed preparation for the January, 1938, presidential election to go ahead until the increasing seriousness of the political crisis, as he said, caused him to decree a postponement.

This postponed election was never held. Instead, the president proclaimed a new and highly authoritarian constitution. This remarkable document, under which Vargas ruled for the next eight years, proclaimed "a state of grave internal commotion." It also established a corporative state. But this structure was not to be erected until the constitution was approved by plebiscite. Since the plebiscite was never held, the president continued to exercise the full power of government granted to him during the "state of grave internal commotion." Meanwhile he faced a rebellion of his palace guard in 1938. For some reason the army was slow in coming to his rescue; but he and his daughter successfully defended themselves with extraordinary courage until their rescuers finally arrived.

Vargas exercised his dictatorial power to carry out many changes. He extended his authority over states and cities by the use of presidential interventors who governed in his name. Control of public lands and natural resources was taken from the states, partly by the device of creating new federal territories. Highways and railroads were built under federal authority. Railroads, packing plants, and two newspapers were nationalized. Municipal, state, and federal appropriations for schools were increased. The most far reaching economic change was a reorientation of national economic policy under which coffee interests took a second place to the promotion of industrialization. Under this policy government credits were extended through development commissions for automotive, electrical, and other industries. With the cooperation of steel interests in the United States, a large steel mill was constructed at Volta Redonda, utilizing rich Brazilian deposits of iron and coal. Textile production grew to the point of making Brazil an exporter of cotton and other fabrics.

For a time Vargas flirted politically with the fascist axis powers, Germany and Italy. But, as the European crisis deepened, he brought Brazil back to its more traditional policy of close cooperation with the United States. His close advisor and Ambassador to the United States, Oswaldo Aranha, engineered this change of policy. Brazil declared war on the Axis powers in August, 1942, and subsequently took an active part in the hostilities. Bases at Recife, Natal, and Belem were made available to the United States for use in the invasion of North Africa and as way stations for the United States planes flying by way of Africa to the Far East. The Brazilian navy and Air Force were enlarged for participation in the anti-submarine war. The production of critical raw materials, guns, and ammunition was increased. A factory for the manufacture of airplanes was established. In July 1944 a Brazilian overseas force entered Italy and participated in the last phases of the war in Europe.

The narrowness of the Vargas power base appeared after the war was over. The enthusiasm for popular government engendered by the defeat of the Axis then made it increasingly difficult for Vargas to operate under the authoritarian structure on which he had relied during the previous decade. As indicated, this structure consisted of the army, the new economic interests created by the industrial development programs, workers' groups (not too well organized), and other loosely organized groups. His support depended even more upon the personal loyalty of the Vargas lieutenants. This political support had a vast potential, but it had not been organized into an effective party. Even the labor syndicates, the most obvious base in an industrializing economy, were poorly developed. National elections were called for 1945, but many Brazilians doubted the seriousness of the president's promise to abide by them. When he appeared in the course of the campaign to be openly courting the support of Carlos Prestes and the newly legalized Communist party, a group of political and army leaders forced his resignation.

The elections which followed were not a repudiation of Vargas, however, for the candidate of the Social Democratic party who won, Eurico Dutra, had been Vargas's candidate and favored the Vargas policies of industrialization and economic nationalism. Vargas was elected to the Senate from his state of Rio Grande do Sul and set about organizing the Labor Party which, with support from the Social Democrats, brought him back to the Presidency with a large majority in the next presidential election (1950). This election was a personal vindication for him, but this second presidency, as suggested, turned out to be a tragic anti-climax to his political career.

The Korean War brought a short period of prosperity in Brazilian international trade, but another economic depression soon followed. This was the central problem in an increasingly difficult political situation as the time for new elections approached at the end of the presidential term. The president's prestige also suffered at this time from charges of gangster connections made against his brother, the chief of police in Rio de Janeiro. As in 1945, army leaders again distrusted Vargas's promise to accept the results of an election. Believing he would again postpone elections and continue in office, they called upon him peremptorily to resign before elections were held. Confronted with this army ultimatum, he committed suicide, leaving the suicide notes, a kind of political testament as mentioned earlier, one of which called upon his followers to continue the populist movement of political and social change he had begun.

Out of the political confusion that followed several Brazilians emerged as Vargas's political "heirs." One of these was the later popular president Juscelino Kubitschek, the builder of Brasilia. But an even clearer heir was the more controversial João Goulart who, like his mentor, was to be forced from the presidential office by a military golpe in 1964.

NOTES

1. See two articles in the *Hispanic American Historical Review*: John V.D. Saunders, "A Revolution of Agreement among Friends," XLIV, No. 2 (May 1964), pp. 197–213; and John W.F. Dulles, "Farewell! Messages of Getulio Vargas," XLIV, No. 4 (November, 1964), pp. 551–553.
2. On the *tenentes* see Robert J. Alexander, "Brazilian Tenentism," *Hispanic American Historical Review*, XXXVI, No. 2 (May, 1956), pp. 229–239.

BIBLIOGRAPHY

Robert M. Levine, *The Vargas Regime: The Critical Years, 1934–1938 (New York: Columbia University Press, 1970)* gives the best critical account, based on Vargas and Aranha archives, of the development of the Vargas system. Other works of particular value include José María Bello, *A History of Modern Brazil, 1889–1964*, translated by Jane L. Taylor (Stanford, California: Stanford Univeristy Press, 1966); John W.F. Dulles, *Vargas of Brazil, a Political Biography* (Austin, Texas: University of Texas Press, 1967); José Jobim, *Brazil in the Making* (New York: Macmillan, 1944); Karl Lowenstein, *Brazil Under Vargas* (New York: Macmillan, 1942); Thomas E. Skidmore, *Politics in Brazil, 1930–1964: An Experiment in Democracy* (New York: Oxford University Press, 1967); Tad Szulc, *Twilight of the Tyrants* (New York: Holt, 1959), ch. iii; and Jordan M. Young, *The Brazilian Revolution of 1930 and the Aftermath* (New Brunswick, N.J.: Rutgers University Press, 1967). The political ideas of Vargas may be read in his *La Pensée Politique de President Getulio Vargas*, French trans. by Hans Klinghoffer (Rio de Janeiro: Imprensa Nacional, 1942).

25

JUAN DOMINGO PERON (1895–   )

As in the case of three other leaders treated in this book, Fidel Castro, Hugo Blanco, and Manuel Gómez Morín, certain distinctive characteristics of Perón as the ruler of Argentina justify risking a comment on the nature of his authoritarian rule while he is still living and still a controversial political figure, or symbol, in Argentine politics. He was a personalist in the Argentine tradition and one of the most authoritarian rulers Argentina or any other Spanish American country has experienced. But he was a personalist of a new kind who does not fit any of the conventional dictator stereotypes.

Although he came to power as the leader of the group of army colonels who engineered a *golpe de estado* in 1943, he remained behind the scenes in subordinate positions during two provisional presidencies of army generals that followed the *golpe*. Thus, he kept himself constitutionally eligible for election to the presidency in 1946, meanwhile laying a broad base of popular support, especially among urban workers. By 1945 he had built this support so effectively among newly organized industry type labor unions, and in a labor-oriented political party, that he was able to defy with success the coterie of senior army officers that sought to prevent his election. The following year he won in what is generally regarded as one of the freest presidential elections ever held in Argentina—a country known for its effective conduct of elections. Later, by sponsoring woman suffrage and a woman's political party, he added another element to a populist political structure that still survives, a decade and a half after his expulsion from office by an army rebellion in 1955.

Ruth and Leonard Greenup described Perón in 1947 as the "most powerful man in Latin America . . . a man with a tremendous grip on the masses of his country."[1] Almost two decades later Arthur P. Whitaker wrote that Perón "married the masses with the military," producing "a new kind of fascism."[2] Arthur Whitaker has also suggested that Perón's leadership suggests parallels to that of Mussolini, Hitler, and Franco, as well as to that of the Vargas of 1930–1945.

But Perón's rule differs from these three models in a number of ways. One of these is Perón's constitutional election to the presidency in a free and highly contested election. Another difference is that Perón did not, like these others, change the basic structure of government, but bent the existing system to his will. Even when his overwhelming majority in Congress made it possible to rewrite the Constitution of 1853, he was satisfied with only such modernizing changes as broadening the Congressional authority for social legislation and authorizing woman suffrage. The major structural change, a disastrous one as it proved, was to provide for the re-election of the president.

Among contemporary European authoritarians, the closest parallel to Perón is probably Franco of Spain. Like Perón, Franco was a professional soldier. But Perón's political style is no blind copy of Franco, or of any European model. Typically he turned to Argentine writers on the subjects of *Argentinidad* and *justicialismo* (social justice) for his ideology, while his style of action was the aggressive political style that Argentines were long accustomed to. What shocked the Argentines, however, was the extraordinary degree of political cynicism Perón displayed in the treatment of the press and in permitting the harassment of political opponents during national elections.

Juan Domingo Perón was born in the small town of Lobos in the province of Buenos Aires on October 8, 1895, the son of modest middle class parents. His father, Mario Tomás Perón, was the son of a physician of Italian origin who had successfully practised medicine in Buenos Aires and of a mother who came from a family of recent Spanish immigrants. Less successful than his physician father, Mario Tomás had moved from one occupation to another. He was a sheepherder in Patagonia for a time before he settled down as a landowner in Lobos. The Perón family was thus rather typical of the emerging and properous middle class of Argentina. While Juan was still a boy the family moved to Buenos Aires, and it was there that he received most of his education.

The education young Juan received was typical of that given a boy of his social background. He was a natural athlete and was encouraged to participate in sports. He was also a good student. In 1911 he entered the Colegio Militar, beginning the military career that led him ultimately into politics. At eighteen he was commissioned a sub-lieutenant and at twenty a lieutenant. In 1930, as a captain in the national army, he participated in the military *golpe* led by General José E. Uriburu to drive President Hipólito Irigoyen from office. Thereafter, during the 1930's, he attended such advanced and specialized military training schools as the Junior Officers School and the Mountain Training Center. He taught military history for five years in the National War College, the nation's highest level professional military school, and served as a military attaché in Chile and later in Italy. While in Europe as an attaché he travelled in Germany, Hungary, and Spain. From this European experience he absorbed some fascist ideas that later found expression in the group of Argentine army officers known as GOU (Government, Order, Unity) in which he found himself, as a colonel, consorting with generals. Within this group, at the age of forty-eight, he emerged as the leader of the "colonels' clique" that challenged the leadership of the older, often political, generals in the *golpe* of 1943.

In that year of 1943 Argentina, in considerable political disarray, was approaching the presidential election to be held the next year. Constitutional government had been restored four years after the Revolution of 1930, but the presidential powers had subsequently been exercised by two essentially weak coalition governments, consisting in both cases of an Anti-Personalist (anti-Irigoyen) Radical party president and a Conservative (National Democratic) party vice-president. President Roberto M. Ortiz, who took office in 1938, had been ill most of the time and had died in 1942, leaving the presidency in the hands of the Conservative vice-president, Ramón S. Castillo.

President Ortiz had maintained a precarious balance of political forces in a country badly divided in the recent past over the issues raised by the Spanish Civil War and now (1943) divided over the issues involved in World War II. Many Argentines, including the army officers in the GOU, which was organized in Mendoza where Perón was stationed, believed that Germany, Italy, Japan and their allies were winning the war. But many other Argentines, of course, sympathized with the anti-Axis Allies. Amid these tensions the Castillo regime had continued Argentine neutrality, despite the recommendation of the Rio de Janeiro (1942) Consultation of Foreign Ministers to break diplomatic relations with the Axis powers. It seemed clear to Argentine opposition leaders that the government coalition intended to secure the election of Conservative and pro-British Robustiano Patrón Costas, despite the fact that he probably could not win in a free election. Some Argentines, therefore, feared that this election would mean a departure from Argentina's long tradition of neutrality and a decision to cast Argentina's lot with the anti-Axis forces in the War.

This was the confused and confusing situation in which the GOU launched the golpe of 1943, overturning the weak regime of Ramón Castillo and installing a provisional government headed by General Pedro Ramírez. Engineering the golpe behind the scenes was forty-eight year old Colonel Perón. Far from a novice in army politics by this time, he had sensed the importance of having a general of prestige at the head of a provisional regime created by the army. Astutely, he also saw that his own road to power (suggested by his observations in Europe) lay in mobilizing the unsatisfied aspirations of the rapidly growing, but poorly organized, urban work force.

Between 1934 and 1943 Argentine industrial production had doubled, although the government had done little if anything to encourage industrialization. Urban population was consequently growing rapidly. The city of Buenos Aires grew from 3.4 millions in 1936 to 4.71 millions in 1947. Much of this urban growth was now coming from the provinces, rather than Europe, as in the past. Because of their provincial origin the workers who were swelling the urban population, and whom Perón was to dub the *descamisados* or "shirtless," lacked the capacity and the motivation to voice their demands through labor organizations. This lack Perón proposed to remedy. He was convinced that the militarist and ultranationalist regimes that had governed Argentina since 1930 were weak in large measure precisely because they had not called into being the potential power in these urban *descamisados*.

With beseeming modesty, but also with rare political intuition, he chose to work from behind the scenes in the non-Cabinet and hence unprestigious post of Minister of Labor and Social Welfare. He combined this post, moreover, with the strategically important but also unpretentious position of chief of the Secretariat of the Ministry of War. From his office a series of decree laws were now issued in breath-taking succession. These laws established a wide range of labor and social welfare programs and gave vigorous leadership in organizing industry-wide and militant labor unions *(sindicatos)*. Labor union membership was around 300,000 to 350,000 in 1943. By 1945 it had increased seven-fold under Perón's urging. Perón personally led the recruiting among packinghouse workers and sugar plantation laborers. The existing Argentine labor organizations in 1943 were already among the strongest in Latin America, but by 1945 Perón had built on this base an instrument of political power that was unprecedented. One of the secrets of this success was that he had taken the function of collective bargaining into his own hands, building control of the labor movement by raising wages and increasing workers' security.

In this labor activity he soon had the collaboration of a remarkable young woman, only about half his age, who became his mistress in 1943, and his legal wife two years later. His first wife, Aurelia Tizón, whom he had married in 1926, had died in 1938. Eva María Duarte was born April 26, 1919(?) in Los Toldos, in the province of Buenos Aires. She was the fourth child of Juan Duarte and Juana Ibarguren. Juan Duarte came from a prosperous and politically conservative middle class family of landowners, but had abandoned his legal wife and children to live in an extra-legal union with Eva's mother and the children of their union.

When Juan Duarte died in 1926, the mother moved with her family to Junín. There Eva attended the Normal School. Eva always remembered her father's death vividly because of the humiliating experience of her family being refused admission to the funeral wake in the home of the legal wife.

Early in 1935, Eva went to Buenos Aires where she slowly gained recognition as an actress. By 1943 she had played important roles in several motion pictures and was conducting her own radio show—a series in which she portrayed prominent women of history. During these years she seems to have had several lovers among actors with whom she worked. She met Perón when they were both engaged in a charity drive to raise funds for the relief of victims of an earthquake in San Juan. Perón quickly recognized her value as a collaborator, particularly her skill in conveying her adulation of him to the public.

At this time Perón was playing a carefully calculated game to secure election to the presidency when regular elections were resumed. In 1944 he engineered the replacement of President Ramírez by General Eldemiro Farrel. Perón now became vice-president; but he also held the key post of Minister of War as well as that of Labor and Security. This golpe of 1944 was widely interpreted outside Argentina as an effort to prevent a declaration of war against the Axis. But within a year he and the new President were forced into a declaration of war, accepting the arrangement worked out by the American Republics at the 1945 Chapultepec Conference that required Argentina to declare war in order to enter the new United Nations. This step cost the Perón regime some of its ultra-nationalist support, but its position was strengthened, on the whole, by eliminating this highly divisive issue of the war.

The presidential election was scheduled for early 1946, and as the time approached Perón had also lost much of his army support by his populist and demagogic appeals to labor. His enemies in the army were strong enough to force President Farrel to order his arrest and imprisonment. To his enemies' surprise, however, Perón proved to be stronger than they were. Eva, now his wife, aided by the head of the packing house workers' syndicate, did a masterful job of organizing a great popular demonstration in Buenos Aires. The demonstration was even supported by the Buenos Aires police, whose morale Perón had built up by giving them better equipment than the neighboring army Campo de Mayo garrison and by improving their pay and working conditions. President Farrel had to give in, releasing Perón to continue his electoral campaign.

His principal opponent in the election was the Radical party candidate, José Tamborini, who was supported by a coalition of the Radical,

Socialist, Communist, and Progressive Democratic parties. Perón's support came mainly from organized labor, upon which he was building his own political party. He also got support from the anti-Personalist Radical and the National Democratic (Conservative) parties. Thus his vice-presidential running mate was an old-line anti-personalist Radical, Juan Hortensio Quijano. Army leaders were divided in their loyalties because of Perón's populist tactics; but a major army faction continued to support him.

Tamborini proved to be a colorless, essentially weak opposition candidate who failed to galvanize his coalition into an effective working combination. The United States Department of State, under the mistaken guidance of Spruille Braden, the Assistant Secretary for Latin America, played into Perón's hands by releasing on the eve of the election a Blue Book charging Perón and Argentina with Axis collaboration. Perón then skillfully turned the election into a campaign against Braden and United States "intervention."

Peronist supporters indulged in some high handed tactics, breaking up a number of opposition meetings during the campaign. But the election was conducted in general in the characteristic Argentine fashion, perhaps even more calmly than usual, and was one of the fairest in Argentine history. Perón was elected with a clear popular majority of 56 percent of a larger than usual vote. In the Electoral College he had a majority of 304 to 72. His followers also won a two-thirds majority in the Chamber of Deputies and made an almost clean sweep in the Senate. In Congressional elections three years later he won an even larger majority, and in 1950, after the adoption of woman suffrage and Eva Perón's organization of the woman vote, his majorities were greater still.

He was inaugurated as president on June 4, 1946, the third anniversary of the 1943 golpe. His presidency quickly brought changes in Argentine social and economic structure and policy. The decree labor laws of the provisional regimes were confirmed by the Congress, which now went even further than the decree laws had gone, increasing the minimum wage, extending paid vacations to workers, providing for inexpensive public housing, and establishing a system of social security that applied to almost all workers. In October, 1946, Perón presented to Congress an ambitious Six Year Plan that included nationalizing the British owned railroads and the U.S. controlled telephone system, the construction of highways, public housing, the sponsoring of a national merchant marine and national airlines, modernization of the armed forces, and national aid to industrialization.

The Congress enacted most of these proposals into law, giving a generous authority to the president to act in many areas by executive decree. But either because of inadequate advice, or because of his ingrained opportunism and devotion to populist politics, Perón somehow failed to translate the broad powers he exercised under these laws into an effective program of economic development.

His basic mistake, probably, was to use the dollar and pound exchange balances ($1.5 to $2 billion, U.S.) accumulated by Argentina during the war to purchase the rundown British railroads and the U.S. owned telephone systems (A.T.&T.). The railroads particularly turned out to be a white elephant—a continuous drain on the national economy. This capital could have been much better used to develop such aspects of the basic economy as electric power and petroleum production, or to finance the import of capital goods needed for his ambitious industrialization plans. The second closely related and even more fundamental mistake of policy was to subsidize the development of industries producing consumer goods, in an import substitution policy, without developing the economic substructure of electric power, raw materials, technological competence, heavy industry and consumer credit.

The high point of his political success came during the years 1946–1949. Using the powers granted by Congress and profiting from his wife's brilliant direction of the labor syndicates, he gave to the organized workers of Argentina during these years a greater share in the national income than they had ever known previously. The María Eva Duarte de Perón Foundation, established modestly in 1948 with Eva's private funds, grew rapidly with "voluntary contributions" from business firms, labor unions, and the income from government lotteries. Its social projects and philanthropy added to the Peróns' popularity among the underprivileged. As time went by, however, it became necessary to hold the line against wage increases in industry in order to encourage capital formation. Under these more stringent conditions, after 1950, the power that had been a major instrument of Perón's authority, his control of collective bargaining, now lost him some of his previous labor support.

He had promised to carry out a program of land distribution during his campaign for the presidency; but he did little after election to carry out such a program beyond sponsoring the unionization of agricultural workers on sugar plantations and expropriating one large estate. Instead, taking advantage of the post World War II food shortage, he undertook to build a program of industrialization on capital derived from the profits of state trading in agricultural exports. For this purpose he created a national trading corporation, the Argentine Institute of the Promotion of Trade (IAPI), giving it a monopoly of agricultural exports. Through IAPI he succeeded for a time in diverting the rich profits from Argentine agricultural exports to finance industrial development. But these high profits lasted only as long as the post World War II food shortages. When prices declined, the resentment of the powerful landowning elite found expression in a boycott that sharply reduced the agricultural exports.

Perón's American style fascism appeared in his treatment of the universities and university student organizations. Argentine university students had been accustomed to great political freedom since their successful demonstration of strength at the University of Córdoba in 1918. In theory, in the past, they had stood with the workers' organizations. But Perón had outmaneuvered them, driving a wedge between them and the workers through control of the national labor organizations. Thus, at the very time the labor unions were rallying to support the election of Perón in 1946 the university students elected to demonstrate in protest against his measures to control them. After his election, Perón met university faculty and student opposition with even greater firmness than during the preceding provisional governments. The student organizations were suppressed and the professors who had supported them against the government were summarily dismissed. Under a new law governing the universities, university autonomy virtually disappeared. Rectors of the universities were appointed by the president for a fixed period of years and they controlled all university appointments.

On the other side of the ledger it should be added, however, that during the Perón years the Argentine universities received much greater financial support. They also became more accessible to students from the lower social classes, and their curricula took on an increasingly practical character. Critics said these changes occurred at the expense of academic standards. His defenders pointed out, in reply, that under his rule higher education was no longer limited to the privileged classes. The Perón measures won some student support, but only many years after the overthrow of Perón (a generation later) did Argentine students in any large numbers begin to support the social and economic objectives of *Peronismo*. Despite their sympathy with the social justice sought by the labor syndicates, they had been turned away by Perón's cynical disregard of Argentina's democratic tradition.

While Perón enjoyed great popularity, he also encountered strong popular opposition, from both the right and the left, in the Argentine style. Demonstrations of university students and professors, as noted, led to the appointment of interventors and to the purge of professors. In part this reaction was due to the influence of such right wing Catholics as

Carlos Ibarguren and Gustavo Martínez Avala (the novelist, better known by his literary pseudonym, Hugo Wast) in the provisional governments. Arthur P. Whitaker has pointed out, however, that Perón's determination to seek popular support soon led him to break with the right wing Catholics who had supported the *golpe* in 1943.

Perón's great capacity for dissimulation enabled him to escape the consequences of this break with right wing Catholicism until near the end of his regime. He accepted without question the agreement of the provisional government to require religious instruction in the public schools. While courting the support of the notoriously anti-clerical labor forces, he urged them to celebrate religious festivals in a way that warmed the hearts of the religious. Eva Perón was a great aid in this respect, particularly because of her audience with the Pope during a dramatic and highly reported visit to Europe. It is interesting to note that only after Eva's death did Church influence turn against Perón.

After the congressional election of 1948, in which he won an overwhelming victory, Perón and his followers adopted a more radical and, as it proved, a more disastrous political course. The Peronists pushed through the Congress a constitutional revision and, in the Senate, impeached the Supreme Court justices who had ruled against Peronist measures. Despite the opposition of a Radical party minority, who withdrew in protest, the Congress adopted constitutional changes that authorized broad social and economic legislation. The century old constitutional provision against presidential reelection was also repealed. After Perón's overthrow, the constitution of 1853 was declared in effect again. But while it was relatively easy to restore the no re-election rule, it was impossible to set aside the other constitutional, social, and psychological changes of the Peronist era. In general, Peronism had become a permanent part of the Argentine social consciousness and institutional structure.

The greatest political mistake of Perón had been to demand revision of the constitution to permit the re-election of a president and then to be a candidate for re-election in 1952. The mistake was compounded by his allowing Eva's name to be proposed for the Vice-presidency, only to be forced by army opposition to withdraw it. Had he abided by the Argentine no re-election tradition he might today appear in Argentine histories as a great president, rather than as the controversial figure he is. He had led the country to choose a progressive course of social and economic action long overdue. He and Eva were popular way beyond the popularity of any rulers of the country since the days of Irigoyen.

The tragic death of Eva Perón may have contributed to his decline, because she had so skillfully managed the labor and social basis of his power and was a powerful link with the Church as well. But in the final analysis it was the Argentine army that brought him down, particularly those elements of the army whose power he had successfully challenged in 1945 and several times thereafter.

One should not underestimate, however, the influence of Argentine public opinion, increasingly alienated by Perón's authoritarian manner and by the financial corruption that appeared to be funneling large sums of money into the hands of the president and his close collaborators. Since 1946 he had been steadily losing the ultranationalist support that had contributed greatly to his rise to power. Loss of this support became more noticeable when he turned to a policy of closer collaboration with the United States to solve some of his economic difficulties. The straw that broke the camel's back was a 1954 contract with the Standard Oil Company of California to develop the nation's petroleum production. He also received a loan from the Export-Import Bank to help finance a much desired steel plant. Advantageous as these arrangements were from the standpoint of his economic development plans, they had the fatal defect of providing his political enemies with an ideal weapon to undermine his popularity—he had sold out to Yankee imperialism!

Church support had been divided since Perón parted company with the rightist advisors of the provisional governments. Eva's philanthropic organization and Perón's encouragement of the syndicates to observe religious festivals gained some support among more progressive Catholics, devoted to the Christian labor movement. But some Catholics of both right and left wings were aroused to opposition by the Perons' increasingly extensive use of Communist labor leaders. After Eva's death, Christian labor leaders seemed to be conducting an aggressive campaign against Communist leaders in the labor unions—a challenge to Perón's control of this major sector of his power structure.

The president's conflict with the Church came to a climax when he gave his approval to a law authorizing divorce. This long overdue social measure had much popular support, but it was interpreted by Church leaders as a betrayal of Perón's presumed support of the Church. What was worse, it was interpreted also as a cynical appeal to the traditional anti-clericalism and "atheism" of the labor movement. Many moderate Argentine Church leaders spoke out against the divorce law, and popular demonstrations against Perón, almost unheard of since the electoral campaign of 1945–1946, were conducted on Corpus Christi Day (1955) with the seeming approval of Church leadership. He finally deported two Church leaders of the demonstrations, an action for which he was excommunicated. By this time the Argentine clergy seem to have turned against him. What is not clear, however, is whether it was the clerical Right, or the Left that opposed his control of the labor unions.

Perón was driven from power in September, 1955, by an army rebellion centering in Córdoba and led by army officers, many of whom he had persecuted and imprisoned. Wisely choosing not to risk a civil war, he resigned and sought political asylum, first in neighboring Paraguay, later in the Dominican Republic, and finally in Spain. But Peronism did not die. In exile Perón became a symbol of the aspirations of the Argentine masses for social justice, and Peronismo remained a major fact in Argentine politics. Peronists were a potential political majority, and no post-Perón government, except the short-lived regime of Arturo Frondizi, has managed to consolidate a power structure without it. Fear of the resurgence of Peronista power increased. After 1962 it seemed to unite army leaders from both the Right and the Left in a series of political interventions that eventually produced the military regime established by *golpe* in 1966. As this sketch is written (1972) it seems unlikely that Juan Perón will ever govern again, although it is not unlikely that he may be allowed to return when he is no longer a potential threat. But Peronism, in one form or another seems to many Argentines to be the political wave of the future.

NOTES

1. *Revolution Before Breakfast: Argentina, 1941–1946* (Chapel Hill: University of North Carolina Press, 1947), pp. 185–186.
2. *Argentina* (Englewood Cliffs, N.J.: Prentice-Hall, Inc., 1964), p. 104.

BIBLIOGRAPHY

One of the more convenient collections of Perón's political statements is *Doctrina peronista* (Buenos Aires, 1948, 423 p.). Eva Duarte de Perón, in *La razón de mi vida* (Buenos Aires: Ed. Peuser, 1951), shows her demagogic character as well as her intense devotion to her husband. On Eva Perón see also Richard Bourne, *Political Leaders of Latin America* (London, Baltimore, and Victoria, Australia: Penguin Books, 1969), pp. 238–270. *El libro negro de la segunda tiranía* (Buenos Aires, 1958) reports the results of a Congressional investigation of the Perón regime. Arthur Whitaker's account of Perón's overthrow in his *Argentine Upheaval* (New York: Praeger, 1956) is good. Other useful works include Robert Jackson Alexander, *The Perón Regime* (New York: Columbia University, 1951) and his *Labor Relations in Argentina, Brazil, and*

Chile (New York: McGraw Hill, 1962); Joseph R. Barager, ed., *Why Perón Came to Power* (New York: Knopf, 1968); George I. Blanksten, *Perón's Argentina* (University of Chicago Press, 1953. Russell reprint, 1967); Ruth and Leonard Greenup, *Revolution before Breakfast, Argentina, 1941–46* (Chapel Hill: University of North Carolina, 1947); Frank Owen, *Perón: His Rise and Fall* (London: Cresset Press, 1957); and Tad Szulc, *Twilight of the Tyrants* (New York: Holt, 1959).

26

FIDEL CASTRO RUZ (1926–   )

It is risky to analyze the political career of any leader still living and active in politics. This risk is even greater if the leader, as in this instance, is to be characterized as both revolutionary and a dictator. The degree of risk is even further increased in the case of so controversial a figure as Fidel Castro, especially if one takes seriously the comment of D. Bruce Jackson, a serious student of Cuban affairs, who has called Cuba's political leadership under Castro "a loose, leader-oriented aggregation of Latin American radicals more noted for revolutionary zeal than for discipline."[1] Fidel Castro is so important an example of present-day Latin American leadership, however, that he demands attention. Nor can he be dismissed with any such simplistic characterization as that of Jackson. It is true that in many ways Castro resembles Latin American revolutionaries of the past more than contemporary European and Asiatic revolutionaries. But his signal importance lies, rather, in the American version of Communist dictatorship he has created and in his persistent efforts to tie the Cuban Revolution to the revolutionary movements of Asia and Africa, while maintaining close ties with the Soviet Union.

This Castro regime, says Bruce Jackson, contrasts sharply with the highly disciplined and bureaucratic post-Krushchev regime in the Soviet Union with which it collaborates and which it copies in many respects. Yet Fidel Castro's concepts of power and of leadership are not too unlike those of his Soviet model. He accepts the basic principle of a dictatorship based on the discipline of a Communist party that consists of the revolutionary elite but derives its power and its legitimacy "from the support of an aroused proletariat." But Castro's Latin American political style is more personalist and flamboyant. It is that of the populist revolutionist-become-dictator. Moreover, he has gone through one metamorphosis, becoming a Marxist-Leninist after gaining control of Cuba, and may well go through another just as striking change before his political career is over.

An argument can be made that Castro's theory of revolution changed, passing through two quite distinct phases as his revolution took over the government of Cuba. These phases accorded with the classical Communist theory. In the first phase, he came to power with the support of a "bourgeois democratic" movement that united a majority of the

Cuban people to overthrow the unpopular regime of President Fulgencio Batista In the second phase, to the utter dismay of his "liberal" friends who believed he stood for the principles enunciated in his *History Will Absolve Me*, after taking power in 1959 he simply threw out such bourgeois-democratic elements while gathering into his hands all the elements of power in the nation. In terms of the history of the Russian Revolution, he was both Kerensky and Lenin.

Fidel Castro was born in 1926 in Mayarí, in the Oriente Province of Cuba. He was the third son of a Spanish immigrant father, Angel Castro, who had gained a small fortune as a sugar-cane planter and timber merchant. His mother, Lina Ruz, came from an old Cuban family. Fidel received the education typical of a child of prosperous parents in Cuba, attending the Jesuit *Colegio Dolores* in Santiago, the *Colegio Belén* in Havana, and the law faculty of the University of Havana, from which he graduated. His life as a university student was characterized by active participation as an aggressive leader in student political movements, usually dominating any group with which he associated. He was too young, however, to participate in the Revolution of 1933 that drove President Gerardo Machado from power and initiated the era of Batista.

His active role began later, during the post-World War II years in which Batista gave way to Ramón Grau San Martín and then to Carlos Prío Socarrás. As a young attorney in Havana Castro gained the reputation of defending causes of the poor. At this time he married good-looking Mirtha Díaz Balart, who bore him one son, José Ramón, better known as "Fidelito." His wife later divorced him and married Emilio Núñez Blanco, with whom she now lives in Spain. In politics, he worked within the Orthodox Autochthonous Party that split off under Raúl Chibás from the Autochthonous Cuban Revolutionary Party of Grau and Prío. In 1952 he was a candidate of this Orthodox party for election to Congress when Batista returned to power by a golpe in the midst of his presidential electoral campaign.

On July 16, 1953, Castro appeared as a revolutionary when he led a group of young rebels in a dramatic display of opposition to the Batista regime—an unsuccessful effort to take over the Moncada army barracks in Santiago. The attack failed and the young rebels were arrested, convicted of treason, and condemned to prison. In his trial Castro pled his case eloquently in a speech later published with the title *History Will Absolve Me*. Both the ideology of this book, a defense of democratic freedom, and the strategy of the putsch employed in the attack on the Moncada barracks provide a striking contrast with the later development of Castro's strategy and ideology as a national leader. Released from prison after President Batista's election in 1954, Castro and a group of fellow rebels went into exile in Mexico. There they met and seemingly came under the ideological influence of the Argentine Ernesto "Che" Guevara who persuaded them to give up the traditional plan of a golpe and to adopt a more fundamentally revolutionary program based on the strategy of guerrilla warfare.

Late in 1956, after careful planning and training for a guerilla campaign in the mountains, Castro and a band of eighty-two followers sailed for Cuba in the small yacht *Granma*, landing on the coast of the Oriente province. All but twelve of the band were killed or captured upon landing. With his brother Raúl, "Che" Guevara, and the other survivors, Castro made his way into the mountains of Oriente Province to initiate the guerilla warfare that eventually led to victory some two years later.

During those two years the original band of twelve guerrillas swelled to number several hundred, operating in three bands or "columns." Castro had put into practice successfully the Guevara (or Maoist) strategy of achieving revolution by guerrilla warfare, relying on the sympathy and support of the peasantry *(campesinos)*.[2] Batista's well equipped army of 30,000 men, ten to fifty times the size of the Castro forces, proved unable to confront the threat, as Guevara had insisted would be the case. Batista himself has admitted as much in his own account of his defeat, *Cuba Betrayed*.[3]

In the 1958 presidential election Batista faced a determined boycott of his all too obvious efforts to control the election of his successor. A well organized underground among university students and professional groups, orthodox autochthonous party leaders, and Christian Democrats supported the Castro guerrillas. The army was no longer the loyal efficient body Batista had built up in the 1930's, and which had been the basis of his power. Political corruption and gangsterism had penetrated its ranks. Some army officers were even participating in the underground. Eventually, the army gave up, turning against Batista and opening the way for Castro's entry into Havana on January 1, 1959.

Once in power, Castro moved rapidly and with the assurance of a born revolutionary leader to grasp almost all the power structures of the nation. He took over the army, imprisoning or executing the officers who opposed him. He nationalized the banks and expropriated the foreign controlled agricultural properties. He took over sugar production, mining, cattle, hotels, and other enterprises. His chosen leaders were imposed on the labor unions and on the university student organizations that had been so active in his underground support. Private schools were nationalized. The Communist party leadership that had only belatedly and half-heartedly supported him was given to understand they must now obey him.

In general, the Church escaped his heavy hand, except for having to accept nationalization of church schools. A rift with the Church developed, however, when a large number of foreign priests were exiled for their opposition to the Castro revolutionary program. Through the underground many church leaders, both Catholic and Protestant, had supported the Castro movement. Christian Democrats had given notable support. When Castro openly embraced Marxist-Leninism and the Communist party, however, he lost most of this Christian-oriented support.

The expropriation of foreign owned agricultural and mining properties, the obvious turn to Communist revolutionary programs, and a bloody purge of opposition military leaders aroused vigorous protests throughout the hemisphere, including the United States. In 1961, these protests eventually resulted in United States' support of the ill-considered and ill-fated Bay of Pigs invasion by the Cuban refugees' Brigade 2506. Spurning U.S. offers to help finance his agrarian reform, Castro had already turned to the Soviet Union and her Eastern European satellites for economic aid and political-military support. In exchange for Cuban sugar, under a Soviet trade agreement, he secured essential petroleum (U.S. refineries refused to handle it) machinery, and technological aid for a program of rapid industrialization placed under the general direction of "Che" Guevara. When this hastily improvised program of industrialization bogged down, Cuba turned back, apparently on Soviet insistence, to an emphasis upon increased sugar production to pay for the Communist bloc aid.

One notable aspect of the Cuban revolutionary development has been a dramatic increase in its armed strength. Universal military service gave Cuba, by 1962, a standing army of some 90,000 men and an armed reserve and militia of several times that size. The placing of Soviet intermediate range missiles on the island in that year produced the most serious United States-Soviet Union confrontation of the Cold War. The Soviet Union backed down, withdrawing its missiles, but only in exchange for a U.S. promise not to intervene in Cuba. The evidence of the withdrawal of the missiles could not be entirely clear, however, and some suspicion remained in the United States, because Cuba refused to permit the inspection that Premier Krushchev had agreed to. In 1970 rumors of the construction of a Soviet submarine base in the Cuban port of Cienfuegos again aroused fears in the United States, but no real threat seems to have appeared. Meanwhile, United States forces remain in the

Guantanamo Naval Base on the island.

As of 1972 it is impossible to evaluate definitely the achievements of Castro's rule of thirteen years. One of his major achievements would appear to be the virtual elimination of illiteracy as part of a great expansion of the national educational system. The large scale emigration of Cuban educational leaders has handicapped this expansion, but Eastern European technologists have partly filled the gap, helping particularly to improve technical and engineering education. Castro himself has publicly apologized for failure to achieve the level of sugar production promised, dramatically offering to resign if the Cubans wished him to!

The final account will doubtless show that the Castro revolution has made very substantial progress in many directions. Above all, it will show that it has gained and retained a high level of popular support. But the price of this success has been high. One out of every fifteen Cubans has left the country. Censorship may not be as vigorous as under some dictatorships, but open disagreement with the regime is clearly out. Superficially, Castro seems to act upon the Lenin theory of achieving socialism under the dictatorship of the proletariat exercised with the power of a disciplined Communist party. But in reality such a party still exists chiefly on paper as of 1972. He has made relatively little use of the leadership of the old Communist party as it existed in Cuba prior to 1959 because of its bureaucratic character and its associations with the Batista regime, especially in control of the labor movement, and because of its luke-warm support for his rebellion.

In his early appeals to the Cuban public on television and radio, Castro rejected representative government, saying that elected congresses merely represented the exploitive interests. The popular interest, he insisted, was in the mass meetings he addressed. As Premier he has acted in accordance with the Bolivarian theory (it is also the Soviet theory) under which the president, as head of state is somewhat above politics, while Castro as head of the government carries the burden of political action. He also appears to be the model of the formula of *la dictadura con respaldo popular* that the former president of the Dominican Republic, Juan Bosch, has presented in his book, *Pentagonism.*[4]

Whatever the years ahead may bring to him, Fidel Castro will have an important place in Cuban history as a dictator led into this role by the success of a popular revolution and by his instinctive populist sense. Historians, of course, will pass the final judgment on him as the political leader of Cuba during his years in power. Without doubt they will see a successful guerrilla leader and a great populist of undoubted charisma, who was either forced or freely chose to accept the role of dictator. They will see a popular university student leader who later succeeded in national politics. They will see a leader swayed by an Argentine ideologue, "Che" Guevara, although their probable judgment will be that Fidel Castro is a much greater Latin American leader than "Che." For they will see that he not only led guerrillas to success, but that he also personified the desires of the Cuban people for a government that would satisfy their burgeoning but imperfectly expressed desires.

NOTES

1. D. Bruce Jackson, *Castro, the Kremlin, and Communism in Latin America* (Baltimore: The Johns Hopkins University Press, 1969), p. 1.
2. Guevara's *Guerra de guerrillas* was published in Havana in 1960. Excerpts in English are found in Jay Mallin, *"Che" Guevara on Revolution* (Coral Gables: University of Miami Press, 1969), pp. 87–102.
3. New York, Washington, Hollywood: Vantage Press, 1962.
4. *Pentagonism, a Substitute for Imperialism*, trans. by Helen R. Lane (New York: Grove Press, 1958).

BIBLIOGRAPHY

Within the voluminous literature on Castro, the following books are particularly useful: Fulgencio Batista, *Cuba Betrayed* (New York, Washington, Hollywood: Vantage Press, c. 1962); Theodore Draper, *Castroism, Theory and Practice* (New York: Praeger, 1965); D. Bruce Jackson, *Castro, the Kremlin and Communism in Latin America* (Baltimore: Johns Hopkins University Press, 1969); Herbert L. Matthews, *Fidel Castro.*(New York: Simon and Schuster, 1969) and *The Cuban Story* (New York: Brazilier, 1961); Jean Paul Sartre, *Sartre on Cuba* (New York: Ballantine Books, 1961); and Robert Tabor, *M-26, The Biography of a Revolution* (New York: Lyle Stuart, c. 1961).

27

AN AFTERWORD

Some-day an ambitious scholar will study much more extensively and thoroughly than this author has been able to the protean forms of Latin American political leadership. In the twentieth century we are belatedly, and despite our psychological and philosophical skepticism, discovering the character and importance of this leadership, at least in its present-day forms, but with little consciousness of its historical roots. What the author has tried to do is something far short of a definitive study in any sense. He has simply tried to give thoughtful readers some historical understanding of how a few more or less typical leaders have acted in the crises of their times, of the factors in their backgrounds and experiences that influenced their decisions, of the validity of their understanding of the problems and choices they faced, and of their consequent successes and failures.

Is it presumptuious to hope that these brief sketches of a few outstanding leaders may have introduced a little more political sophistication into the discussion of revolutionaries, traditionalists, and dictators? The author modestly hopes that at least he may have made apparent to his readers that dictators and revolutionaries are not all of one kind, and especially that dictators may have either revolutionary or traditionalist origins.

No one can deny that the twentieth century charges made by revolutionaries against the "establishment" and the "oligarchy" in Latin America have much truth in them. But the contemporary critics that make these charges do not seem to know how extensively such charges were made in the past—that for nearly two centuries such revolutionaries as Túpac Amaru, Toussaint L'Ouverture, Simón Bolívar, Benito Juárez, "Che" Guevara, and Fidel Castro have inspired rebels, not only in Latin America, but in many other parts of the world as well to effect revolutionary social and political changes. Latin American revolutionary leadership has been recognized worldwide. How else can one explain the fact that guerrillas in Ceylon in the year 1971 adopt the label Guevarists? How explain that the sons of wealthy descendants of European immigrants in Uruguay conduct their urban guerrilla activities as *Tupamaros?*

It must have appeared rather clearly in the preceding pages that the author has hoped, by giving a little more attention to traditionalism and its exponents in this book, to remedy a shortcoming of his two previous volumes of the series which this book continues. The reader will judge how well this objective has been achieved. The author's hope is that the reader will at least have seen the curious paradox or contradiction in the traditionalists here presented. Has the reader, for example, been surprised to find that these traditionalists have usually not defended the existing "establishment"? Or that they have often been revolutionaries in a certain sense? Has he seen that those who have defended the tradition of Roman Catholic Christianity have often been motivated by, or have at least provided a transition to the socialism of the Christian Democratic parties and to the more radical positions of the left-wing Christians of the present day from the orthodoxy and social conservatism of the mid-nineteenth century?

Elsewhere, as in his *Latin American Social Thought,* the author has apologized for giving inadequate attention to traditionalist thought in the history of Latin American thought. This oversight, too, it is to be hoped, has been compensated for somewhat in the present book. It will be compensated for even more in another work, a short history of Latin American thought currently in hand.[1] From the examination of leaders in this present book, however, the conclusion may be drawn that Latin American traditionalism is not so much a part of the European stream as a product of the Latin American historical experience. This Latin American traditionalism is thus a dynamic force for change as it finds expression in such forms as *Argentinidad, Mexicanidad,* and *Peruanidad*—a search for national identity. To some readers its Americanism may obscure its essential traditionalism, causing them to view it as a source of revolutionary ideology merely because it rejects the *European* tradition. This is true, of course, in a certain sense. The author hopes, however, that the reader may now see that such nationalistic ideologies as *Argentinidad* are traditionalist just as truly as if their origins had been European, perhaps even more truly traditionalist because of their American source.

Finally the author approaches the end of this book with another regret quite different from what the reader may have been inclined to expect from the preceding paragraphs. This regret is that he has given inadequate attention to American Negro leaders who have been revolutionaries, traditionalists, and dictators—and numberous examples of all three kinds are to be found. Blacks constitute such a large part of the population of Latin America, and have played such important roles in its history, that they should have been better represented here. In his defense, the author would point out that in his *Latin American Leaders,* in his *The Americas in History* and in his *History of Latin America* he has brought out the revolutionary role of Toussaint L'Ouverture and the history of blacks in general. Moreover, the present volume has sketched two leaders of independence, Morelos and Guerrero, both possibly of mullato origin. It should be added, also, that a major reason for not having more black leaders in this book is the very practical difficulty of writing with confidence about them, given the inadequacy of the biographical studies available.

In the future other scholars, perhaps even this author, may deal more adequately with black Latin American revolutionaries, traditionalists, and dictators. The field is a broad one and one that should be inviting to scholars. One thinks immediately of the need for this kind of study of such figures as Henri Christophe, Alexandre Sabès Petion, and Francois Duvalier of Haiti, of Francisco del Rosario Sánchez of the Dominican Republic, of Antonio Maceo of Cuba, and of countless others, including the leaders of slave uprisings in Jamaica, Venezuela, and Brazil. The elements of traditionalism, it may be noted, are significantly different within the Negro cultural background. The revolutionary psychology also differs. Both revolutionism and traditionalism seem to have given support to dictatorship as well as to free regimes in Black America at different times. Future scholars will pursue these questions further. If this little book has managed to raise a few questions along these lines the author is well satisfied.

One thing, above all others, the author hopes to have said to the readers of this book—that leadership in Latin America is not the exclusive prerogative of any one ethnic group. Criollos, mestizos, Indians, and Negroes have all played this role, as revolutionaries, traditionalists, and dictators. It would be hard to prove that anyone of these ethnic groups tends, more than another, to fall into one of these three categories of leadership.

Finally, the author would return to an observation made in the INTRODUCTION. However one may interpret the role of traditionalists and the phenomena of dictatorship, the outstanding characteristic of Latin American political leadership has been revolutionary. As this manuscript passed through his hands in a final revision the author was pleased to read an agreement with this view in the new work on Latin American political thought by John D. Martz and the late Miguel Jorrín.[2]

NOTES

1. Published by the Louisiana State University Press, 1972.
2. *Latin American Political Thought and Ideology* (Chapel Hill, N.C.: University of North Carolina Press, 1971), p. 16.

INDEX